A History of Independent Television in Wales

A HISTORY OF INDEPENDENT TELEVISION IN WALES

Jamie Medhurst

UNIVERSITY OF WALES PRESS
CARDIFF

© Jamie Medhurst, 2010

All rights reserved. No part of this book may be reproduced in any material form (including photocopying or storing it in any medium by electronic means and whether or not transiently or incidentally to some other use of this publication) without the written permission of the copyright owner except in accordance with the provisions of the Copyright, Designs and Patents Act 1988. Applications for the copyright owner's written permission to reproduce any part of this publication should be addressed to the University of Wales Press, 10 Columbus Walk, Brigantine Place, Cardiff, CF10 4UP.

www.uwp.co.uk

British Library CIP
A catalogue record for this book is available from the British Library.

ISBN 978-0-7083-2213-0
e-ISBN 978-0-7083-2308-3

The right of Jamie Medhurst to be identified as author of this work has been asserted in accordance with sections 77, 78 and 79 of the Copyright, Designs and Patents Act 1988.

Printed in Wales by Dinefwr Press, Llandybïe

Contents

Acknowledgements		vi
Explanatory notes		viii
1	Introduction	1
2	The Pre-history of Independent Television in Wales	15
3	Television Wales and the West, 1956–1963: Organisation and Control	33
4	Television Wales and the West, 1956–1963: Programming and Critical Issues	61
5	Wales (West and North) Television, 1956–1963: Formation and Control	76
6	Wales (West and North) Television, 1956–1963: Operation, Programming and Demise	112
7	Television Wales and the West, 1964–1968: Operation and Programming	129
8	Television Wales and the West: The End of the Road	147
9	ITV in Wales, 1968–1997	169
10	Postscript	180
Endnotes		184
References		221
Index		229

Acknowledgements

I am indebted to a great number of people who have helped me in ensuring that this book has seen the light of day. In particular, I would like to thank Professor Tom O'Malley, colleague, critic, mentor and fellow media historian at Aberystwyth, for his help and support. At ITV Wales, Elis Owen, Shone Hughes, Siôn Clwyd Roberts and Owain Meredith went above and beyond the call of duty by providing a base at Television Centre in Cardiff and answering countless questions related to the project. Lord Roberts of Conwy, former Welsh Controller and Executive Producer at TWW, gave generously of his time and allowed me to access his library, for which I am extremely grateful. I am certain that this book would not have been completed without the help of the aforementioned.

I would also like to thank the following for their help and advice: Professors Deian Hopkin, Adrian Kear, Martin Barker, Elan Closs Stephens, Kevin Williams and Jean Seaton; Drs Hugh Chignell, Cathy Johnson and Rob Turnock; Angela Jones, Library Services, ITV Wales; Hywel Wiliam, Head of Broadcasting and Telecommunications, OFCOM Cymru Wales. The following kindly gave permission to use copyrighted material or allowed me to access personal archives: Sian Eleri, Director of Marketing and Communications, Urdd Gobaith Cymru; Mrs C. M. Harries, Aberystwyth; Mrs Mari Ellis, Aberystwyth; Eleri Huws, Tal-y-bont; ITV Broadcasting Ltd; Punch Ltd. Since completing the research for the book, the archives and records of the Independent Television Authority (ITA), the Independent Broadcasting Authority (IBA) and the Independent Television Commission (ITC) have been deposited at Bournemouth University library and are available to academic researchers once again. Staff at the National Library of Wales, the Hugh Owen Library at Aberystwyth University, the National Archives in Kew, the British Library Newspaper Library in Colindale, the BBC Written Archives Centre and the British Film Institute in London have been patient and generous in their help.

I was fortunate to be granted a semester's research leave from Aberystwyth University during the 2007–8 academic session and, thanks to a research leave grant awarded by the Arts and Humanities Research Council (AHRC), was able to complete writing the book during the first semester of the 2008–9 session. I was also awarded a Sir David Hughes Parry Award from Aberystwyth University, which permitted me to undertake extensive archival work. I would therefore like to record my thanks to the University and to the AHRC.

Commissioner Sarah Lewis and members of the production team at the University of Wales Press have done an excellent job in preparing this book for publication and it has been a pleasure working with them. Needless to say, any mistakes which appear in this book are mine alone.

My family have, as always, been a tremendous support. To Barbara, Iori, Kate and Mari, I say a big thank you for providing support and sustenance (including copious amounts of homemade cake) at just the right times. Ceris and Alice effectively 'lost' a husband and father respectively during my research leave and final stages of writing this book. I am eternally grateful to them for their love, patience and understanding whilst I have been foraging in archives in Aberystwyth, Cardiff and London and locked away in the study at home. I promise to make it up to you and to learn how to use the Playstation. Last, but by no means least, my parents, Heather and Brian Medhurst, have always been there for me. They have been a constant source of support and strength in so many ways. For this reason (and countless others), I dedicate this book to them with great love and affection.

Explanatory notes

Bands and channels in the 1950s and 1960s
International agreements had made available three 'Bands' to Britain (I, III and IV), each of which contained a certain number of channels to be used for broadcasting. The BBC operated in Band I across five channels. This Band was low frequency and allowed for greater penetration via high-powered transmitters and a network of low-powered satellite transmitters. The ITA utilised four channels in Band III (Channels 8, 9, 10 and 11) in Wales. In August 1960, the ITA announced that it would use Channel 8 (from the Preseli transmitter) and Channel 10 (from the Arfon transmitter, which was yet to be completed) to provide a service for west Wales.

Parts of Channels 6 and 7 and Channels 12 and 13 would be available for use by a third UK-wide service (in addition to the existing BBC and ITV services) when it was deemed appropriate. The ITA's request to establish a new transmitter in Flint-Denbigh (on Channel 13 in Band III) had to be made to the Postmaster General. The allocation of Channel 13 to either the ITA or the BBC therefore required a political decision on the part of the Postmaster General over who should be allowed the channel, because its allocation would impact on the technical basis of any third, UK-wide, channel which formed part of government policy.

In the mid 1960s, the Postmaster General permitted the use of Channel 7 for the ITA from the St Hilary transmitter to allow the new 'Teledu Cymru' to be transmitted to south Wales from February 1965, linking up with Channels 8, 10 and 11 to create an all-Wales service. The BBC had been granted permission to launch its own BBC Wales television service on Channel 13 from the Wenvoe transmitter in Glamorgan in February 1964. Channel 5 was used to transmit BBC 1 to south Wales, and Channel 10 was used by the ITA as a general English-language service for south Wales and the west of England.

VHF and UHF

VHF (Very High Frequency) is the radio range between 30 MHz and 300 MHz. British television was launched in black and white on VHF using the standard 405-line system. In 1964 625-line television was introduced on UHF (Ultra High Frequency, 300 MHz to 3 GHz), BBC2 being the first channel to use UHF. Colour television was introduced on UHF in 1967 (BBC2) and 1969 (BBC1 and ITV). The last 405-line broadcast on VHF took place in 1985.

Transmitter/station

During the 1950s and 1960s, the terms 'transmitter' and 'station' were used interchangeably to refer to transmitters which served a particular geographical area. I have tried to regularise this by using the word 'transmitter' apart from in direct quotations from sources.

Quotations

Where original Welsh quotations have been translated, this has been indicated in endnotes.

Abbreviations

The following abbreviations are used in the book:

BBC	British Broadcasting Corporation
GPO	General Post Office
IBA	Independent Broadcasting Authority
ITA	Independent Television Authority
ITC	Independent Television Commission
ITV	Independent Television (brand-name of the broadcasting service)
NLW	National Library of Wales
OFCOM	Office of Communications
S4C	Sianel Pedwar Cymru
TWW	Television Wales and the West Ltd
WAC	BBC Written Archives Centre
WRC	BBC Wales Record Centre
WWN	Wales (West and North) Television Ltd (also known as Teledu Cymru)

For Mum and Dad

1

Introduction

Researching ITV in Wales[1]

Since the mid 1950s, Independent Television (ITV) has entertained, educated and informed the Welsh television audience. It has provided innovative and often pioneering programming and has ensured a degree of plurality within the media in Wales. It has brought ground-breaking programming across a range of genres to homes across the nation and has provided creative opportunities for programme-makers. Now, all this is changing.

On 19 May 2009, the Welsh Conservative Party's spokesman on heritage in the Welsh Assembly, Alun Cairns, argued that the recent restructuring at ITV Wales, which had led to the disappearance of the title and role of National Director, 'essentially downgrades ITV Wales to regional status on a par with those [regions] in England'.[2] The news that a new senior executive in Cardiff would now report to a Director of ITV Wales, Granada and Central effectively ended an era in which ITV in Wales was clearly identifiable as one of the nation's broadcasters. The gradual erosion of ITV's public service broadcasting commitments, coupled with a hostile economic environment, meant that by 2009, ITV Wales was a pale figure of its former self. With a decrease in advertising revenue – the lifeblood of independent television – of 20 per cent by the end of March 2009 and a continuing withdrawal from public service obligations, the future of ITV is bleak.

The motivations for writing this book are numerous. In one sense, the origins can be traced back to a (long) train journey between London and Aberystwyth in 1997. I forget the reason why I was in London, but I clearly remember reading the first volume of Bernard Sendall's history of independent television in Britain on the way back.[3] During the previous year I had joined the staff of the Department of Theatre, Film and

Television Studies at Aberystwyth University and, as a historian, was required to teach aspects of television history and policy. I immediately became captivated by the story of the emergence of commercial television, particularly in Wales. Soon afterwards, I began working on a doctoral thesis which focused on a small but significant episode in Welsh television history, and seven years later, a thesis documenting the history of Wales (West and North) Television, or Teledu Cymru, was submitted and defended successfully.

The second motivation is, perhaps, a desire to redress what I see as an imbalance. There is a dearth of scholarly material on broadcasting history in Wales, in particular on that of independent television. Given the roles that radio and television have played in the development of a national consciousness and community in Wales, one would have expected academic, scholarly writing to be in abundance. However, that was not – and still is not – the case, to a large degree. I have noted in detail elsewhere some of the reasons for this gap, but the key reasons are television's relatively ephemeral nature coupled with a deep-seated mistrust of the medium, particularly in a literary-based society, such as exists within Wales.[4] Access to printed material and documentation is also an issue which may explain the lack of serious historical study of commercial television in Wales. Whilst the historian of the BBC has at his or her disposal the vast resources of the Corporation's Written Archive Centre at Caversham and the Wales Record Centre at Cardiff, the historian of independent television has no such repository to which to turn. There is no one central resource, given that ITV developed as a network of semi-autonomous regional companies. Thus, television (particularly commercial television) has not lent itself to serious academic study until recently,[5] this despite the fact that, as Helen Wheatley argues, 'writing television history often means illuminating aspects of a country's socio-political life in parallel, given that these histories are intertwined and inextricable'.[6]

The original aim of this book was to provide a complete and detailed history of ITV from 1956 up to the takeover of HTV by United News and Media in 1997. However, commercial sensitivities at ITV plc prevented me from accessing any information after 1968 that was not already in the public domain. This included minutes of the Welsh Board of Harlech/HTV and internal company documents which were made available to me in the papers of the late Alun Llywelyn-Williams, thanks to the kindness of his family. I was, however, prevented by ITV plc from using the material. Furthermore, I was required to access the hitherto publicly available (to researchers, at least) resources of the Independent Television Commission Records Centre via a Freedom of Information request to OFCOM. This not only prevented me from searching for information on my own terms, as it were, but I was not allowed to access material after 1991.[7] Such obstacles would naturally have skewed the history, and therefore, in consultation with the University of Wales Press, it was agreed to focus on the key early years of ITV in Wales (1956–68) and provide a broad overview of the years after 1968, based on publicly available material held in various archives. This also allowed for a much more in-depth assessment of these crucial years, when commercial television 'bedded down' (for want of a better term) across Wales. The brief chapter for the years after 1968 is therefore based on secondary source materials, all of which are publicly available.

These obstacles in themselves relate to the third motivation. ITV is changing, not necessarily for the better. Just as Tony Warren, the creator of ITV's long-running soap opera *Coronation Street*, wanted to capture a particular way of life that was fast disappearing in his drama serial, so I sensed that a history of ITV which both narrated and analysed its origins and development in Wales was timely and necessary. The book is a study of the complex relationship and tensions that exist between television, language, identity, public service and commercialism. The key issue for ITV Wales is that many of the problems it now faces – the requirement to make its programming commercially viable, concern over the lack of investment in English-language programming for Wales, the need to attract and maintain audiences – have been there from the outset, as this book demonstrates.

ITV plc faces an uncertain future. Its public service role has been called into question, not only by its detractors (and there have been many over the years), but by those within ITV itself. In addition, the communications regulator OFCOM has, according to Tom O'Malley, 'provided regulatory cover for ITV's withdrawal from its public service obligations'.[8] Michael Grade, ITV's chairman, also wants to see ITV divest itself of the 'millstone' of public service. What better time, then, to revisit the early decades of ITV and to rediscover the driving forces behind the commercial service in Wales?

Archival sources

The main archives for this book have been the National Library of Wales, the National Archives, the British Library Newspaper Library at Colindale, the BBC Written Archives Centre and the former ITC Library and Records Centre (now split between the British Film Institute and Bournemouth University). The primary sources contained within these archives include the minutes of the Welsh Board of TWW, the minutes of the Board of Directors of Wales (West and North) Television, internal company documents, correspondence with government ministers, correspondence between the ITA and the television companies, and documents internal to the BBC which deal with ITV. Furthermore, the 'standard' historical sources have been utilised: newspapers, journals and other secondary sources, all of which are listed in the bibliography at the end of this book. I was also able to interview a number of personnel who were closely involved with ITV in Wales, of whom, again, a list is provided at the end of the book.

The focus of the book is on what could be described as an institutional history of ITV in Wales. One cannot, however, ignore the content of the broadcast media – the programmes which have been produced under specific conditions and within specific contexts. Whilst the focus is on the institution of ITV, this has been located within the overarching framework of discourses on, and arguments relating to, national identity, language and public service broadcasting. The history of ITV in Wales, therefore, sits within political, social, economic and cultural contexts, all of which have helped to shape and develop the service.

Chronology

January 1951   Beveridge Report on Broadcasting published.
May 1952   Government White Paper on Broadcasting establishes the ground for the introduction of a commercially funded television service.
August 1952   BBC Television Service begins in Wales, with the opening of the Wenvoe transmitter in Glamorgan.
November 1953   Second Government White Paper proposes establishment of commercial television service.
July 1954   Television Act (introducing commercial television to the UK) receives Royal Assent.
September 1955   Independent Television (ITV) begins in London.

Introduction

October 1956	TWW awarded the contract for the ITA south Wales and west of England region.
September 1957	Granada Television launches its Welsh-language programme, *Dewch i Mewn*.
January 1958	TWW begins transmissions from the St Hilary transmitter in Glamorgan.
September 1959	First National Television Conference held in Cardiff.
August 1960	Sir Robert Fraser, visiting the National Eisteddfod in Cardiff, announces that the ITA will be establishing an ITV company in the west Wales area.
April 1961	ITA invites applications for the west and north Wales contract area.
June 1961	Licence awarded to the Wales Television Association.
July 1961	Second National Television Conference held in Cardiff.
June 1962	Pilkington Report on Broadcasting published.
September 1962	Teledu Cymru broadcasts for the first time.
May 1963	Teledu Cymru Board of Directors meet in Shrewsbury and decide to end all originated programming because of the financial crisis. As a result, Haydn Williams resigns as Chairman of the Board.
January 1964	Teledu Cymru is officially taken over by TWW.
July 1964	End of TWW's first contract period and beginning of second period.
February 1965	Launch of TWW's television service for Wales (based on the Teledu Cymru network).
October 1966	Aberfan disaster.
May 1967	Licence interviews for TWW and the Harlech Consortium at the ITA in London.
June 1967	TWW loses the Wales and West licence to Harlech.
March 1968	TWW's final programme transmitted.
May 1968	Harlech Television broadcasts for the first time.
May 1970	Opening of Mendip transmitter; creation of HTV Wales and HTV West.
May 1973	Crawford Committee formed to consider establishment of Fourth Channel.
1977	Annan Report on Broadcasting.

5

December 1980	HTV licence for Wales and the West renewed by IBA.
November 1982	Launch of Sianel 4 Cymru (S4C).
1986	Peacock Report on Broadcasting.
October 1991	HTV retains licence for Wales and the West, but at a cost of almost £21 million.
November 1993	Relaxation of ownership rules for ITV companies (further relaxed under terms of 1996 Broadcasting Act).
June 1997	HTV taken over by London-based United News and Media.
July 2000	Granada takes over HTV.
October 2000	Granada sells HTV to Carlton.
2004	Granada and Carlton merge to form ITV plc; HTV rebranded as ITV Wales.

Select review

What follows is a select review of a number of works on the history of broadcasting and, more particularly, the history of ITV. The aim is to suggest how this book fits into the overall historiography, but also to show the scant attention Wales has received within those works.

Two of the earliest works on commercial television were both published in 1961 by American academics, H. H. Wilson and Burton Paulu.[9] The fact that these key works were written by Americans (yet published by British publishers) is significant, as it highlights the interest that the advent of ITV attracted from overseas. Wilson's work is, for many, the starting point for the debate over commercial television in Britain. Described as an 'objective but disturbing account' of the campaign surrounding the advent of commercial television in the UK, Wilson based his work on interviews with key personnel both for and against the commercial service.[10] Based on the evidence to hand, Wilson concluded that commercial television had come about as a direct result of pressure-group activity by a small, but influential, group of Conservative backbench MPs, in union with interests from the radio and advertising industries. His conclusions, however, have not been universally accepted. Asa Briggs draws attention to the fact that the book appeared at a sensitive time in British broadcasting, as the Pilkington Committee was deliberating the futures of both the BBC and ITV. Indeed, as Briggs notes, there were two threats of court action when the book appeared.[11] The main weakness of Wilson's argument, according to Briggs, is that he underplayed the parliamentary debates and the complexity of the arguments, and did not give enough attention to the compromises which emerged as Britain moved into a period of duopoly.[12] Wales does not feature in Wilson's account, apart from a brief reference to Mark Chapman-Walker, secretary to the Conservative Parliamentary Broadcasting Committee and later managing director of TWW.[13]

Burton Paulu, Director of Radio and Television Broadcasting at the University of Minnesota, had already written on British Broadcasting – his *British Broadcasting: Radio and Television in the United Kingdom* was published in 1956.[14] As in the case of his first publication, Paulu's second book was aimed at readers on both sides of the Atlantic, as '[t]hinking Americans are questioning their broadcasting system as never before, and some knowledge of what is done elsewhere may suggest solutions to a few of their problems'.[15] Described by Sendall as 'a lucid, scrupulously fair, brief but scholarly assessment of the impact of competition on television', the book is a study of the British television system in the first years of the duopoly.[16] The author saw Britain as 'an excellent laboratory in which to observe the relative advantages and disadvantages of monopoly and competition.'[17] He also noted that the scenario would allow an observer the opportunity to study the thorny issues surrounding commercial broadcasting regulation, particularly in terms of programme standards and quality. Drawing primarily on official documentary material, annual reports and accounts, government publications, interviews and memoirs, Paulu came to the clear conclusion that British television had been improved by the advent of commercial television. 'Competition', he wrote, 'has been an incentive to the BBC at the same time that Independent Television has greatly enriched the country's program fare.'[18] The only reference to Wales appears when the author discusses the notion of regional broadcasting, regional diversity and Welsh-language output. The account is factual, with no comment or critique, and there is no specific reference to independent television in Wales.[19]

One further work published in 1961 was Clive Jenkins's *Power Behind the Screen*, which was a detailed study of those who owned British commercial television and a list of their other business interests. The book also aimed to explain the motivation of those behind the ITV network companies.[20] The research was based on reference books, company information and interviews with certain key figures in ITV at the time, for example Norman Collins, who spearheaded the Popular Television Association's campaign for commercial television, and Mark Chapman-Walker. Jenkins, an occasional newspaper columnist, set out to expose the fact that in the ITV companies:

> Behind the show-business people, the theatre controllers and the impresarios lay a tangled, but beautifully effective, intertwined control by the investing groups in society. In brief, the same banking, insurance and industrial interests that make up the nerve and motor centres of the British economy, also control the heartbeats of the commercial television programme contractors.[21]

Although the book was written in 1961, there is no mention of Wales (West and North) Television. However, the chapter on TWW shows Jenkins's awareness of Welsh nationalist sentiment. He states that he is in agreement with Gwynfor Evans's arguments about the potential of television to maintain and stimulate the Welsh language and culture, and quotes from a pamphlet written by Evans and the Plaid Cymru party organiser, J. E. Jones, in 1958, entitled *TV in Wales*.[22] Jenkins ends this section by observing that 'in Wales more than anywhere else, the deplorable impact of a profits drive upon a national cultural situation can be seen'.[23] Allied with Jenkins's support for Evans's views is a strong anti-American and anti-Conservative thread running through the chapter, which is notable, given that TWW had a heavy preponderance of Conservative Party members on its Board and was also being advised by the American broadcaster NBC.[24]

Peter Black's *The Mirror in the Corner* was published in 1972.[25] The significance of the book lies in the subtitle – 'People's Television'. Black picked up on a phrase used by the ITA's first Director-General, Sir Robert Fraser, in a speech to the Manchester Luncheon Club in December 1960. In the speech, Fraser referred to the commercial television service in these terms, believing in the good judgement and sense of the ordinary viewer. Black devotes very little attention to Wales, beyond two pages which discuss the reasons for the loss of the TWW contract to the Harlech Consortium in June 1967. According to Black, there was a contemporary rumour that Harold Wilson, the Prime Minister at the time, was seeking revenge for the anti-government line taken by the *News of the World*, a major shareholder in TWW, over Rhodesia. Black suggests that this was a key factor in TWW's losing the contract. However, there were a number of other matters at stake (as discussed in chapter 8), including the accusation that the company was too 'London-based'.[26]

The work of Asa Briggs is noted in the field of television history. His five-volume history of British broadcasting has been the cornerstone of research in this area for many years. Briggs was commissioned by the BBC to write the work in 1957, at a time when the monopoly had only recently been broken, and the work tends to focus on the 'official' viewpoint, revealing its reliance on official BBC sources. The author clearly demonstrates an understanding of the complexity of the relationship between broadcasting and cultural politics in Wales (and, indeed, Scotland).[27] Wales is not positioned so much as a 'problem', but as an issue to be addressed, with needs that require answers. There is no mention in Briggs of ITV in Wales or Teledu Cymru, despite the fact that the BBC and Teledu Cymru were in discussion on several occasions over the possible sharing of transmitters and programmes.[28]

In 1982, Bernard Sendall published the first of what were to become six volumes covering the history of independent television in the UK. The first volume focused on its origin and foundations between 1946 and 1962, whilst the second volume, published in 1983, covered the period 1958–68, a period defined by the author as 'expansion and change'.[29] Sendall was a senior member of the Independent Television Authority, serving as its Deputy Director-General for many years, and his studies serve to echo that loyalty and adherence to the ITA. Just as Asa Briggs had been approached by the BBC, Sendall was asked by the Independent Television Companies' Association, in association with the Independent Broadcasting Authority, to write the work. What emerges from Sendall's history of the first decade of ITV is, firstly, an indication of the willingness on the part of the Authority to address the specific linguistic and cultural needs of Wales and, secondly, an awareness within the Authority of the complexity (in political, linguistic, cultural and geographical terms) of achieving this. 'The rightness of establishing national companies outside England was . . . even more patent in the case of Wales with its live spoken language and cultural tradition' notes Sendall. 'Yet nature had made the job much more difficult.'[30] These sentiments are echoed in the minutes of the first meeting of the ITA's Advisory Committee for Wales, where Jenkin Alban Davies, the Welsh member, underlined the ITA's 'sympathy with the cultural aspirations of Scotland, Ulster and Wales'.[31]

In their work, James Curran and Jean Seaton do not isolate developments in broadcasting, but place them within the wider social, cultural, political and economic spheres of which broadcasting is a part.[32] However, Wales does not figure in the history of British broadcasting as written by Curran and Seaton. John Davies's work on the history of the BBC and broadcasting in Wales does not even appear in the bibliography, and in the discussion on the establishment of Channel 4, there is no reference whatsoever to the campaign to there is no reference whatsoever to the campaign to establish S4C.[33] In this respect, the account could be accused of being a rather Anglocentric one. There *is*, however, a reference to the award of the ITV Wales and West licence to Harlech Television in 1967, together with a comment that the regionalism of ITV was 'less firmly rooted in popular needs than in the convenience of the market', a point underlined by Kevin Williams in his history of mass communications in Britain.[34]

In summary, the attention devoted to Wales, and commercial television in Wales in particular, in the broad spectrum of broadcasting historiography has been minimal.

Organisation of this book

The second chapter contextualises the emergence of ITV in Wales by tracing the development of broadcasting in Wales from the advent of radio broadcasting in the 1920s until the early years of the 1950s, and placing this within the context of contemporary debates about the need for the recognition and representation of Wales within UK broadcasting; it then outlines the emergence of the ITV service in the UK and Wales, noting the political, economic and cultural debates surrounding its introduction.

The third and fourth chapters trace the history of Television Wales and the West (TWW) from its inception and award of licence in 1956 until the end of the first licence period, in 1963. In addition to a study of the company's institutional history, the chapter considers the relationship between TWW, the ITA and the government, as well as studying the programming of the first period of operation. The period was one of financial success for the company, with large profits from the outset. In addition to financial success, TWW also had successes in programming terms, being a pioneer in news and current affairs (in particular in Welsh) and setting a new 'tone' for the viewer.

Chapters 5 and 6 focus on the history of the ill-fated ITV company which served west and north Wales between 1962 and 1963, Wales (West and North) Television/Teledu Cymru. However, it places the history of the company within the wider debate over nationhood and the struggle for representation, for it is the history of WWN which exemplifies this, more than that of any other company. In many ways, WWN can be seen as an answer on the part of the government and ITA to increasing Welsh demands for a separate television service for Wales. The reasons for the demise and financial collapse of the company in 1963 were complex, and raise a number of issues in the context of the relationship between ITV, the government, the BBC and the Post Office at this time.

The seventh and eighth chapters return to TWW and consider the company's 'second phase', between 1964 and 1968. This period saw TWW provide a service for the whole of Wales, in addition to the west of England, following the demise of WWN, but it also signalled the beginning of the end for the ITV contractor. Increasing criticism came from the ITA on a range of issues (primarily concerned with programming), and in 1967 the company lost its licence to a rival consortium, led by Lord Harlech.

Chapter 9 is a very broad overview of the history of ITV in Wales (and, by default, Harlech Television/HTV) from 1968 onwards. The overarching issue during the 1970s was a campaign for a separate Welsh-language channel, spearheaded by the Welsh Language Society, Cymdeithas yr Iaith Gymraeg, but supported by both Welsh and non-Welsh speakers for different reasons. The 1980s were a decade of mixed fortunes for HTV, culminating in a large bid for the Wales and west of England licence in 1991 (under a new franchise auction system introduced by the Conservative government of the time). The bid did untold damage to HTV, and the story of the 1990s is one of cutbacks and eventual takeover. ITV in Wales today is a pale shadow of its former self.

Key themes

Cathy Johnson and Rob Turnock evoke the notion of a 'battle' or 'struggle' surrounding the advent and subsequent development of ITV in the UK. They argue that the battle was fought between those who had commercial and ideological interests in expanding the television service and those who had deep-seated fears about the impact of commercial forces on British cultural life and public service broadcasting.[35] On a Welsh level, both historically and in contemporary terms, it is possible to develop Johnson and Turnock's notion of 'tensions' within the ITV framework by noting five themes that will be developed further in subsequent chapters.[36]

Firstly, tensions emerged between a public service broadcasting remit (under the 1954 Television Act) and commercial pressures, such as those which exist in any business which has a duty to secure returns for shareholders in a competitive market. During the lifespan of ITV in Wales, this tension was a prominent feature in the histories of the various companies that operated the Welsh commercial service.

Secondly, linguistic tensions dominate the history of broadcasting in Wales, and ITV was no exception. As will be seen in chapter 2, the Welsh language had been politicised and tied up with the politics of broadcasting since the earliest days of radio. Although not laid out in the Television Act of 1954, public service requirements for the provision of Welsh-language and English-language Welsh-interest programming were later placed upon all ITV companies which operated in Wales. Each company had to balance these requirements against the commercial imperative to maximise profits for shareholders (primarily by placing mass-appeal, English-language programmes at peak times and relegating the minority-interest Welsh-language programmes to less prominent hours). In the case of a company such as Wales (West and North) Limited, as we shall see later, where an ideological commitment was given greater weight than commercial considerations, the outcome was financial disaster. The history of ITV in Wales is one of constant dialogue with the regulatory authority over the amount and nature of Welsh-language programming. This raises another significant issue, that of the place of English-language programming about Wales on commercial television. Barlow et al. raise the issue of the ambivalence or confusion in the campaigns surrounding Welsh broadcasting about whether there should be a separate broadcasting regime for the whole of Wales or just one for the Welsh language.[37] This lack of clarity about what should be provided continued in the context of a situation where the voices of Welsh-language campaigners were significantly stronger than those of the English-speaking majority. As a result, ITV companies in Wales were often criticised by the ITA, by politicians and by the viewers for focusing on Welsh-language programming at the expense of English-language provision.

This leads on to the third issue which dogged ITV from the launch of TWW in 1958, the tension between Wales and the west of England. As will be seen in chapter 2, the BBC's regional radio policy was based primarily on technical and economic necessity, in particular where the location of the transmitters was concerned. Only after pressure was put on the Corporation did a separate Welsh Region come into existence. In 1952, when the television service was launched in Wales, the country was again tied to the west of England, as this area was reached by the signals of the Wenvoe transmitter. When ITV launched its service in south Wales, an alliance, based on economic reasoning as opposed to cultural understanding, was forged with the west of England (see chapter 3). This 'yoking' of Wales and England into a dual region inevitably caused tensions on either side of the Bristol Channel, as both Kevin Williams and John Davies note.[38] A related factor is the fact that, throughout ITV's history, Wales has been subject to significant overlap, in terms of neighbouring ITV companies, and has not, therefore, been able to operate as a fully coherent broadcasting unit. Granada Television, which began broadcasting in May 1956, transmitted from the Independent Television Authority's Winter Hill transmitter and its signals could be received as far away as Anglesey. In mid Wales, the signals of ATV in the Midlands could be picked up by viewers with ITV receivers. When HTV split its programming for Wales and the west of England in 1970, many non-Welsh-speaking viewers in south Wales decided to 'avoid' Welsh programming by turning their aerials towards the Mendip transmitter. The situation changed in 1982 when the Welsh fourth channel, S4C, began broadcasting. Thus, tensions between Wales and the west and overlap areas have created a difficult environment in which ITV companies in Wales have had to operate.

The fourth issue, which is unique to ITV in Wales, is the tension between the regional and the national. Whilst TWW, WWN and Harlech/HTV were all considered regional programme contractors by the ITA, they also had a national role within Wales, and even an international role beyond that. This often placed great demands on the companies, but it also allowed them to take advantage of the fact that, unlike the BBC, they were not at the behest of 'Head Office' in London, and as such could promote themselves as national broadcasters.

Finally, the tension between the popular and quality in terms of programming plagued ITV from the outset. Although independent television had a clear public service remit, its emphasis was always to err on the side of the popular whilst maintaining a certain quality of programming. ITV has always been associated pejoratively with so-called low-quality programming, such as quiz shows and soap operas, and, as will become clear later in this book, the ITV companies in Wales were often castigated for the lack of 'quality' drama. However, I hope to show that much of the ITV programming in Wales was innovative, pioneering and achieved a certain standard of quality.

Within Wales, as in the United Kingdom as a whole, I believe that there is a common perception that commercial television is 'not as good' as the BBC and that there exists an almost automatic predisposition towards the Corporation. This is reflected in the fact that very little academic writing exists on the history of commercial television. It is as though within what little writing does exist on Welsh television, the BBC has 'stolen the limelight', which, it could be argued, reflects a general BBC-focused view of broadcasting in Britain as a whole.[39] I hope that the chapters that follow will go some way to redressing that imbalance, by giving the history of ITV in Wales the attention it deserves.

Writing this history has been a fascinating experience, and I hope that it will stimulate you, as it has done me. A *Western Mail* journalist, on the eve of the opening night of ITV in Wales over fifty years ago, wrote:

> Someday someone will write the history of independent television in Britain . . . The Welsh chapter will certainly make the most interesting reading. For what has ever made good entertainment without containing a quota of trials, tribulations and ups-and-downs. And those, independent TV in Wales and the West has certainly had . . . The author of that history will have quite a job on his hands![40]

The author of the 'Welsh chapter' *has* had 'quite a job on his hands', but that job has been a most pleasurable and enlightening one. I have spent over ten years researching and writing on the history of ITV in Wales and, indeed, have had my 'quota of trials, tribulations and ups-and-downs'. My only hope is that what you have in front of you now makes 'the most interesting reading'.

2

The Pre-history of Independent Television in Wales

Introduction

The aims of this chapter are twofold: firstly, to contextualise the emergence of Independent Television (ITV) in Wales by tracing the development of broadcasting in Wales from the advent of radio broadcasting in the 1920s until the early years of the 1950s, and to place this within the context of contemporary debates about the need for the recognition and representation of Wales within UK broadcasting; secondly, to outline the emergence of the ITV service in the UK and Wales, noting the political, economic and cultural debates surrounding its introduction.

Broadcasting in Wales, 1923–1956

There are three phases in Welsh broadcasting history, prior to the arrival of a specifically Welsh ITV company, which help shed light on some of the particular nuances of ITV's operation in Wales thereafter. The first period spans from 1923, when the British Broadcasting Company opened its Cardiff Station, to 1937, the year when Wales was established as a BBC region in its own right. This followed demands from various sectors of Welsh society, demanding Wales be separated from the 'West Region', of which it had been a part since late 1926. The second phase runs from 1937, through the years of the Second World War, and up to the publication of the Beveridge Report on the future of broadcasting, in January 1951. The final phase runs from the years after the publication of the Beveridge Report up to the point when a consortium was formed to apply for the commercial television licence for south Wales and the west of England, in 1956. This period saw the introduction of television on Welsh soil and growing calls for a separate television service for Wales.

1923–1937

BBC broadcasting in Wales began on 13 February 1923 at 5 p.m. when the British Broadcasting Company opened its 5WA station in Cardiff.[1] Three months had passed since the British Broadcasting Company had been established by six companies, all with a vested interest in selling wireless sets to the listening public. As John Davies states, 'public broadcasting came into being, not because of a desire to enlighten, educate and entertain the citizenry, but because manufacturers of wireless receivers were concerned to sell their products'.[2] Soon after, in December 1924, the company opened its Swansea station, 5SX. During the early days of radio in Wales, very little Welsh was heard on the medium; the only Welsh of a substantial nature was transmitted by Radio Éireann in Dublin, presumably as the broadcaster was aware that the signal reached the Welsh heartlands of west Wales.[3] Programmes broadcast followed the pattern set by the London headquarters of the company, as there was no commitment to 'regional' or 'national' provision at the time; indeed, a feeling prevailed amongst John Reith and his senior staff that the 'best' programmes were broadcast from London and that every effort should be made to imitate their style and content.[4] In order to ensure that the British Broadcasting Company was made aware of the language and culture of Wales, Cylch Dewi (a group of cultural nationalists with Saunders Lewis[5] as one of its founders) arranged the first broadcast of a Welsh-language religious service, and by the mid 1920s were producing programmes of their own, following consultations with E. R. Appleton, the Cardiff Station Director.[6]

Concerns about the impact of the wireless on life in Wales were apparent in the early years of broadcasting. In 1927 a report commissioned by the President of the Welsh Board of Education – *Welsh in Education and Life* – was published, and contained a damning attack on the BBC:

> Wireless is achieving the complete Anglicisation of the intellectual life of the nation. We regard the present policy of the British Broadcasting Corporation as one of the most serious menaces to the life of the Welsh language ... nothing short of the full utilisation of the Welsh language in broadcasting will meet the case.[7]

The report was to raise issues that would emerge over the following half-century. The heart of the problem, it was noted, was the fact that Wales, in broadcasting terms as well as in political life, was ruled from London, and that understanding of, and empathy with, Welsh language and culture was virtually non-existent in the higher echelons of the Corporation. This attitude was exemplified by the response of E. R. Appleton to the *Welsh in Education and Life* report, which appeared in the *Western Mail* on 30 August 1927:

> Wales, of her own choice is part of the commonwealth of nations in which the official language is English . . . If the extremists who desire to force the language upon listeners in the area . . . were to have their way, the official language would lose its grip.[8]

On 30 November 1928, a deputation from the University of Wales went to the BBC in London to press for increased recognition for the nationhood of Wales. Described by Rowland Lucas as 'an important confrontation', the BBC's officials (including Sir John Reith) were left in no doubt about the level of discontent in Wales regarding reception, provision and quality of programmes.[9] This was the first in a long line of deputations and meetings which would characterise the history of Welsh broadcasting for the next fifty years or more.

The 1930s witnessed increased pressure from many parts of Welsh society (most notably the University of Wales and local authorities) for the BBC to recognise Wales as a nation, with its own cultural and linguistic needs. Much of the anger was targeted at the BBC's insistence that both the geography of the country and the scarcity of wavelengths made establishing a separate Welsh region difficult. Added to this was the nature of the scattered population of Wales, which the BBC used as an argument for not providing the country with a separate broadcasting system. As the BBC Handbook of 1931 stated, 'Wales cannot be considered technically in one piece.'[10] However, a scientist, E. G. Bowen, had however already put forward a plan to overcome these perceived technical problems – his ideas had appeared in the *Western Mail* on 12 March 1930.[11] The BBC ignored these ideas and continued with its regional plan (adopted by the BBC's Control Board in November 1926), which fused Wales and the south-west of England into one 'Western Region'. Much was made at that time of the apparently favourable treatment given to Scotland (which was afforded the status of a full region), and accusations abounded that the BBC was more sensitive to the needs of Scotland than to those of Wales.[12] The reasons given by the Corporation for not establishing a similar Welsh region were based on the lack of available wavelengths and the mountainous terrain of the country. This prompted J. E. Jones, then secretary of Plaid Cymru (the Welsh Nationalist party) to write sardonically that everybody knows, of course, that Scotland is flat.[13]

Welsh-language journals published during the 1930s provide evidence of the nature and strength of feeling. In 1932, one correspondent writing in the Plaid Cymru newsletter, *Y Ddraig Goch*, stated that: 'The majority of the material broadcast is alien to our traditions, damaging to our culture, and is a grave danger to everything special in our civilisation.'[14] An article in the same journal in September 1932 referred to the BBC's 'lies', and deplored the fact that the Corporation insisted on calling the Welsh a minority, whereas in fact they were a nation.[15] These sentiments were to be echoed in 1949 at the time of the Beveridge Committee on Broadcasting, in 1960 at the time of the Pilkington Committee's deliberations, in the 1970s during the Crawford and Annan Committees' deliberations on broadcasting and the fourth channel, and at all points in between and later. In Wales, broadcasting was turning into a political battleground. Saunders Lewis referred to the fact that the BBC administered Wales as a conquered province, and the language of contemporary discourse highlighted the feeling that as the BBC increasingly centralised power in London, so the dissatisfaction amongst Welsh speakers in particular increased.[16]

In 1935 Wales was given a measure of independence in broadcasting terms (or rather, as the *Times* later put it, the BBC 'grudgingly acceded' to Welsh demands for full regional status).[17] A number of Welsh speakers, such as T. Rowland Hughes, Tom Pickering, Alun Llywelyn-Williams (later to become a director of Harlech Television/HTV) and Arwel Hughes, were also appointed to key positions in the Corporation, and Sam Jones was appointed to head the team at the newly opened Bangor studio, laying firm foundations for broadcasting from north Wales.[18] The slow process of separating Wales from the south-west of England had begun, and the Liberal politician Rhys Hopkin Morris was appointed as Director of the Welsh Region on 1 September 1936. Although the transmitter in Penmon was opened in February 1937, it was not until 3 July 1937, when Sir John Reith, the Director-General of the BBC, visited Cardiff for an inauguration ceremony, that the Corporation fully acknowledged Wales as a separate region. The importance of this milestone is noted by John Davies, who argues that the establishment of the Welsh Region was an important concession to nationalist sentiment, on a par with the disestablishment of the Church of Wales in 1920 and the formation of the Council for Wales and Monmouthshire in 1948.[19] Indeed, Davies argues that the establishment of the Welsh Region had wider repercussions:

> In the history of BBC broadcasting in Wales, the importance of the victory won in sound radio can scarcely be exaggerated. All the subsequent recognition of Wales in the field of broadcasting (and, it could be argued, in other fields also) stemmed from that victory.[20]

1937–1951

The 1930s also saw the advent of a new medium, television. The BBC's television service was launched on 2 November 1936, and by the following year the BBC was broadcasting approximately twenty-two hours of live television per week in the London area, as well as showing films every morning. The service, however, was halted at the outbreak of war on 1 September 1939. In the words of the BBC Handbook of the time, 'The BBC was on a war footing.'[21] During the War, the Welsh-language radio service was extremely limited – three hours a week at most. It was during this time of restrictions on the broadcasting service to Wales that Gwynfor Evans, in a speech to the cultural nationalist society, Undeb Cymru Fydd, called for an independent broadcasting corporation for Wales.[22] His argument was that the needs of Wales were being overlooked by the BBC's management in London, and that 'the only system that will remove that possibility of a clash between the needs of Wales and the BBC's policy is an independent Welsh Corporation.'[23]

The BBC television service resumed broadcasting on 7 June 1946. At the time, the service was available only to 15,000 households in the London area. Soon afterwards the service spread as transmitters were opened across the UK – in the West Midlands in 1949, in Manchester in 1951, and in 1952 in Scotland and south Wales.[24] However, as Kevin Williams notes, '[it] struggled to establish itself in a hostile environment'.[25] There was a deep suspicion amongst many senior executives at the BBC as to the value of television, and William Haley, the Director-General, shared with his predecessor, John Reith a mistrust of the medium. However, as

Briggs notes, Haley's overall attitude to television was, on the whole, more positive.[26] Despite this, television remained relatively underfunded and underdeveloped during the immediate post-war period. In 1947–8, television accounted for only one-tenth of the BBC's total expenditure, and even by 1950 the budget for television was only half of that of the Home Service.[27] There can be no doubt that the attitude of the Corporation's senior management in the early days of television influenced its development in two ways: firstly, in arguing that television was merely an extension of sound (as Haley did, in an article reprinted and submitted as written evidence to the Beveridge Committee), the early exploitation of television was stifled.[28] Secondly, in following this approach, and in mishandling the appointment of a Director of Television in 1950, the BBC lost one of its key players, Norman Collins, who resigned from the Corporation and went on to spearhead the campaign for commercial television.[29] The heart of the problem was the distrust amongst senior management of the visual. As Grace Wyndham Goldie, former Head of Television Talks, writes in her book on television and politics:

> their speciality was the use of words; they had no knowledge of how to present either entertainment or information in vision, nor any experience of handling visual material. Moreover, most of them distrusted the visual; they associated vision with the movies and the music hall and were afraid that the high purposes of the Corporation would be trivialised by the influence of those concerned with what could be transmitted in visual terms.[30]

In 1946, at the point when the BBC Charter was due for renewal, the Labour government under Clement Attlee deferred the appointment of an independent commission of enquiry and extended the Corporation's charter for a further five years. John Corner argues that the primary reason for this course of action was as a result of the 'more immediate and pressing political tasks' of post-war social and economic reconstruction.[31] It was also a decision based on the wartime achievements of the BBC at home and overseas in gaining worldwide acclaim for the service provided.[32]

By 1946 there were the beginnings of a move to question (if not remove) the BBC's monopoly on broadcasting. Winston Churchill, the Leader of the Opposition, questioned the wisdom of allowing the Charter to be extended without an inquiry, and the former Director-General of the BBC, Frederick Ogilvie, wrote a letter to the *Times* on 26 June 1946:

> Is monopoly of broadcasting to be fastened on us for a further term? Is the future of this great public service to be settled without public enquiry, by Royal Commission or otherwise, into the many technical and other changes which have taken place in the last ten years. Freedom is choice. And monopoly of broadcasting is inevitably the negation of freedom, no matter how efficiently it is run, or how wise and kindly the boards or committees in charge of it . . . In tolerating monopoly of broadcasting we are alone among the democratic countries of the world.[33]

As Ogilvie's letter indicated, there was also concern over the appropriateness of monopoly control over a channel of communication, especially one which had formed such a close relationship with the government during the war.[34] These murmurs of discontent formed the backdrop to the Broadcasting Committee.

In June 1949, the Labour government appointed a committee of enquiry to consider the future of broadcasting in the UK. Sir William Beveridge, architect of the post-war Welfare State, chaired the committee, and in January 1951 it presented its report to Parliament.[35] Although the committee recommended that the BBC's monopoly should continue, it did so with certain reservations concerning the nature of the monopoly and the London-centric approach of the BBC. This was to influence the eventual shape of ITV, which became a series of regionally based companies rather than one central corporation. More importantly, one of the members of the committee, the Conservative MP Selwyn Lloyd, produced a minority report in which he distanced himself from the majority recommendation of the committee that the monopoly should be maintained; instead, he argued for some form of competition for the BBC. It was this report that the newly elected Conservative government seized upon when it came to power at the end of 1951.

The report's main recommendations were to have a long-lasting effect on broadcasting in Wales. The issue of monopoly was one of the main preoccupations of the committee, and it had encountered objections to the monopoly on a number of counts, including the notion of the danger of excessive power in a single organisation and the resentments expressed by organisations in Scotland and Wales, in particular, to 'Londonisation'. Although the committee recommended the continuation of the BBC's monopoly, they did so with what they termed 'safeguards' against the perceived dangers.[36] One of these safeguards was to ensure that three of the BBC's Governors represented Scotland, Wales and Northern Ireland, respectively. The report also recommended that regional commissions be established in Wales, Scotland and Northern Ireland, under the chairmanship of the relevant national Governor, to oversee broadcasting developments in the respective nations and to 'secure their effective autonomy'.[37] Whilst Beveridge did not see these commissions as leading to complete autonomy within (or without) the BBC, it called for what it termed a 'federal delegation of powers', which would include a degree of financial independence.[38] The committee's role in the formation of Wales (West and North) Television is discussed in chapter 5.

1951–1956

In October 1951, the Conservative Party won the general election and within seven months had introduced a White Paper on broadcasting, which not only provided for an element of broadcasting devolution for Wales in the form of the Broadcasting Council for Wales, but also would give the Council oversight of the policy for, and content of, the Welsh Home Service. Its members were drawn from Welsh local authorities, together with representatives from cultural, religious and other bodies. In a radio talk by Lord Macdonald of Gwaenysgor, the Council's chairman, on the Welsh Home Service on 29 December 1952, he referred to the Council's intention to pay 'full regard to the distinctive culture, interests and tastes of the people of Wales'.[39]

Television first came to Wales when the government's Postmaster General (who had overall charge of broadcasting matters), the Earl de la Warr, opened the Wenvoe transmitter near Cardiff on 15 August 1952. As a result of the transmitter's range, once again the BBC in Wales was tied to the west of England. Prior to this date, those with television sets in certain parts of Wales could receive a signal from the BBC's Sutton Coldfield transmitter, which had opened on 17 December 1949. By 1954 over thirty-four hours of television per week were being broadcast in Wales, and by 1959 half the households in Wales possessed television licences.[40] The early 1950s saw the advent of the opt-out system, whereby a region could opt out of the national (British) network and broadcast programmes of a regional interest. However, in broadcasting Welsh-language programmes during this opt-out period, the BBC would have deprived the English-language majority of programmes in English. Consequently, programmes in Welsh were broadcast at off-peak, often very unsociable, hours, such as Sunday lunchtime.

Running parallel to the advent of the BBC's television service was the 'birth' of a rival television service in the UK, Independent Television (ITV). Debates over commercial television began in the immediate post-war period, and the Conservative government's White Paper on television in November 1953 proposed the establishment of a television service funded by advertising revenue.[41]

The reasons behind the setting up, and the eventual shape, of the rival independent commercial television network are complex and have been discussed in detail elsewhere.[42] As has been noted earlier in this chapter, the roots of ITV can be traced back to the Beveridge Committee's report, published in 1951, in particular Selwyn Lloyd's minority report. The report also helped ensure that ITV was based on a federal structure, with semi-autonomous companies operating in each region. In the political arena, the Prime Minister, Winston Churchill, harboured a deep-seated suspicion of the BBC, believing it to be riddled with communists, and relished the opportunity to break the monopoly. Although not backed by the vast majority of his party, pressure was brought to bear upon the leadership by an influential grouping of backbench Conservative MPs. These MPs worked closely with Lord Woolton, the Lord President of the Council, himself an advocate of commercial television, and Mark Chapman-Walker, Woolton's chief publicity officer in Conservative Central Office and a protagonist of change in government thinking on broadcasting.[43] Further factors to consider include societal changes, a shift from paternalism to democratization, and economic patterns of change from a period of austerity to one of increased affluence.[44] The somewhat negative attitude of the BBC towards the development of television (as noted earlier in this chapter) should not be underestimated, particularly in the context of those who saw within the medium a great potential for mass information, entertainment and information. This gave impetus not only to those who left the Corporation, such as Norman Collins, but also to the advertising and business sectors, who could see no way forward in developing a new market through BBC television.

The factors leading to the establishment of ITV and its subsequent shape were therefore complex and interweaving. Suffice to say that two camps emerged during the debate over the introduction of commercial television – those who were in favour of commercial television (whose focus was provided by the Popular TV Association, supporters of which included the Earl of Derby, later to become Chairman of TWW, who argued that an alternative service would provide an additional outlet for creative talent) and those who were against, embodied by the National Television Council.[45] The former had the support of the advertising industry, who were keen to see an alternative outlet for reaching the mass audience, and television-set manufacturers, who had a vested interest in an additional television service. The latter were backed by a substantial part of the British press (due to fears of declining advertising revenue in the face of competition from television) and certain members of the British cultural establishment, who feared for the 'vulgarisation' and 'Americanisation' of television. Lord (John) Reith, in a debate on commercial television in the House of Lords on 22 May 1952, even went so far as to compare the impending arrival of commercial television with the introduction of dog-racing, smallpox, the bubonic plague and the Black Death to the UK.[46]

In essence, there were two main points of debate: firstly, how desirable it was to permit one medium of broadcasting (that is, television) to be dominated by one organisation, namely the BBC; secondly, whether a medium such as television be exploited for commercial purposes. In a letter to the *Times* newspaper on 4 June 1953, several members of the National Television Council stated that their aim was to resist the introduction of commercial television and develop public service broadcasting in the national interest. 'The development of this new medium of information and entertainment', they wrote, 'calls for the exercise of the highest sense of responsibility.'[47] The Labour Party was also a key part of the movement which opposed commercial television, although Des Freedman, amongst others, argues that there was a myriad of positions held within the Party.[48]

What emerged from the period of intense debating in the early 1950s were two government White Papers, in May 1952 and November 1953, and a Television Act which was passed in 1954, breaking the BBC's monopoly and introducing terrestrial competition for the first time.[49] To a large degree, the fears of those who opposed the idea of commercial television were allayed by the eventual shape and form of independent television. The new service was to be regulated by a public authority – the Independent Television Authority – a body which bore the markings of a public service broadcaster. As John Corner comments, this had the effect of 'conferring on the newcomer an immediate aura of responsibility and institutional rectitude'.[50] The overarching framework of the new commercial network, therefore, was a public service one. In addition, the proposed method of advertising ensured that programme 'editorial' and advertisements were separated. The ITV companies would follow a 'spot advertisement' system, whereby adverts would appear at convenient breaks in the programme, as opposed to the American – style sponsored programme. This also placated those opponents of commercial television who feared for the manipulation of programmes by advertisers. The Act required that advertisements be clearly distinguishable from programme content. It also emphasised the public service remit of the new service: 'The amount of time given to advertising in the programme shall not be so great as to detract from the value of the programme as a medium of entertainment, instruction and information.'[51]

ITV went on air for the first time on 22 September 1955 and broadcast to the London area through the recently appointed licence holder for that area, Associated-Rediffusion. The opening night consisted of a grand opening ceremony at the Guildhall in London, with inaugural speeches by, amongst others, the Lord Mayor of London, the chairman of the ITA, Sir Kenneth Clark, and the Postmaster General, Charles Hill. There followed a 'sparkling' variety show, excerpts from three plays, a boxing match, the news and a gala night from the Mayfair Hotel. The night concluded with a preview of programmes to come on ITV over the following months.[52]

The emergence of ITV in Wales

On 9 December 1953, following a question from the Welsh Labour MP Raymond Gower, the Assistant Postmaster General confirmed that none of the initial ITV stations was likely to be in Wales.[53] The first ITV stations were to be established in the populous, metropolitan areas of London, Birmingham and Manchester. Doubts were raised at this early stage about the commercial viability and general desirability of commercial television in Wales. In a House of Commons parliamentary debate on government television policy on 15 December 1953, Ness Edwards, the Labour MP for Caerphilly (south Wales) and former Postmaster General, raised doubts about the general desirability of commercial television: 'Do they [the government] really think that education, religion and subjects of social importance will really be supported by beer, pools and pills?'[54] He then turned his attention to Wales:

> Does the Minister for Welsh Affairs think that there will be a commercial programme in West Wales? Does he think that there will be one in North Wales? ... [A]ll the applications for commercial licences are in the best market areas – London, Manchester and Birmingham . . . This Government of Tory businessmen at least ought to know that advertisers only advertise where it pays to advertise, and it will not pay to advertise in Montgomery or Meirioneth or West Wales or North Wales . . .[55]

The following year, during the debate on the Second Reading of the Television Bill on 25 March 1954, Eirene White, Labour MP for Flint East (north-east Wales), drew the House of Commons's attention to the scale of the objections to commercial television that she had received:

> Since the Government's proposals to have commercial television were first mooted, I have had a larger correspondence from outside my own constituency on this subject than I have had on any other subject since becoming connected with politics. I have had a number of constituency letters on the matter which is natural enough, but I have had from all over North Wales letters from educational bodies, from teachers, from associations such as the Workers' Educational Association, from religious bodies, from cultural bodies, and from Women's Institutes. Every single one without exception has implored me to oppose commercial television.[56]

She went on to state that she had not received any communication in support of commercial television from a Welsh source, and that there was 'a very strong feeling indeed in Wales against this proposal for commercial television'.[57] The reasons given for this were twofold: firstly, that the Welsh people respected the 'cultural standards' established by the BBC, and secondly, that the Welsh-speaking population would not be considered a mass audience by advertisers, and therefore would not be served by commercial interests: 'They feel they would be far better served by seeing the money to be devoted to commercial television interests devoted to the extension of the services of the B.B.C.'.[58]

Further Welsh interventions were made at the committee stage of the Bill's progress through Parliament. On 5 May, Eirene White again stated that she felt that Wales would be getting a less adequate service – a 'raw deal', as she stated – from commercial television under the government's plans to introduce commercial television to Wales (and Scotland) within six months of its introduction to parts of England. She argued that Wales might be better served if the BBC were allowed to improve its service, on the grounds that the population was too thin in Wales to offer an attractive market to commercial broadcasters. At the same time, she echoed many of the submissions to Beveridge in rejecting commercial broadcasting, but demanding, at the same time, an alternative to the BBC. The argument was put forward that Wales should be treated on an equal footing with England. A clear lack of consensus or agreement was apparent.[59]

David Llewellyn, Conservative MP for Cardiff North, mocked the Labour Party for rejecting commercial television, on the one hand, and for arguing that Wales should be treated as any other part of the UK, on the other:

> For a considerable period we have heard from the Opposition of the debasement of cultural standards and the danger to public morals, especially in connection with advertisements for drink, and we have heard that the Welsh language may be drowned in a sea of commercial English ... We have been told that the new Authority [the ITA] is to be regarded as an altar of Mammon, and yet fellow-countrymen of mine and a fellow countrywoman have suggested that the Golden Calf itself must be set up in Wales.[60]

Roderic Bowen, Liberal MP for Cardiganshire, voiced his concerns over the effects of commercial television programmes on the Welsh language: 'I do not believe for a moment that the people who will control commercial television programmes will show much consideration for the Welsh language.'[61] The final Welsh contribution from a Welsh perspective was that of Goronwy Roberts, Labour MP for Caernarfon, who argued that all sections of Welsh life – educational, industrial, religious and social – were against the Television Bill and the proposed introduction of commercial television. In demanding a safeguard against what he called the 'worst excesses of commercial television', Roberts warned that the Bill would 'unleash on our way of life influences against which we shall find very difficult to fight back'.[62]

The parliamentary debate over ITV, from a Welsh perspective, therefore, focused on the idea that damage would be inflicted on the language and culture of Wales by a market-driven service. The arguments, however, appear to have been confined to Parliament, as, during the period 1952–6, there is little evidence (for example, in contemporary newspapers and journals) to suggest that the population at large, together with the main cultural organisations in Wales, were overly concerned with developments. This was to change, however, with the announcement from the Independent Television Authority (ITA) of an ITV licence area for south Wales and the west of England in 1956 (see chapter 3).

ATV/ABC, Granada and Wales

On 17 February 1956, the ITA began transmitting from the Lichfield transmitter in the Midlands. The programme contract for the region was shared between Associated Television (ATV) during weekdays and ABC Television at weekends. Because of the location of the transmitter, homes in east Wales along the English border could receive a signal and were amongst the first Welsh households to see commercial television.

On 3 May 1956, transmissions from Granada Television in Lancashire began via the Winter Hill transmitter (Yorkshire followed on 3 November, when the Emsley Moor transmitter was opened).[63] Bernard Sendall, whose volumes on the history of independent television in Britain provide a full and comprehensive account of the history of the first fifteen years of ITV, has noted that by 1958 the Northern Region extended over Lancashire, Yorkshire and into north Wales – 'it was a heterogeneous region, sometimes called "Granadaland" in an effort to give it a basic sense of identity'.[64] The Granada area covered large parts of the Welsh-speaking north as well as the more Anglicised towns of the north-east of Wales, and this fact was openly recognised and acknowledged by the Manchester-based company.[65] The commercial benefits of providing a Welsh-language programme to attract viewers from an area hitherto without a commercial television operator must have been paramount in the minds of those who launched *Dewch i Mewn* in September 1957. This was certainly the view of Oldfield-Davies at the BBC.[66] However, Graeme McDonald, who was a trainee director with Granada in the early 1960s and who eventually went on to become Controller of BBC2, has referred to *Dewch i Mewn* as 'some sort of sop to Welsh viewers on the Welsh borders of Granadaland'.[67] It is difficult to ascertain the exact motives of Granada in providing a Welsh programme, as Sendall does not refer to the programme in the context of Granada's programme strategy, neither does it feature, beyond a factual reference, in the early Granada annual reports. There are, nevertheless, two possible answers. Firstly, the only programming permitted to be broadcast outside the government-prescribed fifty hours per week of broadcasting was Welsh-language programmes. By transmitting *Dewch i Mewn* two to three times a week, Granada succeeded in increasing its airtime. The company could 'bank' the minutes devoted to advertisements during the transmission of the 'Welsh Programme' – as it was known in Granada – and add them to peak-time viewing, since *Dewch i Mewn* fell outside the standard hours. The commercial benefits for the company were obvious – increased advertising revenue, as a result of extra advertising time during the premium-rate peak hours.[68] The second explanation is also advertising-related. The ITA had allowed television companies to charge more for advertisements within 'foreign-language' programmes. In Sidney Bernstein's eyes, Welsh was a foreign language for a Manchester-based television company, and so it was a shrewd business move as opposed to any cultural sympathy which led to the launch of *Dewch i Mewn*.[69]

The first edition of *Dewch i Mewn* was transmitted on 19 September 1957 at 4.20 p.m. on the Granada Television network via the ITA's Winter Hill transmitter. The total spent on the programme was £768, which was a slight overspend on the set budget of £751, and the programmes for the remainder of 1957 were budgeted at an average cost of £654 per programme.[70] The archival material in the Rhydwen Williams Papers in the National Library of Wales and the Granada Television Archive underlines two things: firstly, the Welsh-speaking audience's interest in, and desire to partake in, Welsh-language television. There are countless letters offering items for the programme, such as a talk on harps and harpists from Mr Joseph Hughes of Ormskirk. Another suggestion came from Valmai Owen of Tregaron, who recommended Islwyn Jones of Tregaron, an expert on nylon who had made 'wool' from monkey nuts during the Second World War!derived[71] Secondly, the topics discussed in the *Dewch i Mewn* programme reflect a high degree of concern for a changing Welsh society. The programme running orders note that there were talks on the role of a national theatre for Wales, the demise of the 'Welsh way of life', and calls for Welsh-medium education.[72]

The programme was produced by Warren Jenkins and later by Rhydwen Williams, who also devised and presented much of the material.[73] It was the first of its kind – a light, mid-afternoon, Welsh-language magazine programme. As one of its early presenters, the actor Meredith Edwards, noted: 'This was the first Welsh programme of its kind and from England!'[74] At the same time, it provided a service to viewers through its Welsh-language news bulletin. *Dewch i Mewn* proved to be very popular with Welsh-speaking viewers in north Wales and was broadcast, not only by Granada, but also eventually by TWW in south Wales, once the company had begun transmissions. A year on from the start of the programme, the *Caernarfon and Denbigh Herald* informed its readers that 'Independent Television is now providing all Wales with a full-length programme every weekday'.[75] A letter in the May 1958 edition of the journal *Y Cloriannydd* also welcomed Granada's Welsh output, stating that, 'Where the prayers of the Welsh have failed, Mr Bernstein has succeeded'.[76]

Conclusion

The idea of a 'battle' or 'struggle' has been central to the history of the broadcast media in Wales since its inception in 1923, when the British Broadcasting Company opened its Cardiff Station. Indeed, David Barlow notes that:

> It is difficult to see how any account of the history and development of the media in Wales can be given without recourse to the idea of a struggle. The veracity of this observation is evident in the widely supported, lengthy and sometimes vitriolic campaigns to establish the BBC radio Welsh region and S4C.[77]

In a BBC radio lecture on 8 November 1972 entitled *Darlledu a'r Genedl* ('Broadcasting and the Nation'), Aneirin Talfan Davies, then the recently retired Head of Programmes at the BBC in Cardiff, argued that the history of broadcasting in Wales had always been a 'battle for the nation's rights'.[78] Fourteen years later, Michelle Ryan asserted that '[t]elevision in Wales has been defined as one of the key areas in the struggle for a national identity'.[79] The Welsh historian John Davies used the phrase 'The Struggle for the Welsh Region' in his history of the BBC in Wales, published in 1994.[80]

There are three major themes relating to the notion of a struggle which surfaced around the structure of early broadcasting and which have been discussed in this chapter: the structure of early broadcasting; the

Welsh language; and nationhood. Firstly, although the initial structure of early radio broadcasting was 'local' and decentralized, by the end of the 1920s, John Reith (Managing Director of the British Broadcasting Company, 1922–6, then Director-General of the British Broadcasting Corporation, 1927–38) implemented a policy of central control of broadcasting in the UK, with the result that the BBC's strategy and outlook were predominantly London-centric. By 1930, local identity had been all but eradicated, and the dominant 'National Programme' and subservient 'Regional Programme' were the two services on offer to the listening public. As Kevin Williams argues, Reith's major contribution to British broadcasting was 'the imposition of a certain set of cultural values on the whole of Britain and the centralisation of these values at the expense of local, regional and national differences'.[81] The promotion of a unified sense of national (that is, British) identity was at the heart of the Reithian endeavour. To many this was an affront to the national character of Wales and, indeed, to the Welsh way of life (a phrase that will appear many times in this book, but which is notoriously difficult to define precisely). 'A radio system was forced upon the nation', argued Talfan Davies, 'with no consideration whatsoever for the differences between two nations.'[82]

In terms of the BBC's structure, Wales formed part of the 'West Region' under the Regional Scheme implemented in 1927, Cardiff being the main production centre of the region. The regions, as Scannell and Cardiff note, were determined primarily by economic and technical factors, as opposed to any real sense of what regionalisation meant to the BBC.[83] Whereas south Wales formed part of the West Region, the north of Wales fell under the auspices of the North Region, whilst mid and west Wales were not affiliated to either.[84] The 'marriage' of Wales (or at least parts of it) to other regions riled those who viewed the BBC's policy decisions as derisive to and contemptuous of the Welsh nation. The 'struggle' over structure surfaced again in 1952 and 1958, when the BBC and ITV (respectively) launched television services for Wales which were part of 'Wales and the West' regions.

Secondly, the Welsh language has been at the heart of the 'struggle' over broadcasting in Wales. Talfan Davies argues that 'the language was the foundation for the battle over Welsh rights in the broadcasting world, because in the end, the language is the foundation of our identity'.[85] This, of course, is a problematic issue in a nation where almost 80 per cent do not speak the language, and, as will be seen later in this book, Welsh broadcasters have been castigated for focusing on Welsh-language programming at the expense of the non-Welsh-speaking majority. Nevertheless, the Welsh language dominated struggles over broadcasting in Wales. The language forms part of the 'Welsh way of life', which was, in the 1920s and 1930s, perceived to be under threat from a tide of Anglicisation emanating from the London-based medium of radio. The BBC was accused in the early days of being ignorant of the needs of the Welsh-speaking audience, and, as a result, a vigorous campaign was mounted in the late 1920s and early 1930s to exert pressure on the Corporation to educate it about the language issue.

Finally, issues of nationhood and national identity help to explain the notion of a struggle. Aled Jones has argued that:

> some of the general assumptions regarding the functions of media in society and political life were also carried over from nineteenth-century newspapers to twentieth-century broadcasting. Among them was the idea that, if employed in the right way, forms of communication could help maintain a sense of nationhood and protect the integrity of the Welsh language.[86]

This argument – which relates to a large degree to ownership of the media – came to the fore at various points during the history of the broadcast media in Wales, in particular during periods when committees were appointed by government to review broadcasting (for example, Beveridge in 1949–51, Pilkington in 1960–2, Crawford in 1974 and Annan in 1974–7). The 'struggle' in broadcasting articulated by various sections of Welsh society reflected a wider struggle for representation and recognition of Wales as a *nation* with *national* rights, as opposed to a *minority* within a *region*.[87] The media, in this respect, could be seen to play a vital role in the creation of what Benedict Anderson calls 'imagined communities', whereby nationality, nation-ness and nationalism are cultural artefacts, and a sense of belonging is manufactured by, inter alia the media.[88] This is an approach adopted by John Davies when he suggested, somewhat provocatively, that Wales could be defined as an 'artefact produced by broadcasting'.[89] In this light, the 'struggle' to ensure a Welsh broadcasting service which was – to use a modern phrase – fit for purpose, can be understood.

3

Television Wales and the West, 1956–1963: Organisation and Control

Introduction

This chapter traces the history of Television Wales and the West (TWW) from its inception and award of licence in 1956 until the end of 1963. In addition to a study of the company's institutional history, the chapter considers the relationship between TWW, the ITA and the government. The period between 1956 and 1963 witnessed the 'rolling out' of the ITV service across the UK as new transmitters were opened and new regions created. It also saw the transformation of the commercial service from one which struggled initially to one which, in Roy Thomson's now infamous phrase, was a 'licence to print money'.[1] Indeed, it was the often excessive profit margins of the ITV companies which led to the government imposing a levy on the pre-tax profits of the companies in 1963, a decision which riled many of them.[2] In Wales, the years between 1956 and 1963 saw TWW establish itself as a credible rival to the BBC's television service, the number of homes in south Wales and the west of England with access to TWW programmes growing from 191,000 in 1958 to 802,000 in 1963.[3] They also witnessed the arrival (and departure) of a new Welsh television station serving the west and north of Wales.[4]

The chapter is divided into two parts. The first is a narrative account of the period leading up to the launch of the TWW service in January 1958, and the second provides an overview of TWW during the period between 1958 and 1963.

1955–1957

At its twenty-eighth meeting, on 5 April 1955, the Independent Television Authority stated its intention to open an ITV station in Wales.[5] Given the available channels allocated to it by the government in Band III, the ITA had made the initial decision to prioritise the location of three high-power transmitters in the populous areas of London, the Midlands and the north of England.[6] Its strategy was to roll out the service to the rest of the UK, with the aim of ensuring that 90 per cent of the population were able to receive the ITV service by 1960.[7] When the time came to establish the region, Wales and the west of England were 'married' once again.[8] The ITA, in creating a new licence area for this part of the UK, was driven by technical and economic considerations. As Sendall notes:

> It was a hybrid area determined in part by what was considered the necessary population coverage to sustain a viable independent company and in part by the ineluctable fact that no transmitter located near the Bristol Channel and, as technical factors dictated, near the Wenvoe transmitter of the BBC, could throw a signal to the north and west of the estuary without also reaching south and east.[9]

At a later date, Charles Hill, former Postmaster General and later Chairman of the ITA, referred to Wales as an 'awkward area' in his memoirs.[10] The reason for this was that TWW had to serve Wales and England in both the Welsh and English languages. Hill recounts how the Welsh Parliamentary Group urged him to establish a purely Welsh company, on the grounds that Wales was a country in its own right. However, several days later, one of the MPs saw Hill privately and told him to ignore what his fellow MPs had said. As Hill wrote:

> Wales needed the English 'rump', for without it and the advertising income derived from it a Welsh company would be too poor to put on an acceptable service. This, indeed, was the snag. The English part of the area supplied the larger share of the income, although its population was but a minority of the population of the whole area. Wales would have to pay for its nationalism and the price would be high.[11]

The nature of the dual region and the problems that stemmed from this coloured much of the wider debate on television in Wales during the 1960s and beyond, and are discussed at the end of chapter 4.[12]

What is interesting to note is that in one of its early meetings the ITA initially planned to establish two stations in Wales – one in the north-west and one in the south of the country, with a separate station for the West Country.[13] The minutes of the Authority following that meeting do not elaborate on the point and, apart from a reference to the broadcasting of Welsh programmes, the issue of the Welsh station was not discussed again until 6 December 1955. At this point, Robert Fraser, the ITA's Director-General, noted that the plans for Wales had fallen behind schedule, due to the trouble in finding a suitable site and the subsequent delay of the Post Office in establishing a link to the station.[14] The developments planned for Scotland and Wales were also slowed down, by restrictions on capital expenditure imposed by the government.[15] In February 1956, the Labour MP for Aberdare, Arthur Probert, wrote to the Postmaster General, Dr Charles Hill, asking where an ITA transmitter for south Wales would be sited. Hill replied, stating that no decision on a site for a transmitter for south Wales and the west of England had yet been reached.[16]

Even before the ITA had advertised for the contract area, there was conjecture as to who would apply, and by April 1956, the London-based press was speculating that three rival groups would be battling for the licence.[17] An advertisement inviting applications for the area was published in the press in July 1956, and by the end of August, fourteen groups had contacted the ITA for application forms, amongst them the Cambrian Broadcasting Service (which included the Welsh poet and writer Keidrych Rhys and John Eilian, editor of the *Caernarfon and Denbigh Herald*), Associated-Rediffusion (who owned the London weekday licence) and a group which had the backing of the *News of the World*.[18]

The Welsh regional press also paid close attention to the competition. The *South Wales Echo and Evening Express*, for example, referred to the 'Welsh TV Stakes' that were becoming more intriguing by the day.[19] The weekly Welsh-language newspaper, *Y Cymro* ('The Welshman') highlighted the fact that Wales would be attached to three English counties under the new ITA region and suggested that the whole commercial enterprise would make for an interesting marriage between culture and industry.[20] Both these points would feature heavily in debates about television in Wales in the years that followed.

The deadline for applications was 14 September, and ten groups applied to provide ITV programming for the region.[21] The Authority had stipulated that the licence-holder would be required to provide not less than 15 per cent of the total programme output, the remaining programming coming from the larger ITV network companies. The other key requirement was that the company must appeal to regional tastes and outlook. The rental for the station would be £185,000 a year, based on a regional population of 2.72 million, plus an additional

£6,000 to cover what the ITA called 'additional costs, not known when the Authority first calculated the rental, of an improvement in the "network"'.[22]

Press speculation about the companies continued after the closing date. The *Western Mail* discussed three groups which, in its opinion, were favourites for the licence. These included the group which eventually became TWW, a group headed by Roy Thomson (the Canadian owner of Scottish Television) and a Wales-based group, led by Sir Godfrey Llewellyn.[23] The main concern for *Y Cymro* was the fact that two of the leading contenders had American involvement (the 'TWW' group and Thomson's group), but in the case of the former, this was tempered somewhat by the presence of Welshmen, such as Sir Ifan ab Owen Edwards and Huw T. Edwards, on the group's board of directors (see below).[24]

The Authority decided to interview three groups: one led by Tom Arnold (which included amongst its directors Lord Aberdare, former Welsh member of the ITA); TWW (which included Lord Derby, Jack Hylton and the American broadcasting network, the National Broadcasting Company); and the group headed by Sir Godfrey Llewellyn. All three were interviewed on 16 October. On 24 October the licence was awarded to TWW, although this was conditional on the withdrawal of the American shareholdings of NBC.[25] The group agreed to the condition and reassured the ITA that alternative sources for the £85,000 capital could be found.[26] Two days later, the news was warmly received by local press on both sides of the Bristol Channel.[27] There were two main reasons for the success of the TWW group, headed by Lord Derby. Firstly, it had the financial backing of the *News of the World*, and secondly, the ITA were impressed with the expert knowledge of the television industry shown in the application. This was due in no small part to the advice given by Herbert Agar of NBC.[28] It also reflected the input of Mark Chapman-Walker, TWW's Managing Director. Chapman-Walker was a member of the management team at the *News of the World* and had been seconded to work on the TWW project. Furthermore, he had previously worked as Director of Publicity at the Conservative Party's Central Office and had been closely involved with – and was indeed a founding member of – the Popular Television Association with Lord Derby, the pressure group which had campaigned for commercial television in the early 1950s.[29]

The directors of the new company included the President of the company, the Earl of Derby, who had been an active member of the pro-commercial television lobby group, the Popular Television Association; Lord Cilcennin, former First Lord of the Admiralty, who became Chairman of the company in March 1957; Herbert Agar, Sir William Carr, Chairman and owner of the *News of the World* newspaper; Alfred Francis, Administrator-General of the Old Vic theatre in London; Sidney Gilliat, the film producer and director; Colonel Harry Llewellyn, the former captain of the British show-jumping team; Sir Grismond Philipps, Chair of the Historic Buildings Council for Wales, who also became Chair of the company's Welsh Committee; Mark Chapman-Walker, Manager of *News of the World*; Sir Alexander Maxwell, a Bristol businessman; and Sir Ifan ab Owen Edwards (founder of the Welsh League of Youth).[30] Other directors who joined the company at a later date included the impresario Jack Hylton and the educationalist and trade unionist Dr Huw T. Edwards.[31] They were, to quote Wyn Roberts, 'a motley band'.[32] The reasons for this were primarily financial. As noted earlier in the chapter, the first year of independent television was a lean one for the original ITV companies. Both Associated-Rediffusion and ABC had made losses, and so there was little hope of securing the £500,000 required to establish a regional commercial television station from within Wales. As Roberts noted in a speech in April 1961, 'It was just before the end of that lean period of investment and no appreciable return that T.W.W. first went on the air and I remember the time when very few people indeed would have invested a penny in I.T.V.'.[33] However, three groups from outside the country were considering applying for the licence: one led by the *News of the World*, one led by Herbert Agar, and another involving Jack Hylton and Lord Derby. As none of the groups was able to raise sufficient investment capital on their own, they eventually merged to form the winning consortium.

Crucially, overall control of the company did not rest in the hands of either Welsh or west of England directors. The vast majority of the financial backing for the company came from outside the region. The main shareholders were Lord Derby and Jack Hylton (25 per cent between them), the *News of the World* (20.5 per cent), Berrows Newspapers of Worcester (4 per cent) and, later, the *Liverpool Daily Post* (14 per cent).[34] Indeed, as a government memorandum noted in January 1959, the south Wales and west station was not Welsh-controlled, not as a result of any failure on the part of the ITA, but because 'no qualified Welsh group sought the contract'.[35]

Nevertheless, the founder members of the group ensured that board members were as representative as possible from the outset. Huw T. Edwards was one such person. He had once signed a letter opposing the introduction of commercial television and was initially approached to join a group which was considering bidding for the Wales and West licence, but declined.[36] It was only after the intervention of Aneurin Bevan, who had dropped his opposition to the idea of commercial television, that Huw T. (as he was more widely known) agreed to join the group.[37] Both Huw T. and Sir Ifan ab Owen Edwards joined for reasons relating to the preservation and maintenance of the Welsh language. As Gwyn Jenkins has stated, '[Huw T. Edwards] and many other Welshmen saw the threat to the Welsh language from the coming of this new, entirely English, medium to the homes of Wales'.[38] In a letter to Lord Derby in September 1956, Edwards gave his reason for joining the board as 'a desire to see that Welsh matters and particularly the Welsh language are given a fair deal by Commercial Television'.[39] Likewise, Sir Ifan was 'interested in Wales, and in the impact independent television must have upon the life and culture of the people of Wales'.[40] The addition of Sir Ifan ab Owen Edwards and Huw T. Edwards gave the board (and commercial television in general) a degree of respectability within Welsh-speaking Wales. As one writer in *Y Cymro* admitted, 'my first reaction upon first hearing of the intention to mix culture and soap [opera] was that it would do no good for Welsh life'. However, upon hearing that Huw T. Edwards and Sir Ifan ab Owen Edwards were members of the company, he was somewhat relieved.[41]

The Welsh Committee of Directors of TWW met for the first time at the Royal Hotel in Cardiff on 29 November 1956. Sir Grismond Philipps, Lord-Lieutenant of Carmarthenshire, took the chair, and other members, in addition to Sir Ifan ab Owen Edwards and Huw T. Edwards, were D. V. P. Lewis from Brecon (who was later to become Minister of State for Welsh Affairs in Harold Macmillan's government), Percy Jones (a Newport councillor and businessman) and Colonel Harry Llewellyn. The first meeting highlighted two things: firstly, the fact that the Committee aimed to be more than just a 'cultural committee'. It had been charged with overseeing all Welsh aspects of the company's operation (although, as will be seen later, it tended to focus on Welsh *language* matters alone). Secondly, the importance of the company's associations with the United States was emphasised. The relationship with the US had been cemented through the services of Bob Myers, one of NBC's senior representatives, who was seconded to TWW in an advisory capacity. His extensive experience in the field of television operations was invaluable to TWW.[42] It is clear that Chapman-Walker, in particular, was drawing on the American experience in the field of commercial television, not only in terms of operations, but also in the context of training new staff in the latest production techniques.[43]

Pre-transmission matters

TWW had been awarded the licence on 24 October 1956, but between then and 14 January 1958, when the first programmes were transmitted from St Hilary, there were several matters, some of an urgent nature, which demanded the company's attention. The first of these was the company's title. The Television Programme Contractors' Association had contacted the Authority in October 1956 to draw attention to the anomaly in this – Television *Wales* and the West – since the area served was, in fact, *south* Wales and the west of England. The letter also pointed out that north Wales was already covered by Granada Television.[44] The ITA's response to the letter suggests that the Authority had not been clear enough in its thinking about the overlap areas. There is also a suggestion that planning in the early years was driven by technical considerations. For example, in considering the contractors' letter, Robert Fraser, in an internal memorandum, noted that:

> '[A]part from the North Wales complication, there is West Wales. There is an established West Wales television region with Aberystwyth as its centre. We shall be opening a station there, *I suppose*. Alternatively, we may cover all West Wales from two stations, one in Pembroke and one in Anglesey.[45]

This also indicates that in 1956 the ITA was considering establishing a west Wales station when permitted by the Post Office and when the transmitters allowed. The point was confirmed when, on 5 November 1956, Sendall wrote to Mark Chapman-Walker requesting him to refer to the TWW region as 'South Wales and the West' in its literature and promotional material (and not 'Wales and the West'), as Granada was already reaching 200,000 people in north Wales and 'because eventually there will be a station covering West Wales'.[46] Chapman-Walker reassured Sendall that TWW would now emphasise that its remit covered south Wales and the west of England alone.[47] However, in May 1957, Howard Thomas, the Managing Director of ABC Television, wrote to the ITA complaining that TWW's press announcements constantly referred to 'Wales and the West'. Thomas was at pains to emphasise that parts of north Wales were within reach of the ITA's transmitter at Winter Hill and out of reach of St Hilary. Despite the protestations, 'Television Wales and the West' passed into common currency.[48]

The second issue which required resolving prior to transmission was that relating to programme-sharing. As has been noted, TWW was expected to provide no less than 15 per cent (seven and a half hours per week) of its total programme output, the remainder coming from other network companies. Although negotiations began with Associated-Rediffusion in London, they were soon abandoned, as the terms offered by that company were in breach of the Television Act.[49] By March 1957, Chapman-Walker was in negotiation with Granada Television, with a view to offering a wholesale price to account for 70 per cent of the TWW output, with an option to purchase a further 15 per cent and a right to reject programmes deemed to be unsuitable for the regional audience. This, argued Chapman-Walker, would prevent Cardiff from becoming what he called a 'tap outlet' for other stations, such as Scottish Television had become for the London ITV stations.[50] The deal with Granada was, however, not without controversy. On 24 May, Granada announced that it had, in effect taken TWW under its wing and that TWW was heavily dependent on Granada for its advertising operation. This led to a swift rebuke from the ITA, in the form of a letter to Chapman-Walker on 28 May. 'It is not suitable', wrote Robert Fraser, the Director-General, 'that one programme company should be ensuring the effectiveness of advertising in the programmes of another programme company.'[51] In reply, Chapman-Walker assured Fraser that Granada would operate only as an agency, and that the TWW sales and advertising operations were completely autonomous.[52] As will be seen, the relationship between TWW and Granada would develop on a different level in the future, through the sharing of Welsh-language programmes.

The third issue requiring resolution before broadcasting began related to Welsh language programming. There was no stipulation in the 1954

Television Act or in the contract for TWW that there should be any Welsh-language programming. There was, however, in Section 3(1)(e) of the Act, a provision that programme contractors should offer a suitable amount of programming designed to appeal specifically to those people served by the station.[53] The first reference to the Welsh language in the ITA minutes was on 6 November 1956, and the issue remained high on the agendas of both the ITA and the Welsh Committee of TWW. Jenkin Alban Davies, a London businessman (originally from Cardiganshire), was the Welsh member on the ITA, having replaced Lord Aberdare in early 1956.[54] Davies suggested to the Authority that attempts should be made to ascertain whether or not TWW was willing to accept a contractual provision that, as far as was economically possible, a certain amount of programming would be in Welsh.[55] The company agreed, but it was not until 30 July 1957, however, that the ITA formally notified TWW of the requirement to transmit at least one hour per week of Welsh-language programmes.[56] These programmes would not have to be shown within the government-prescribed limit of fifty hours per week, and could therefore be shown during the 'closed' time between 6.15 p.m. and 7.30 p.m. on Sundays. Chapman-Walker had, in the meantime, applied for financial assistance towards the costs of these programmes. The request was rejected by the authority, on the grounds that if the programmes were attractive to non-Welsh viewers, TWW would be getting additional time (and, presumably, advertising revenue) not available to other ITV contractors.[57] Despite the lack of additional financial support at the outset, in the years that followed TWW was to produce innovative and pioneering Welsh-language programming (see below and chapter 4).

The fourth matter related to the location of the TWW television studios. In January 1957, the company was considering converting a skating rink in Cardiff into the two studios that would be needed to produce the required 15 per cent of original programming. Another possible site was Cefn Coed House in Cyncoed, Cardiff.[58] However, the local council refused permission for the Cyncoed site, and the skating rink location disappeared from the agenda altogether. The company focused its attention on land adjacent to a farmhouse in Pontcanna in the centre of Cardiff, and in a letter to Huw T. Edwards on 19 February, Chapman-Walker asked him to concentrate his efforts (and influence, presumably) on ensuring that the Pontcanna application did not get referred to the

Minister for Housing and Local Government for approval, as this would result in further delays at a time when the start date of 25 November was fast approaching.[59] Much to everyone's relief, the application did not need to go to the Minister.[60]

Although planning permission for the Pontcanna studios was not delayed, the final issue – a long delay in the opening of the transmitter mast – caused major problems for TWW. The process of selecting a site for the region's transmitter began in July 1955 and several sites on both sides of the Bristol Channel were considered. The best site in terms of population coverage was St Hilary, on the outskirts of Cardiff, and the ITA gained the necessary permission to commence erecting the mast.[61] However, in December 1956, the Minister for Housing and Local Government halted construction, following objections to the 750-foot mast from Cambrian Airlines and Aer Lingus, two of the companies operating out of nearby Rhoose Airport. At its meeting on 13 February 1957, the Welsh Committee of TWW noted its concerns at the delay. The main worry was that if the mast could not be sited at St Hilary, then a site in Somerset would have to be considered. A transmitter located in south Wales was, in the Committee's opinion, of paramount importance in order for ITV to succeed in the area. So passionate were the members' feelings that Sir Ifan ab Owen Edwards threatened to resign if Wales was not given the transmitter it had been promised. In addition to the delay in getting programmes on air, the Committee stated that further delays would result in the company missing out on a peak period for advertising (Christmas). The Committee concluded its discussion on the matter by underlining that the ITA was responsible for the mast, and not TWW. It was further decided to issue a statement to the press to this effect.[62]

A public enquiry was held to investigate the siting of the mast, on 7 March 1957. A fortnight later, the Minister rejected the claims made by the airlines that the location of the mast was dangerous in terms of navigation and aviation. Although the ITA and TWW agreed (albeit reluctantly on the part of the latter) to a new start date of 17 December, tensions between the Authority and the contractor remained. There was a possibility that TWW would have to go on air with a weaker signal than had previously been envisaged, as a result of the transmitter not being up to full capacity. This would, inevitably, cause reception problems in the hills and various 'black spots' of south Wales, and the company was concerned that if the picture was not good from the outset, then it would be extremely difficult to redeem its position at a later date.[63]

Late October brought more bad news for TWW. A technical problem with the transmitter's aerial meant that the start date had to be moved from 17 December to mid January 1958. Lord Derby, who was unveiling a plaque at the Pontcanna studios, described being 'badly let down' by the ITA.[64] The delays would result in a projected loss for TWW of approximately £50,000 in revenue and artists' salaries.[65] Such was the anger in TWW that a claim was made for compensation from the ITA, but the Authority did not admit liability.[66]

The events noted above did not make for the most auspicious start for TWW in its relationship with the ITA. Wyn Roberts, in his memoirs, talks of a need to 'improve our standing with the Independent Television Authority', and Bernard Sendall, in an internal ITA memorandum in October 1958, referred to 'making a fresh start with T.W.W.'.[67] The evidence suggests that after a shaky start, TWW *did* manage to improve its standing in the eyes of the ITA, although the relationship could often be strained (see chapter 4).

Meanwhile, the BBC was becoming increasingly aware of the likely competition from ITV in Wales. Realising the potential threat posed by commercial television, the BBC's Alun Oldfield Davies (Controller Wales) wrote to the Director of Television Broadcasting, Gerald Beadle, on 4 October 1957, asking for a revenue increase of £30,605 to meet the competition in Welsh-language programmes from Granada and from the likely offerings from TWW. '[T]he two hours a week in Welsh televised by Granada from September 19', wrote Davies, 'have added point and force to the complaints that too little in Welsh was being done by the BBC.'[68] He also feared that the situation would get worse when TWW began to broadcast from the studios in Pontcanna. In reply, Beadle suggested the consideration of a form of cooperation between the Corporation and commercial television, an issue that was to arise several times in the late 1950s and early 1960s. There was also a suggestion by the BBC's television directorate in London that the BBC, TWW and Granada might discuss the possibility of sharing programmes.[69] This was subsequently ruled out by Robert Fraser, the ITA's Director-General, and later, in 1962, by the BBC.[70]

At a lunch to mark the launch of TWW on 30 October 1957, Thomas Mervyn Jones, Chairman of the Wales Gas Board, proposed a toast to the company:

May T.W.W. be profitable, very profitable, there's nothing to be ashamed of in that. But to be profitable, does not prevent her being purposeful, and pleasurable . . . Purpose, pleasure, profit, and in that order, are not conflicting but complementary aims of this or any other I.T.V. company.

He then went on to talk about the dual nature of the region:

Her career she must pursue in Wales (South) and in England (West). As a wise young lady she will already have recognised that they are, in some senses, two countries . . . Of course our countries are linked indissolubly . . . King Arthur successfully united Wales and the west of England. Saint Mark, as your Managing Director, now has the same job.[71]

In a light-hearted speech, Jones succeeded in laying out some of the key issues that would dominate TWW for the next decade, namely the tensions between the public service aspect of television and the profit motive, and the tensions that would emerge between Wales and the west of England.

1958–1959

By the time TWW was ready to go on air for the first time, there was a good deal of anticipation amongst the prospective audience. The *Liverpool Daily Post*, for example, reported that television dealers in parts of south Wales were having difficulty coping with the demand for additional aerials in preparation for the new service.[72] The area covered by the St Hilary signal included the major centres of Swansea, Cardiff, Newport, Bristol, Weston-super-Mare and Bridgwater. Towns and villages in the 'secondary area' (where a satisfactory signal could be received) included Merthyr Tydfil to the north, and Bath, Taunton and Tiverton to the south. Places further afield, such as Monmouth to the east, Carmarthen to the west and Yeovil to the south, would get a reasonable signal.[73]

After a number of setbacks and delays, TWW finally broadcast for the first time on 14 January 1958. As the 1958 edition of the *Television Annual* noted: 'Independent television . . . grows like a lusty adolescent, rapidly increasing its frame. The network is now spreading to . . . South Wales and the South-West. Its "flesh", the audience within reach of the network, waxes fatter each month.'[74] The opening evening began with the aptly named *Production One*, a fifteen-minute programme in which Mark Chapman-Walker, the Managing Director, and Bryan Michie, the

Programme Manager, introduced the station and forthcoming programmes. The next hour and a half were filled with ITV network programmes (*Jolly Good Time* with Jimmy Hanley, *The Buccaneers* and a Granada production, *Youth Wants to Know*). After the Independent Television News at 6.30 p.m. (delivered by Llanelli-born ITN newscaster, Huw Thomas from the Pontcanna studios), Lord Derby, Sir Ifan ab Owen Edwards and Alfred Francis gave introductory speeches. Sir Ifan's speech was in Welsh. This was followed by Jack Hylton talking to Shirley Bassey and the opening-night show, *The Stars Rise in the West*. This was hosted by Jack Train and included Stanley Baker, Petula Clark, Tommy Cooper, Donald Houston, Tessie O'Shea, Ralph Reader, Sir Ralph Richardson, Harry Secombe, Donald Sinden and Naughton Wayne – all of whom had associations with Wales or the west of England. A special edition, especially for TWW viewers, of ATV's *Emergency – Ward 10* followed, and at 8 p.m. 'TWW's own exciting quiz-show', The *£1,000 Word!*, was broadcast. The remainder of the evening consisted of sport, variety and news. After the news, Robert Sarnoff, President of the US broadcasting network NBC, broadcast a special message to TWW, highlighting the good relationship between the two companies. The evening ended with a Jack Hylton production of *Love and Kisses*, starring Arthur Askey.

Surprisingly, very little was said about the opening night at the meeting of the Welsh Committee of TWW on 10 February 1958. The reaction in the press was generally good, but somewhat muted. The *Daily Herald's* headline stated that TWW was 'good in parts', noting at the same time that in some areas the picture could hardly be seen because of poor reception.[75] The *Western Mail* described ITV as 'livelier, more in tune with the times, and particularly with the demands of the young viewer, and excelling in light entertainment'. The editorial finished by saying that 'in Wales, particularly, anything which can broaden the outlook and experience of the community can only be welcomed'.[76] The *Western Daily Press* quoted Roy Ward Dickson, host of *The £1,000 Word!*, who said that TWW acted like an electronic bridge between Wales and the West.[77] The South Wales Echo felt somewhat let down by the lack of pomp, and highlighted the commercials which peppered the evening's viewing (much to the annoyance of the writer): 'Two bottles of stout sang an operatic duet, a pack of chimpanzees advertised tea, a contented looking gentleman spoke up in Welsh for a brand of headache tablets. All clever. But too much of it.'[78] An editorial in *Y Cymro* stated that the coming of ITV would mean competition for the BBC and a resulting improvement in the fare on offer. The editorial also touched on another issue, that of the timing of programmes. It was hoped that Welsh programmes would be transmitted during the evenings, in addition to the afternoons, so that the working audience could have access to the programmes.[79] In the February 1958 edition of the Plaid Cymru official newspaper, *Y Ddraig Goch*, the 'Cribinion' column thanked ITV for commercial television (in particular TWW), noting that the BBC had done little for Wales and the Welsh language and that now attention was being paid to the needs of Wales. 'We have the ITV programmes for free', the columnist noted, 'but have to pay £3 per annum for the rationed BBC programmes.'[80]

After the excitement of the launch and first night, the company set about establishing itself firmly within the area. In technical terms, it had an excellent starting-point. It had the biggest and most modern television studios in Britain and had spent a considerable amount on equipment – the four cameras in one studio alone cost £5,000 each. Yet, regardless of the high specification of the equipment, TWW found itself facing reception problems from the outset. The complaints about reception difficulties on the opening night did not abate, and the nature of the terrain within the TWW area exacerbated the problem. The ITA explained the difficulties in terms of the fact that signals in Band III (as used by the ITA) were more easily deflected than those in Band I (used by the BBC).[81] On 14 February, TWW announced on the front page of *Television Weekly* that it would be meeting with the ITA and television-set dealers in south Wales to discuss the issue.[82] The situation was no better on the other side of the Bristol Channel. In early March 1958, fifty television-set dealers in the Bristol area grouped together to form a protest group about reception issues. The situation also prompted the Lord Mayor of Bristol to comment that placing the transmitter in Wales, rather than in the west of England, had been a mistake.[83]

Despite these problems, TWW made good headway in grounding itself within its territory within the first few years of operation. Even prior to launching, local advertising revenue in December 1957 stood at £38,828, with a further £42,000 being negotiated, and during the first fortnight of transmission, a total of 1,513 advertisements were broadcast.[84] However, by May, it was reported that income from advertisements in the west of England was low, due to a perception of TWW as being 'Welsh'. The company had made a concerted effort from the start to promote itself to both English and Welsh audiences. It had placed a supplement to the *Bristol Evening Post* in June 1957 which stressed the equality of Wales and the West: 'Although the station is sited near Cardiff . . . there will be no greater emphasis on South Wales than on the West of England. The intention is to present balanced programmes of interest both sides of the Bristol Channel.'[85]

By June 1958, TWW was confident enough to indicate to the ITA that its ultimate aim was to offer an ITV service for the whole of Wales. Given that Granada operated in much of north Wales, it conceded, however, that an all-Wales plan might not be possible. The company therefore requested to be given either a separate channel in Band III, to provide a Welsh service separate from the English service, or a satellite station in Aberystwyth, to serve mid Wales. The satellite station would be built by either TWW or the ITA, should the ITA wish to give the company the capital to do so.[86] The ITA responded by pointing out that current capital expenditure restrictions imposed by the government prohibited any expansion to Aberystwyth, and that the Authority did not wish to commit itself, one way or the other, to a west Wales contract area.[87] Nevertheless, TWW staked its claim to a separate channel within Band III again in July, in order to provide an all-Wales service. From this point onwards a wider campaign for the establishment of a television service for Wales gathered momentum, and involved a wide range of cultural bodies and organisations. The campaign is discussed in detail in chapter 5 as it forms an important context for the emergence of Wales (West and North) Television Ltd. A further sign of TWW's confidence came in September 1958, with the announcement that it would be opening new studios within eighteen months in Bristol. The main purpose, according to Mark Chapman-Walker, was to affirm that the company was associated with Wales and the West in equal measure.[88]

The year 1959 continued to be a successful one for TWW. By the beginning of the year, 445,000 homes were tuning in to the ITV station, and a company press statement issued by the Welsh Committee argued that there was 'no evidence to substantiate the fears of those who were reluctant to see Independent Television come to Wales'.[89] The Welsh Committee also continued their call to expand coverage to other parts of Wales, a call that saw them write to the ITA in February 1959. The members of the committee estimated that 500,000 people were currently out of reach of independent television, 180,000 of whom were Welsh speakers. The solution proffered was to build satellite stations, which would be linked with the TWW operation at Pontcanna.[90] There is no evidence of the ITA's reply, but given the Authority's response to the letter in July 1958, it is reasonable to infer that it would be on the same lines as previous replies to Chapman-Walker. Meanwhile, TWW was steadily gaining financial strength. Thus, by June 1959 it was in a position to plan extension work to the Pontcanna studios, designed to allow for a likely increase in originated hours in the future. Local advertising sales revenue for the first quarter of 1959 saw £24,481 from south Wales out of a total of £35,603, with an increase in short seven-second spots for local advertisers.[91] By this time, TWW had its own facilities for producing commercials and in June 1959 the company produced a two-minute commercial 'selling' Wales, which was shown at peak time in ITV regions in London, the north of England and the Midlands.[92] By August, TWW's audience had grown by 160 per cent, to over half a million homes, signalling the most rapid growth of audience in any ITV area. As ownership of television sets was higher in the region than the national average, the attraction for advertisers was obvious.[93] September 1959 saw TWW become a pioneer, or 'make television history', as the *Bristol Evening World* put it. On 16 September, TWW became the first ITV company to broadcast news from its two studios in the same programme. Not only did this create television history, but it formed part of TWW's offensive to appease viewers in the west of England. As the paper's reporter stated: 'Last night's programme made it quite clear that the West Country is going to get its fair crack at the whip. Those people who claim that TWW screens too much Welsh content will soon be eating their words.'[94] The timing of the newspaper article was helpful for the company, for only the previous month, the new Managing Director, Alfred Francis, had written in the *Bath Chronicle* that one downside of TWW's success at Cardiff was the assumption that the company and its policies were predominantly Welsh.[95] By the end of 1959, TWW had established itself as a confident, self-assured and financially successful company. It was not without its concerns (for example, the transmitter at St Hilary had been operating at a lower level and had been more problematic than other ITA transmitters)[96] but the general picture was good. The *Financial Times* reported that shareholders had received large returns on their investments: 480,000 non-voting shares, which had been sold at 5s. each when the company was established, were now selling at 35s. each. In short, the paper concluded, TWW was a 'money-spinner'.[97]

1960–1963

The success story continued in 1960. As TWW's pre-tax profits rose to over £1 million, the company had to decide on the best way forward in terms of advertising. On 14 March, the Welsh Committee agreed that steps to promote local advertising would be beneficial to the company, not only in terms of revenue, but with a view to negotiations in 1963 for the renewal of the licence.[98] However, there appeared to be a shift of opinion at the meeting of 17 May, when it was noted that national sales were increasing to a very healthy level, so much so that the company had to decide whether or not the time devoted to local advertising should be reduced in favour of the more profitable national advertising.[99] As this was a matter for the whole company, the Welsh Committee spent no more time on the matter.

On 13 July 1960, the Conservative government announced its decision in Parliament to establish a Committee of Inquiry into broadcasting in the UK.[100] The committee was to be chaired by Sir Harry Pilkington, an industrialist and former president of the Federation of British Industries. The committee's terms of reference, as set out by the Postmaster General, Reginald Bevins, were:

> to consider the future of the broadcasting services in the United Kingdom, the dissemination by wire of broadcasting and other programmes, and the possibility of television for public showing; to advise on the services which should in future be provided in the United Kingdom by the BBC and the ITA; to recommend whether additional services should be provided by any other organisation; and to propose what financial and other conditions should apply to the conduct of all these services.[101]

There were several reasons for the establishment of the committee at this point. Jean Seaton locates the origins of the Pilkington Committee and its report in the context of post-war affluence and changes in the nature of what was becoming a mass television audience. She also highlights the moral debates of the time, which 'demonised' television as a destructive force.[102] Jeffrey Milland notes more reasons: the BBC's Charter expired in

June 1962 and the 1954 Television Act, which had created ITV, was to expire in July 1964. Both issues necessitated a review. In addition, it had become apparent from 1958 onwards that new frequencies would become available, and different interested parties – the BBC, the ITA and the advertisers – were also beginning to make demands on the government. Two further, more 'negative', issues which triggered a review of broadcasting were the concern over the large profit margins of many of the ITV companies and the general concern over the influence of television on the viewing public.[103] In September 1960, the Postmaster General announced the membership of the committee, which included Richard Hoggart, Professor of English at Birmingham University, the actress and broadcaster Joyce Grenfell and Elwyn Davies, Secretary to the University of Wales Council and Treasurer of the National Library of Wales.

TWW submitted a memorandum in November 1960 and made it clear that 'the problem created by its two-fold territory [was] not a handicap but a stimulus'.[104] The commitment of the company to the dual region was emphasised by a list of donations (totalling over £14,000) made by TWW to the arts and sciences in the region. As might be expected from a company whose licence was due for renewal in 1964, TWW made proud claims about its success in integrating Wales and the west of England. The tone of TWW's submission was self-congratulatory and reads almost like a submission for a renewal of the licence. There is no doubt that the company recognised the importance of the status of Pilkington and its place in the future formation of broadcasting policy. In a somewhat different mode from the other Welsh submissions, TWW took a line which, when read in a certain way, had the tone of a company attempting to convince itself of its own strengths:

> South Wales and the Bristol areas supplement each other in a unique way. TWW believes that it is helping to forge a cultural bond between two peoples possessing many affinities, and who are destined to progress together in the industrial centres either side of the Severn estuary. We know that we have only begun to develop this splendid opportunity.[105]

Nevertheless, TWW drew the committee's attention to the fact that it had 'no empire-building ambitions and had no desire to expand its territory merely for the sake of expansion and possible further profit'.[106] However, it clearly stated that should the ITA call upon the company to extend its remit in Wales, it would gladly do so. Some degree of empire-building was, after all, on the minds of the Welsh directors, at least. The written memorandum ended with a carefully worded statement on the future possibility of the creation of an all-Wales ITV company:

> TWW ... is very conscious of its present responsibilities, especially to its Welsh-speaking minority, and finds ample satisfaction in the duty and privilege of serving its existing territory. If, however, it was called upon to undertake any extensions of that territory in the future it would assume this task in the same spirit with which it has approached the present venture.[107]

The Independent Television Authority's memorandum on 'Independent Television in Wales', which was submitted in April 1961, gave a factual account of the development of ITV in the country. In slight contrast to TWW's statement, it stated that the ITA policy of programme companies identifying themselves fully with the life of the regions might have been compromised or 'complicated' (as the submission notes), because of 'its having to serve an English-speaking region' in addition to the bilingual population of south Wales.[108]

In May, TWW was given the opportunity to present oral evidence before the committee. Lord Derby, Grismond Philipps, Alfred Francis and Arnold Goodman, the company's solicitor, represented the company. Asked to comment on what the committee called the 'present agitation' in Wales and the argument that Wales should be served primarily by Welsh-language and Welsh-interest programmes only, Philipps replied: 'I think academic people always speak for Wales and they do not really represent the great Welsh people who are just as interested in sport and musicals and that sort of thing, as the mass of people in any part of the country.'[109] This was, in fact, borne out by the ratings (see chapter 4).

The Pilkington Committee's report was published in June 1962. According to Jean Seaton, '[t]he committee had been asked to review the development of television. In fact they did much more, producing a report which judged the nation's culture.'[110] The report effectively castigated independent television for trivialising television's output.[111] It also underlined what it saw to be ITV's 'organic weakness': the fact that it had a dual purpose. On the one hand, it was to provide a public service, and on the other, it was required to provide a service to advertisers. According to the report, the two did not coincide.[112] The Pilkington Committee's report contained a number of key recommendations relating to Wales, primarily, though not exclusively, relating to the BBC. With regard to commercial television in Wales, the committee suggested that the ITA establish an Advisory Committee for Wales to advise the companies in the franchise area. This was not, according to the committee's recommendations, a statutory requirement, though the ITA were urged to 'continue to see the need' for such committees in Scotland and Ireland, as well as in Wales.[113] In fact, this recommendation, together with the extension of the ITV service to cover almost the whole of Wales and the appointment of a second ITV company in Wales (WWN), prompted the ITA to act. On 1 February 1963, the Committee for Wales met for the first time under the chairmanship of Jenkin Alban Davies, the member of the ITA with special responsibility for Wales. Other members of the committee included Norah Isaac (headmistress of the first Welsh-medium primary school in Wales, which had been established at Aberystwyth), Revd D. R. Thomas and the children's author, Enid Watkin Jones.[114] At the outset, the Chairman noted the ITA's 'sympathy with the cultural aspirations of Scotland, Ulster and Wales', and he noted that the ultimate aim was to establish an all-Wales ITV television service.[115]

There is little evidence that the Welsh Committee of TWW discussed Pilkington's recommendations in great detail. The first reference appears in the minutes of the meeting held in Cardiff on 18 April 1962, when a paper by Sir Ifan ab Owen Edwards was circulated amongst members. It noted that whilst the BBC had created one broadcasting unit in sound, the ITA had divided Wales into four areas, each covered by a different company: TWW, Granada, Westward and now WWN.[116] Edward's warning to the committee was that the BBC was now in a position to become the dominant television authority from Holyhead to Land's End.[117] However, in the light of Pilkington's recommendations, Edwards also noted that the company could face the future with hope founded on experience, the prestige of its Welsh-language programmes, the company's financial reserves and the densely populated dual region.

One of the main concerns of TWW's Welsh Committee during the latter part of 1960 and in early 1961 was the emergence of the Wales Television Association, the group that would eventually become Wales (West and North) Television.[118] In a special meeting, held at Sir Ifan ab Owen Edwards's home in Aberystwyth on 29 August 1960, the Welsh Committee discussed its involvement in the area. Members were circulated with a copy of a paper written by Sir Ifan which highlighted four 'trump cards' which TWW held, and which might be played should the company wish to apply for the licence: Cardiff studios; a land-link with London; half of the Welsh-speaking population being already in the TWW area; and the high esteem in which TWW was held by the ITA and the people of Wales.[119] Rather caustically, Sir Ifan also described the new region as 'a sparsely populated seabound mountainous land', noting that 'if fish and sheep were televiewers, it would be a television operator's dream'. He went on to say:

> I cannot see that it is at all feasible as a Commercial Venture. This view is supported by the fact that the only serious Welsh Company which has yet seemed to be taking any shape is one based upon patriotism and not business – it is non-profit-making and charitable in character.[120]

Nevertheless, despite the dismissal of the emerging company as ideologically driven and lacking in financial nous, by the beginning of 1961, the Welsh Committee was concerned that TWW staff might wish to join the new company. In September that year, one of the company's senior officers, Nathan Hughes, left his post as Chief Engineer to work as General Manager for the Wales Television Association.[121] On 21 April, Lord Derby wrote to Sir Ivone Kirkpatrick informing him that TWW would not be applying for the west Wales contract, in view of the fact that three all-Welsh groups were considering applying. The letter went on to reiterate the point made in the written submission to Pilkington, that TWW, however, would be willing to 'step into the breach' should the need arise.[122] The contract for the west Wales area was awarded to the Wales Television Association on 6 June 1961, and at its meeting on 12 June, TWW's Welsh Committee considered the implications of the decision. Sir Ifan ab Owen Edwards wanted as much of the operation to be 'in TWW's hands', whilst others noted that the BBC would now undoubtedly seek to extend its Welsh programme production as a result of the new ITV company. It was made clear at the meeting that TWW would have to 'keep up'.[123] The Welsh Television Association (or Wales Television, as it was becoming known) continued to take shape over the summer of 1961. At the same time, tensions between the two companies were apparent. The Chairman of Wales Television, Dr Haydn Williams, had stated that he wished the ITA to locate a transmitter within TWW territory. This clearly annoyed Sir Ifan ab Owen Edwards, who wrote to Huw T. Edwards on

10 August urging him to talk with Haydn Williams and ask him to withdraw the transmitter idea. Only then, he asserted, could the two companies move forward in a spirit of harmony and cooperation.[124]

Harmony and cooperation were not words which could be used to describe the relationship between TWW and Westward Television. Although the latter did not begin broadcasting in the south-west of England until 29 April 1961, the first three months of 1961 were spent in a vigorous publicity campaign, and this highlighted what Sendall has called 'a dormant problem which was to prove a continuing source of irritation and concern', namely the overlap between the area served by TWW and that served by Westward.[125] Derby had mounted a campaign to attract the 190,000 overlap population to TWW, much to the annoyance of Peter Cadbury, Chairman of Westward. He declared that TWW was a Welsh company without any claim to viewers in the Bristol area, and so he embarked on a campaign to attract Bristol viewers to Westward. Following the threat of legal action by TWW, the ITA intervened and relative calm was restored, but not before Cadbury had written to Fraser suggesting that the west Wales contract be offered to TWW, as he had 'received so many letters from people in Bristol pointing out that Bristol and Wales are uncomplementary and such a solution might resolve all our difficulties in the West'. The letter ended with a strong suggestion that Westward might then take over the whole of the west of England.[126] In November, the issue surfaced again briefly when the Welsh Committee of TWW noted that the strength of Westward's signal from the transmitter at Stockland Hill was such that it reached Abergavenny in south-east Wales. However, no further action was taken.[127] The year ended well for the company in financial terms. Profits before tax in 1961 were £1,277,648, which prompted Alfred Francis to comment (rather defensively) that TWW liked to think of itself as a television company which made profits, and not as a profit-making company that made television.[128]

The end of 1961 was dominated by the new company for west and north Wales, Wales Television. The emergence of another ITV company in Wales, supported as it was by some of the most eminent Welsh men and women (see chapter 5), caused consternation amongst some staff at TWW. Writing to Huw T. Edwards in October 1961, Wyn Roberts voiced his concern that the Welsh leadership of the TWW was in danger of fading away. Although not made explicit in the letter, the company's chairman, the Welshman Lord Cilcennin, had died the previous year and his place had been taken by Lord Derby, TWW President, on a temporary basis.[129] Roberts wanted to see TWW develop a Welsh policy with teeth, led by someone who would speak for TWW in Wales.[130] In a later letter to Edwards, Roberts noted his worries about the critical and unimaginative spirit which he thought now pervaded the Welsh service, and he berated the company's focus on profit. He called again for a real policy on Welsh programmes, stating that although the company had once had one, it had been pushed to one side in order to please the ITA and Pilkington.[131] Clearly, Roberts had one eye on the emergent new company at this stage.

There were concerns about two main issues at the beginning of 1962: firstly, the claims that were being made by Wales Television over TWW's vulnerability in fringe or overlap areas which were refuted by TWW (in fact, as will be shown later, where the population and relay companies had a choice, they would often either stay with, or revert to, TWW).[132] The second issue was that of Wales Television's title. The Welsh Committee objected to the implication that the company served the whole of Wales and made it clear, in a meeting on 6 February, that it would raise its objections with the ITA.[133] By April, TWW was discussing terms for cooperating with WWN. The Welsh Committee felt it was in rather an invidious position, in the sense that if it didn't cooperate, it could contribute to the failure of the company, 'forfeit popularity in Wales' and lose favour with the ITA. The committee recommended that Welsh-interest and Welsh-language programmes be made available to Wales Television, on condition that the new company stopped recruiting from amongst TWW staff and stopped 'coveting T.W.W. territory'.[134] The tensions between the two companies were discussed at the May meeting of the ITA, the relationship being described as 'strained'. The Authority had received TWW's complaint about the use of 'Wales Television', and insisted that the new company use 'west and north' in addition; neither should the new company use 'Wales Television Centre' on its headed paper and rate card.[135] By 14 May, WWN, TWW and the ITA had reached agreement over the supply of programmes to WWN, and the strained relationship relaxed somewhat. The existence of two ITV companies in Wales prompted Goronwy Roberts, Labour MP for Caernarfon, to ask the Postmaster General, Reginald Bevins, in July 1961 what steps were being taken to appoint an ITA Advisory Committee for Wales. Bevins replied, stating that this was a matter for the ITA, but that the Pilkington Committee had recommended the establishment of such a committee.[136]

The ITA formally announced the establishment of a Welsh Advisory Committee on 12 December 1962, and on 1 February 1963 the committee met for the first time, at the Park Hotel in Cardiff. In addition to the chairman of the committee, Jenkin Alban Davies, other members were Norah Isaac (drama lecturer at Trinity College, Carmarthen, and former headmistress of the first Welsh-medium primary school at Aberystwyth), the children's author Enid Watkin Jones, Dr I. H. Davies, Mr J. Jeffreys-Jones, Major-General L. O. Pugh, Leslie Richards and the Revd D. R. Thomas. Secretarial support was provided by Lyn Evans, the ITA's Regional Officer for Wales and the West. The committee recorded the ITA's 'sympathy with the cultural aspirations of Scotland, Ulster and Wales' and discussed the character of WWN, inviting members 'to give it time to settle down before passing judgements'. At the outset, the ITA's policy for Wales was noted as the organisation of an all-Wales service.[137] In its second meeting in March the support for WWN was made clearer: 'The Authority should help WWN as far as it possibly could.'[138] Subsequent meetings demonstrate that the Advisory Committee was willing to make a determined effort to secure the future of the company, which by this time was facing financial difficulties (see chapter 6).[139]

On 14 September 1962, WWN went on air for the first time. Although the TWW Welsh Board did not devote much time discussing the new service, it did air concern over the continued use of 'Teledu Cymru' ('Wales Television') on the service, and referred the matter to the company's solicitors.[140] The tensions between WWN and TWW continued throughout the first part of 1963. In April, Frank Brown, the TWW Public Relations Manager, wrote to the ITA complaining about Haydn Williams's statement in his company's annual report, which, in effect, told the company's shareholders that it aimed to secure the all-Wales contract for itself after 1964 (when contracts would be renewed and a new frequency would become available).[141] A further missive was sent from Derby to Robert Fraser on 22 April, underlining TWW's anger at Williams's statement. He also pointed out that TWW had not received a single payment for programmes since 1 January 1963 (when the agreement over programming between WWN, TWW and the ITA came into force), and that it was now 'becoming harder and harder for us to continue to bestow benefits on his Company when we receive this kind of reward'. Furthermore, Derby stated: 'When we undertook to give him the maximum possible assistance over programmes it was on the understanding that he would cease from making public remarks as to the future of his Company in our area.'[142] In this, Derby had the support of a fellow Conservative, the MP for Cardiff North, Donald Box, who, on 21 May, called for TWW to be allowed to take over WWN and provide a service for the whole of Wales. He also tabled a motion in the House of Commons to protect TWW from encroachment by WWN into their area and to prevent the further strengthening of WWN at the expense of TWW.[143] However, a visit by Sir John Carmichael (Acting Chairman of the ITA) and Jenkin Alban Davies to the Minister for Welsh Affairs, Sir Keith Joseph, the Minister of State for Welsh Affairs, Lord Brecon, and the Postmaster General, Reginald Bevins, on 23 May 1963 convinced the government that the ITA was considering the option of extending the Teledu Cymru franchise to cover the whole of Wales. At the beginning of the meeting the Postmaster General suggested that the only option available to the ITA was a takeover of Teledu Cymru by TWW; yet he also noted that the political implications of doing this were 'disturbing'.[144] Carmichael and Alban Davies stated their wish that Channel 7 be allocated to the ITA, in order that Teledu Cymru be allowed to provide a south Wales service in competition with TWW. According to the minutes of the meeting a lot of 'inconclusive discussion' took place, the outcome of which was that the ITA was adamant that competition with WWN would not be harmful to TWW, but admitted at the same time that the issue had not been raised with the company.[145] The minutes of the meeting included the following important sentence: It was difficult to avoid the impression that the members of the I.T.A. were really assuming a priori that WWN would be the company that would take over the eventual all-Wales service and that TWW would become a wholly West of England Company.[146] Whether intended or not, the impression given to government ministers was that the ITA was keen to see Teledu Cymru as the ITV service for Wales.

The financial situation of WWN was dire at this point, and on 31 May, the company's board of directors decided to end originated programming. By 21 June, Eric Thomas, the Managing Director, was convinced that the only way forward would be an alliance with TWW, as there was no prospect (in financial terms) that the company would be able to produce its own programmes again. The main reason given for this decision was that the company had expected a rate of revenue of between £240,000 and £270,000 per annum, yet by May 1963, this had totalled only £16,000 since January.[147]

One of the problems facing Teledu Cymru was that the company's bank, Martin's Bank, was unwilling to extend the company's overdraft from £130,000 to £180,000. Following a meeting between Eric Thomas and the bank in Bristol on 28 June, this was extended to £165,000 as a compromise.[148] Further to this meeting, Thomas met with Lord Derby and John Baxter, the joint Managing Director of TWW, to discuss Teledu Cymru's difficulties. According to Thomas, Derby had 'promised to use his good offices with Martin's Bank (of which he is a director) to see whether their rather firm stand can be loosened in our favour so that we can avoid circulating our own creditors'.[149] On 9 August, Eric Thomas and fellow director P. O. Williams met with the TWW Finance Committee. TWW was willing to offer 12s. 6d. for every £1 share (voting and non-voting). This would be paid for by the issue of TWW non-voting shares at the market price of 15s. per share.[151] The meeting was followed by a letter to Eric Thomas from Alfred Goodman, the TWW solicitor, who noted that the transfer to TWW was conditional upon the ITA granting TWW a renewed licence for the south Wales *and* the west of England and the west and north Wales areas from July 1964 onwards. It was also conditional upon satisfactory arrangements being made with regard to Channel 7 at St Hilary (which would allow the separation of a Welsh service from the English service).[151] The financial offer from TWW was placed before the Teledu Cymru directors on 17 August: TWW would acquire the whole of the issued share capital of Teledu Cymru, a total of 304,000 voting and non-voting shares of £1 each. Despite Gwynfor Evans's opposition to selling to TWW (the reason for which was not minuted), Emrys Roberts argued that the board had no alternative but to accept the offer.[152] For the remainder of 1963, Teledu Cymru operated as a relay company, transmitting the Welsh-language and Welsh-interest programmes of TWW together with the ITV network programmes, and on 16 October, Teledu Cymru shareholders voted in favour of the TWW takeover bid.[153]

Meanwhile, the ITA was awaiting a decision from the government as to whether or not it was to be given Channel 7 in Band III for use at St Hilary, which would allow the new contractor from July 1964 onwards to provide a service for Wales apart from the service to the west of England.[154] It is clear from a letter from the Postmaster General, Reginald Bevins, to Sir Keith Joseph, the Minister for Welsh Affairs, on 4 November 1963 that the government was minded to give Channel 7 to the ITA.

Bevin's personal view was that the ITA proposal had 'obvious attractions', although he was aware that there was nothing extra on offer for the west of England. He was also concerned that some, such as the BBC, would see the move as offering too much to the ITA.[155] Nevertheless, by the time TWW representatives attended their first contract interview with the ITA, the issue had been resolved and the ITA had Channel 7.

In the Wales section of their application for the contract, TWW emphasised the company's aim of producing more Welsh-language programming than the BBC, in a wide variety of formats. The company drew attention to its experienced Welsh staff, in particular Wyn Roberts, Dorothy Williams and Owen Roberts (all of whom had joined TWW from the BBC), Owen Griffiths, Emyr Edwards, Eirwen Davies; and Rhydwen Williams (who had joined TWW from Granada) and Meurig Jones. The pioneering aspect of Welsh programming was also emphasised, and the aim of popularising the language through game and quiz shows was described as 'a pioneer effort' (see chapter 4).[156] A rival application was submitted by a group called Independent Television Ltd. However, the company had no representation on its board from Wales or the west of England, and neither was there any reference to Welsh language or culture. In fact, there was little awareness of the cultural and social make-up of the region as a whole. The ITA also commented that the company had not given a satisfactory picture of its financial arrangements. Needless to say, the interview did not go well and the contract was not awarded to the group.[157]

On 4 December 1963, Lord Derby, Alfred Francis, Huw T. Edwards, John Baxter and Alfred Goodman from TWW were interviewed by the ITA for the new Wales and West contract area. The contract was offered to the company on condition that they avoided clashing with the BBC on Welsh and Welsh-interest programmes. The new programme requirements were laid out in terms of five hours of Welsh-language programming and six hours of English-language, to cover Wales, the west of England and mixed viewing.[158] The same day, Derby wrote to Charles Hill, the ITA's Chairman, and noted that he was unwilling to let any WWN director join the 'new' TWW board, as they had let Wales down and would be a 'disaster'.[159] The ITA agreed to this, and instead required TWW's Welsh Committee to be redesignated a Board and to gain three members from the WWN area.[160] A second interview was held at the ITA on 2 January 1964, which Lord Derby, John Baxter, Alfred Francis,

Huw T. Edwards and Wyn Roberts attended. The Authority confirmed that from 1966 onwards the company would have to produce a total of twelve hours of locally originated programming and would need to collaborate with the BBC in terms of scheduling the programmes.[161] There being no objections to this, the ITA announced that TWW would be the ITV contractor for the Wales and West region from July 1964 onwards. At the final Teledu Cymru board meeting, the directors were to learn that TWW would not be requiring the services of any of their staff and on 27 January 1964, WWN was officially taken over by TWW.

4

Television Wales and the West, 1956–1963: Programming and Critical Issues

Introduction

This chapter studies TWW's programming and audiences during its first contract period, discussing issues such as scheduling, programming decisions, the programmes broadcast and audience responses. The company not only produced its own particular brand of programming for Wales and the west of England, but also carried the ITV network's popular programming to the region. In Welsh-language programming, TWW pioneered quiz shows and magazine-style programmes, and also provided programmes for learners of the language. The second part of the chapter is a thematic section on the critical issues that dominated TWW during the period between 1956 and 1963. One of the main issues stemmed from the nature of the dual region itself – the seemingly strained relationship between Wales and the west of England. Yet, this did not seem to prevent the company from demonstrating a pioneering attitude in its programming and from becoming a commercial success in its early years.

Programmes, 1956–1963

Unfortunately, very few of TWW's programmes still exist, as they were either broadcast live and not recorded or (for those for which there was a record) were disposed of, as a result of the loss of the ITA contract in 1967. However, there is a handful of complete programmes and several film inserts in the ITV Wales Archive, and from these pieces of evidence it is possible to gauge from the presentation format that a more 'relaxed' attitude was taken towards the audience, in comparison with the approach taken by the BBC. This is borne out by a piece written for the TWW weekly listings journal, *Television Weekly*, by Wyn Roberts, the station's Welsh Controller and Executive Producer: 'The BBC had been rather highbrow in its programming: TWW decided to be popular. Instead of treating the audience as a bunch of college graduates, TWW treated the people as they really were, ordinary working men and women.'[1] Not everybody welcomed the introduction of ITV programmes to south Wales, however, in particular those programmes which emanated from the larger network companies. In 1961, for example, *Blodau'r Ffair*, the journal of Urdd Gobaith Cymru (the Welsh League of Youth) published a poem by the Cefneithin poet David Henry Culpitt. The poem was entitled 'Yr Oes Olau Hon' ('This Enlightened Age') and, although one can possibly detect a tongue firmly placed in a cheek, it does resonate with certain fears surrounding the influence of television on a particular Welsh way of life which were prevalent at the time:

> Mae ffyrch y diawl i'w gweld yn awr
> Ar gornel simnai'r Hendre Fawr;
> I fangre dethol geiriau da
> Daeth roc an' rôl a'r tsha, tsha, tsha,
> A merched glandeg coesau noeth
> A leinw le y Salmydd doeth;
> Mae Rhys a Marged yn gytûn
> Yn gwneud y tango, clun wrth glun;
> Daeth 'Take your Pick' a 'Treble Chance'
> I dŷ cymydog gŵr y Mans,
> Ac yn lle dameg gwidw dlawd
> Ceir sôn am hap a 'pools' a ffawd,
> A crŵno oerllyd a geir beunydd
> Yn lle salmau'r Pêr Ganiedydd,
> A Tommy Steele mewn trwser melyn
> Yw'r darlun geir ar wal y gegin;
> Mae Shirley Bassey o Gaerdydd
> Yn awr yn ffrâm hen gewri'r ffydd,
> A siarad geir am Peri Como
> 'Mhlith hysbysiadau 'Teid' ac 'Omo';
> I'r aelwyd gynt lle bu y gân
> Daeth dyfeisiadau uffern dân,
> Ac ym mythynnod Cymru Wen
> Mae'r diawl unllygad heddiw'n ben.
> Daeth barn ar fyd! Gyfeillion, dowch
> I'r encilfeydd! O bobol, ffowch![2]

The poem loses something of its impact in translation, but the gist can be seen below:

> The Devil's forks can now be seen
> On the corner of the chimneys of Hendre Fawr;
> To the place of good words
> Came rock 'n' roll and cha, cha, cha,
> And pretty girls with naked legs
> Fill the space where the wise Psalmist used to be;
> Rhys and Marged are happy
> Doing the tango, thigh by thigh;
> Take Your Pick' and 'Treble Chance'
> Came to the home of the neighbour of the Manse,
> And rather than the parable of the poor widow
> All that is heard is talk of gambling and 'pools' and fate,
> And daily crooning can be heard
> Rather than the hymns of the Pêr Ganiedydd,
> And Tommy Steele in yellow trousers
> Is the picture on the wall of the kitchen;
> Shirley Bassey from Cardiff
> Now fills the frame where the fathers of the faith used to be,
> And we hear talk of Perry Como
> Amongst adverts for Tide and Omo
> To the hearth where once the song reigned
> The devices of hell now reign,
> And in the cottages of Wales
> The one-eyed devil is now in place.
> Judgement day is here! Friends, come
> To the retreats! O people, flee![3]

Despite concerns over the impact of commercial television on the Welsh way of life, and on the Welsh language in particular, the nature, amount and location in the schedule of Welsh-language programmes featured high on the agendas of TWW's Welsh Committee, the ITA and the Authority's Committee for Wales throughout the period covered by this chapter. Indeed, as will be discussed later, it could be said that too much time was spent on Welsh-language programming, at the expense of English-language programmes for non-Welsh speakers in Wales.

Pre-transmission discussions at the Welsh Committee focused on the type, nature and scheduling of Welsh programmes. The company were required to produce seven and a half hours per week of original material overall and had agreed with the ITA that a 'suitable proportion' would be in the Welsh language.[4] Following a discussion on Welsh-language policy, the ITA decided that there was a 'cultural obligation' to the almost half a million people in the TWW region who spoke Welsh. Since TWW was obliged to originate 15 per cent of its programming, it would be 'fair and reasonable' for the company to provide 15 per cent of this (that is, approximately one hour) in Welsh.[5] The Authority and TWW faced a dilemma at this point. Welsh-language broadcasting was permitted outside normal broadcasting hours, and therefore the Sunday early evening closed period would be the ideal location for such programming. However, both the ITA and TWW were keenly aware of what they termed 'chapel time', which conflicted with the time allocated for Welsh programmes on a Sunday evening. Wyn Roberts and Sir Ifan ab Owen Edwards both stressed the importance of securing a Welsh-speaking audience for its programmes from the outset, and so the Welsh Board proposed using the 7 p.m. to 7.25 p.m. Sunday slot, just before the ITN news.[6] There followed a series of discussions between the ITA and TWW with regard to the location of Welsh programmes in the schedule. Any Welsh-language programme broadcast during the day, albeit of only half an hour's duration, could cause problems for the region as the transmitter was shared with the west of England; not only would part of the audience be alienated, but advertising revenue would suffer as a consequence. The Welsh Committee took a pragmatic view of this, exemplified by Sir Ifan ab Owen Edwards's argument that Welsh-language programmes should be broadcast only in off-peak periods.[7] A compromise was reached, following a Welsh Committee meeting on 7 October 1957, whereby a half-hour programme would be broadcast mid-week during normal broadcasting hours and another on Sundays.[8] TWW wished to put its Sunday evening Welsh programme on the network in order to recuperate some of the costs of production. However, in November that year, the company learned that the ITA had authorised the transmission of a teenage Sunday School programme from ABC Television during closed hours (on grounds of religion, and therefore not covered by the fifty-hour normal broadcasting hours restriction). TWW's programme would therefore be impossible to network, due to advertisers clearly preferring a potentially larger audience for an English-language programme than for a Welsh one. Failure to network would make the programme economically unviable for TWW. The committee also felt that a mid-week Welsh programme without a Sunday one would be a liability, in that it could ruin the ratings (and hence the revenue) for the whole evening.[9] The matter was discussed by the ITA on 10 December together with a proposal from TWW that the company transmit two Welsh-language programmes from 4.20 p.m. to 5 p.m. in addition to Granada Television's *Dewch i Mewn*, which went out at the same time. There would therefore be a Welsh-language programme during this time on four days of the week. Alban Davies was not happy, as the timing precluded a large audience for the programmes.[10] Nevertheless, a week before TWW was due to go on air in January 1958, the Authority and the company had agreed that TWW would transmit Granada's programme on three afternoons a week and produce its own on one afternoon. Eventually, TWW would add a further programme and there would also be a monthly 6.15 p.m. to 7 p.m. Sunday evening networked programme.[11]

The first edition of the networked programme, *Gwlad y Gân/Land of Song*, went on air on 9 March 1958. Set in the fictional village of Llantelly, it provided a platform for the singer Ivor Emmanuel and was primarily music-based. The first programme included the soprano Mary Thomas, the Royal Welsh Male Voice Choir from Treorchy, the TWW Children's Choir and the violinist Granville Jones. Norman Whitehead was the musical director and the show was produced by Chris Mercer.[12] Almost immediately, though, the programme ran into difficulties, and Mark Chapman-Walker had to inform the Welsh Committee that he was engaged in 'a somewhat acrimonious exchange of correspondence' with the ITA, which was threatening to discontinue the programme in its present form. The issue revolved around an interpretation of the 1954 Television Act. Under the terms of the Act, Welsh-language programmes were allowed in the closed period only in order to support and maintain the language. Any programme which included a percentage of English music translated into Welsh did not constitute a Welsh-language programme, as the entire programme, according to the Authority, should be of Welsh indigenous material.[13] The matter was resolved, and by the beginning of 1960 *Land of Song* was being watched in an estimated 2,874,000 homes across the UK, and was particularly popular in Scotland.[14] Nevertheless, the programme was further criticised by the

ITA's Welsh Committee during 1963, when it was accused of not representing the Welsh musical tradition, of no longer fulfilling its original purpose, of being too contrived and artificial, and of 'masquerading as a Welsh programme'.[15] Yet, during this time, it remained one of TWW's flagship programmes, placing the name of the company on the wider UK network until its final show in July 1964.

The BBC was clearly keeping a close eye on the competition and was ready to intervene in what it saw as attempts by ITV to steal audiences. One such instance is illustrated by a letter about *Land of Song* written by Sir Ian Jacob, Director-General of the BBC, to Robert Fraser at the ITA on 9 April 1958. In it, Jacob draws Fraser's attention to the fact that two recent editions of the programme 'unavowedly [tried] to attract a non-Welsh audience;' this, despite the agreement that Welsh-language programmes could be broadcast on a Sunday, as they were to provide 'a small and localised section of the community with a token recognition of their claims'. Jacobs noted that the programmes had been prefaced with an announcement that 'all viewers, i.e. other than those for whom the programme is permitted, would enjoy it and captions in English were introduced at a number of points'.[16] Further memoranda were sent from Cardiff to London in 1959, sometimes betraying a more desperate tone. On 11 March 1959, Oldfield-Davies wrote to Cecil McGivern, the BBC's Deputy Director of Television Broadcasting, offering suggestions for programme ideas in English for a non-Welsh-speaking audience in Wales. The *local* nature of TWW was emphasised time and time again: 'Poor though much of [TWW's] output may be, it is being increasingly regarded by the man in the street as "our" programme . . . We do little or nothing.'[17] In response, McGivern wrote to Gerald Beadle, the Director of Television, noting that 'TWW is becoming more of a force in Wales' and admitting that he would like a programme such as *Land of Song* to be part of the BBC's output. In essence, he agreed with Oldfield-Davies's assessment of the situation.[18]

Once established, the pattern for Welsh-language programmes became fairly routine. The weekday would start at 4.20 p.m. with either *Dewch i Mewn* or TWW's *Amser Te* ('Tea Time'). The latter, presented by Newport-based Myfanwy Howell, was aimed at the female audience and became an instant hit in the region; it was also taken by Granada for its north Wales viewers. The programme was a mix of studio-based and filmed items, and Howell's homely style of presenting endeared the audience to her. There is evidence to suggest that the programme was watched by non-Welsh speakers, as *Television Weekly* had to print an English translation of a recipe, following several requests from women who did not speak Welsh.[19] From early 1959 onwards, this slot was preceded by a daily five-minute bulletin of news in Welsh. When Granada 'rested' *Dewch i Mewn* (for example, during the summer months), TWW would replace it with programmes such as *Cipdrem ar Fywyd* ('A Glance at Life'), a filmed programme which showed various aspects of industry, culture and important events in Wales, or *Orig Yr Ifanc* ('Youngsters' Hour'), a programme aimed at young people. Other programmes included *Trysor o Gân* ('Treasury of Song') and *Troeon Gyrfa* ('Career Turns'), in which a distinguished Welsh woman or man met with pupils from her/his old school. The essence of these Welsh programmes, transmitted daily in the afternoon, was encapsulated in TWW's written submission to the Pilkington Committee in 1960:

> Mostly they are designed so that viewers as well as Welsh men and women of distinction can participate: to encourage interest in the exchange of articulate opinion; to further the enjoyment of music, poetry, homecrafts, leisure pursuits and of all forms of activity and behaviour characteristic of the Welsh way of life.[20]

In an internal document published in July 1962, TWW underlined its commitment to the whole of Wales, as opposed to just the south of the country or a certain section of the population: 'TWW has always regarded its responsibilities as covering the whole of Welsh life, and our programmes reflect the nation as a whole rather than any one geographical or intellectual group.'[21]

Throughout the period 1956–63, TWW broadcast a weekly average of two hours and forty minutes of Welsh-language programming. It should be noted that for commercial reasons, to do with maximising the audiences for programmes, and thus advertisers, no Welsh programmes were transmitted after 5 p.m., thereby depriving a large part of the audience of the chance to see them (an issue raised by the ITA, as noted previously). This point was also raised by Elwyn Davies, the Welsh member of the Pilkington Committee, when the TWW representatives met with the committee in May 1961. Davies commented that whilst there was a 'good deal' of Welsh-language material, none of it was in peak hours. Lord Derby retorted and pointed out that the BBC did not broadcast Welsh programmes at peak-time but late at night, and that putting Welsh programmes at peak hours would be providing a programme for a minority within a minority. At this point in the argument, Harry Llewellyn intervened by adding that within the TWW area in Wales (essentially Glamorgan and Monmouthshire), there was no demand for Welsh at peak-time viewing hours, such as there would be in mid Wales or Carmarthenshire (neither of which was within the TWW area).[22]

One area in which TWW was a pioneer was Welsh-language quiz shows. Programmes such as *Taro Deg* (which was later adapted for the non-Welsh speaking audience as *Try For Ten*) and *Pwy Fase'n Meddwl* ('Who'd Have Thought It') broke new ground in Welsh entertainment. The company was aware that Welsh-speaking audiences wanted programmes which entertained, as well as those which sought to inform and educate. Lighter programmes were often suggested; for example, on 5 May 1961 a literary programme was dropped and replaced by a 'light-hearted discussion programme' on interesting items from local newspapers.[23] Again, in 1962, Sir Ifan ab Owen Edwards suggested to Wyn Roberts that Welsh-language programmes could be less serious and more entertaining. 'Theological and literary discussion programmes over forty minutes', he suggested, 'could desirably be changed for items of more general interest.'[24] TWW was also a pioneer in the key area of programmes for Welsh learners. *Camau Cyntaf* ('First Steps') showed how television could be used as a medium for language teaching and saw Cassie Davies, a former teacher and schools inspector, use a variety of novel teaching methods. The programme's success was followed by *Croeso Christine* ('Welcome Christine'), more of which in the next chapter. One area of weakness, in terms of programme output, was Welsh-language drama, a topic which was to feature prominently during the second contract period between 1964 and 1968. The reason given by the company was a lack of production facilities, but it could also have been that TWW was aware of the commercial value of 'lighter' shows, in terms of attracting larger audiences, and thus larger advertising revenues. As noted in one Welsh Committee meeting, Welsh speakers were already a minority, and it was not considered desirable to design programmes to appeal only to a few of the minority.[25]

TWW was also required to provide programming to the majority non-Welsh-speaking population of south Wales. Despite some notable series, such as *Here Today* (a light current affairs programme which 'bridged' Wales and the west of England) and *Wales and the West* (in which John Betjeman and Gwyn Thomas travelled around the region, in another clear attempt to present it as a coherent unit), there were several calls from a number of Welsh directors for English-language programmes about Wales from the outset.[26] TWW did make a number of English-language programmes, but their status as reflecting, or being grounded in, the particular region was questionable.[27] *Discs-a-Gogo* was a pop music show which was taken by a number of regional ITV companies (such as Westward, Channel Television, Grampian and Anglia Television, where the programme appeared at number seven in the top ten ratings in October 1962).[28] Its 'Welshness', however, is somewhat doubtful. A weekly variety show hosted by the Welsh entertainer Wyn Calvin, *New Airs and Faces*, aired for the first time during TWW's first week on 16 January 1958. The show gave a chance to new artistes to make their debut on television. Again, the Welsh dimension of the show is not clear, but it did give one new pop group a chance to impress the audience. They were called the Rolling Stones.[29] The company went on to produce long-lasting quiz shows in English, such as *Three Little Words*, which were hosted by a TWW regular, Roy Ward Dickson. It also led the way in the field of documentaries, broadcasting the first-ever documentary on Dartmoor prison on 28 November 1962.[30] TWW also spearheaded efforts to challenge the dominance of the 'Big Four' network companies (Associated-Rediffusion, ATV, ABC and Granada). In 1961, the company signed singers Joan Sutherland and Geraint Evans to perform at the Royal Opera House for a thirty-minute programme which was offered to regional companies only (Scottish Television and Southern Television took the programme).[31] In 1963, TWW undertook to challenge at the dominance once again by drawing together six other regional companies (WWN, Scottish, Grampian, Ulster, Border and Westward) and the Irish station, Telefis Eireann, in creating a project entitled *Celtic Challenge*. The programmes were recorded in the regional studios in turn and featured a local personality being questioned on a topic of current interest by four students.[32]

Sport was another programme area in which TWW did well. TWW's production panel noted in May 1962 that the British Featherweight Championship between Winston and Carroll was 'well worth the fee paid for it' and that the company had been instrumental in gaining exclusive rights for the ITV network for other boxing matches. In addition, the live television rights to the inter-Celtic swimming contest which was held in the Empire Pool in Cardiff on 29 September 1962 were offered to TWW.[33] TWW's regular *Sports Preview* was broadcast on Thursday evenings for a number of years, and the company also broadcast filmed football highlights, such as the Bangor vs. Naples match in September 1962.[34] In the political arena, in addition to programmes such as *In the News*, which took a detailed look at topics of current interest, TWW covered the 1959 General Election in its area, and during the ITN election night special programme, TWW fed into the network at least eleven times.[35] The company also kept a detailed count of airtime given to the various political parties since reporting on the election had begun on 8 September 1959, in order to maintain political balance. The one slight error on the part of the company was when Jack Hylton appeared in a Labour Party political broadcast.[36] Overall, therefore, TWW provided English-language programming across a range of areas or genres, although the amount of Welsh-interest programming was a cause for concern both within the company and within the ITA.

In terms of the audience, TWW were aware from the outset that they had to embark upon a campaign in order to persuade people to convert their sets to receive the Band III signal which would emanate from St Hilary carrying the TWW programmes. Although the audience was slow to convert initially [37] (a case of waiting to see what the station had to offer before investing in a new aerial, perhaps), its size soon grew:[38]

Year	Number of TWW homes
1958	191,000
1959	449,000
1960	571,000
1961	698,000
1962	769,000
1963	802,000

Once the audience had converted, TWW relied on Television Audience Measurement (TAM) ratings to gauge the popularity of its programmes, as did other ITV companies. These showed the percentage of households watching a particular programme at a particular time. However, TWW did not rely exclusively on this method of assessing viewer satisfaction or attitudes. The company also used the letters pages in *Television Weekly* to gather opinion, although invariably the letters were positive or complimentary, rather than critical. There is very little evidence in newspapers and journals of viewers writing to discuss commercial (or BBC) television programmes, particularly in the Welsh-language press. Correspondence is sparse, what there is tends to focus on larger issues, such as a campaign for a separate television service for Wales (see chapter 5).

Viewer loyalty to TWW came to the fore when the WWN service commenced, in late 1962. In certain overlap areas, it was possible to choose between TWW and WWN, as one case in the west Wales town of Llandovery, Carmarthenshire, highlighted. The television signal to the town was carried via a television relay company and had space for one commercial channel only. Initially, the service carried TWW programmes and proved to be popular, but at the end of January 1963, the town council voted by seven to two to change to WWN. The decision caused uproar in the town and the relay service was inundated with complaints.[39] Eventually the situation was resolved, by the demise of WWN, but the case underlines the popularity of TWW by 1963. A similar case was reported in Lampeter, also in west Wales, where a local dealer had to revert to TWW programmes after relaying the WWN service.[40]

What is apparent from the TAM ratings and from letters to *Television Weekly* is that the network programmes were by far the most popular: only on rare occasions did locally originated programmes (such as *Here Today*) reach the top ten for the TWW region. That is not to say that viewers were not loyal to TWW, rather that they used the station more as a vehicle to view mass-appeal programmes, such as *Coronation Street*, *Sunday Night at the London Palladium* and *Emergency – Ward 10*. Given that 85 per cent of TWW output consisted of network programmes, perhaps this is not surprising. What is a little more surprising is that TWW did not make an impact on the ITV network. Although some ITV network programmes, such as *Double Your Money* and *Take Your Pick*, were recorded at the Pontcanna studios in early 1962, TWW's contribution to the network was restricted to the monthly *Land of Song*, *Discs-a-Gogo* and occasional inserts into news programmes. The main reason for this was the dominance of the big four companies, hence TWW's efforts to rally the regional stations in *Celtic Challenge* and other shared programming, as has been seen. It also put a good deal of effort and energy into Welsh-language programming and, as has been noted, was a pioneer in this area.

Critical issues, 1956–1963

One of the key issues that dominated this period was the relationship between south Wales and the west of England. The strains and tensions which existed between what the ITA called the 'widely differing areas' were, in a sense, of the Authority's own making, as the transmitter located in St Hilary served a wide area, as noted earlier in this chapter. When the geographical nature of the region was made public, J. C. Griffith Jones, writing in the *Western Mail*, commented that:

> In the pioneering radio days the B. B. C. suffered many qualms and heartburnings through striving to maintain and uneasy marriage between Wales and the West of England. It was with a deep sigh of relief that the B. B. C. eventually pronounced the divorce! Will I. T. V. match these well nigh unmatchables?[41]

The same concern was expressed in the *Western Daily Press*: 'The directors of the new group are men of eminence, knowledge and experience in many walks of life, but they include none who has any apparent qualifications to represent Bristol or the West Country.'[42] Later, in 1961, the ITA was forced to issue a statement in response to Westward's Peter Cadbury who, as was seen earlier, suggested that TWW should retreat to Wales, given the company's alleged lack of attention to the west of England, thus leaving the whole of the West Country to Westward.[43] TWW was at pains (at board level, at least) to emphasise the unity of the region. During the interview with the Pilkington Committee in May 1961, Lord Derby argued that 'we have found that both areas on the whole . . . like pretty much the same thing'.[44] In its written submission to Pilkington, as noted earlier, TWW underlined the cohesive nature of the region. Yet Alfred Francis, the Managing Director, during an address to staff at Pontcanna in May 1959, admitted that whilst the company had established itself well in south Wales, 'it has a big recovery job to do in the West of England'.[45] By 1961, Welsh Members of Parliament were calling for a 'divorce' between Wales and the West, and when this became possibly technically, there was relief from both sides of the Bristol Channel.[46] The dual nature of the region meant that TWW had to serve the Welsh-speaking population of south Wales, the non-Welsh-speaking population of south Wales and the population of the west of England. It was also required to provide programming that would appeal to the tastes of the region as a whole. In being pulled in many directions, fundamentally because of the nature of the region, it had to compromise, and it would appear that English-language programmes for Wales were neglected.

The second dominant issue during this period was TWW's attitude towards an ITV service for the whole of Wales. As has been noted, the company had indicated its interest in, and willingness to, expand its territory westwards and northwards at an early stage. The matter overtook the company somewhat from 1958 onwards, when a campaign spearheaded by Undeb Cymru Fydd gathered momentum and resulted ultimately in the creation of the Wales Television Association (which later became WWN).[47] TWW's expansionist aims were not only culturally driven by a desire to serve the whole of Wales. An increased territorial area would result in a larger potential audience, which in turn would result in increased advertising revenue and profits. When the opportunity came about, however, TWW decided not to apply for the west and north Wales licence, citing the reason that three all-Welsh groups had already applied. The letter stated that, should the new company find itself in difficulties, then TWW would be willing to 'step into the breach'.[48] It is possible that by this time the TWW board was aware of the financially unstable nature of the new company and was biding its time, waiting for what it saw as the inevitable collapse. It should be said, however, that when WWN did encounter severe problems, TWW was on hand to offer programming free of charge, which, in the eyes of the ITA, was an admirable move.

The relationship with the ITA is another critical issue which dominated the period. From the outset, the relationship between TWW and the Authority was often strained. The root of the problem was in the fact that control of the group lay in the hands of men from outside the region, primarily Lancashire and London. The regional dimension was provided only in the form of individual directors, who had very little share capital with which to wield power. TWW had proved to be intransigent with regard to the Sunday evening programme slot, to the point where Jenkin Alban Davies, the ITA member for Wales, was 'very disappointed' with the company.[49] Further occasions incurred the wrath of the ITA. TWW had been using the phrase 'Your free television service' to promote its programmes, and the Authority gave the company three months to remove the phrase from circulation.[50] The ITA were also concerned at the use by TWW of what it perceived to be subliminal methods to keep the audience, by transmitting a 'Keep Watching' slogan during viewing times.[51] Whilst criticism abated for a period of years at the beginning of the 1960s, the establishment of the ITA Committee for Wales led to an increase in criticism of TWW, some of it justified, some not, which continued into 1964 and beyond (see chapter 8).

Not even the ITA, however, could argue that TWW had not been a pioneer in its operation and its programming. It was one of the first ITV companies to make use of the new video-recording equipment and pioneered its use during the Montgomery by-election in 1962.[52] The company also pioneered the use of colour television, giving demonstrations at the Royal Welsh Show and at the National Eisteddfod of Wales in Llanelli in August 1962. In programming, TWW introduced new formats in the Welsh language, such as quiz shows, light magazine programmes and regular television news bulletins. At the time of the contract renewal in late 1963, Lyn Evans, the ITA's regional officer, wrote that TWW had a 'good record' over the years and had maintained a high quality in all its Welsh programming. Moreover, it had popularised the Welsh language and had 'created a most favourable image in the public eye', even though the ITA had previously pointed out that over the five-and-a-half year period there had been no *significant* increase in the amount of Welsh-language programming being produced.[53]

In addition to the pioneering spirit, TWW was also a resounding commercial success between 1956 and 1963. The ITV system had effectively created a monopoly of television advertising in each region (hence the tensions in overlap regions, such as that between TWW and WWN or TWW and Westward). The establishment of TWW coincided with industrial growth in the area of the Severn estuary, later to be dubbed 'Severnside' by TWW, which comprised the coastal strips of Glamorgan, Monmouthshire and Avon.[54] With industrial growth came prosperity and disposable income, all within the TWW area. A survey in March 1958 by Television Audience Measurement Ltd noted that 41 per cent of ITV homes in the TWW area were within the ABC socio-economic classes compared with 39 per cent the previous year.[55] The area continued to grow, both in terms of population and industry and in terms of attractiveness to advertisers.[56] In April 1961, the ITA was able to claim that '[TWW] has been able to claim almost every week the highest percentage and number of local advertising spots of all the provincial contractors.'[57] Such was the success of the company, and so large the profits, that a House of Lords debate on the Television Bill in 1963 used TWW as a case study in arguing for the reduction of the advertising time allowed on television.[58] The increases in TWW's net advertising revenue (NAR) and dividends to shareholders can be seen below:[59]

Year	NAR	Dividend rate
1958	£2,191,292	58.5%
1959	£2,597,233	110%
1960	£3,271,634	110%
1961	£3,521,503	110%
1962	£3,580,914	95%
1963	£3,715,116	95%

For TWW, Roy Thomson's 'licence to print money' was a reality, and the company entered its second contract with confidence.

Conclusion

Although TWW's relationship with the Authority had been shaky from the outset (and became tenser with the advent of the ITA's Committee for Wales in 1963), the period between 1956 and 1963 was one of growth and financial success for TWW, as has been shown.[60] As Sendall states: 'They were one of ITV's golden boys: not only immensely profitable but lively and adventurous in their programmes and eager to expand'.[61] Control of the company was in the hands of a few from outside Wales, and the reasons for this have been given. The fact that in 1956 nobody from within Wales wanted to invest heavily in ITV (or was able to venture financially) reflects the cautious nature of the Welsh in venturing into the capitalist, commercial field. Yet when the WWN project, led as it was by ideological and cultural nationalist aims, was mooted, hundreds of people invested, and control was set firmly in Wales, much to the delight of the ITA – and that is the subject of the next chapter.

5

Wales (West and North) Television, 1956–1962: Formation and Control

Introduction

This chapter focuses on the history of Wales (West and North) Television (WWN), or Teledu Cymru, as it was known in Welsh. It places the history of the company within the wider debate over nationhood and the struggle for representation, for it is the history of WWN which exemplifies this more than that of any other ITV company. Unlike TWW, WWN emerged as the result of a coordinated campaign led by cultural and political groups in Wales, and in many ways WWN can be seen as an answer (albeit a partial one) on the part of the government and ITA to increasing Welsh demands for a separate television service for Wales. The origins of WWN can be traced back to the Beveridge Committee on Broadcasting (1949–51), but the campaign to establish a separate television service for Wales gathered momentum in 1956, at the time when commercial television arrived in Wales. The company had a long gestation period and a turbulent history, yet despite the intensive lobbying and campaigning which eventually secured its existence, and despite the involvement of some of the major figures in Welsh cultural, political and educational life at that time, WWN ended less than a year after it had gone on air.[1]

The campaign for WWN

The roots of the campaign which eventually led to the establishment of WWN can be traced to the Beveridge Committee on Broadcasting, in 1949–51. Amongst the memoranda submitted to the committee during its deliberations were five which focused on broadcasting in Wales. These were submitted by the BBC in London, the BBC's Welsh Advisory Council, Undeb Cymru Fydd, Plaid Cymru and the Welsh Parliamentary Party (a grouping of Welsh Labour, Liberal and Conservative Members of Parliament). All the submissions, whilst not forming a clear consensus on the best way forward, called for a measure of broadcasting autonomy for

Wales in the form of an independent corporation (apart from the submission of the BBC Welsh Advisory Council, which called for a national broadcasting unit within the existing structures). Undeb Cymru Fydd demanded a separate, independent broadcasting corporation for Wales which would offer programming in both Welsh and English. The corporation would be independent of the BBC, and commercial broadcasting was rejected outright. The Welsh Parliamentary Party also called for an independent corporation, but the proposed relationship with existing broadcasters was not considered. Plaid Cymru demanded a separate corporation, independent of existing structures, which would oversee programming in Welsh and English. No reference was made to any form of commercial broadcasting. In calling for an independent broadcasting corporation, the various Welsh groups founded their arguments primarily on grounds of language and the separate national identity of Wales. The Welsh Parliamentary Party submission, for example, highlighted the distinctiveness of the (undefined) 'Welsh way of life'; the BBC's Welsh Advisory Council evoked a certain type of nationalist discourse, one which emphasised the role of the broadcaster in the maintenance of a cohesive national identity.[2] On the subject of control, the Welsh Members of Parliament were emphatic: 'We are confident that placed in the hands of Welsh men knowing their audience, and sympathetic to our Welsh way of life, broadcasting would become a far more powerful influence for good than it is at present.'[3] The message from the groups was unambiguous: that control of Welsh broadcasting should lie within Wales, and that, if this did not happen, the indigenous language and culture would be placed at a greater risk than they already were.

The debates during 1949–51 surrounding issues of culture, language, national identity and broadcasting organisations formed the framework out of which WWN emerged. These issues persisted throughout the 1950s and emerged again during the evidence-gathering stages of the Pilkington Committee's deliberations in 1960. The key issue, in this respect, was the lack of consensus over the way to achieve the goal of a separate television service for Wales. An added problematic was to emerge after the advent of commercial television in 1955, when debates surrounding the most appropriate framework for advancing the cause – public service, under the BBC, or commercial, under the ITA – became apparent.

The period 1956–7 witnessed an increase in campaigning activity, prompted by the ITA's announcement that a contract for the south Wales and west of England area was to be advertised. Although concerns had been raised in various meetings of Undeb Cymru Fydd regarding the amount of time devoted to Welsh-interest and Welsh-language programmes on television, it was not until July 1956 that the Union began its campaign in earnest to try to secure a separate television service for Wales. By August that year a deputation had visited the BBC's Controller in Wales, Alun Oldfield-Davies, and the Chairman of the BBC's Broadcasting Council for Wales, Lord Macdonald of Waenysgor.[4] Following this meeting, a meeting was held between Undeb Cymru Fydd and the Postmaster General, Charles Hill, on 19 November 1956, which was also attended by representatives of Urdd Gobaith Cymru, the Honourable Society of Cymmrodorion and the National Eisteddfod Council. As a result of this joint deputation, the Joint Television Committee was formed, containing members from the aforementioned groups.[5]

The level of activity on the part of various groups in Wales intensified in 1958 and, at the same time, increased pressure was put upon the ITA and the government to act to create a television service for the whole of Wales, whilst the BBC came under increasing pressure as ITV began broadcasting in south Wales. There is no doubt that the ITA was aware of the growing feeling amongst Welsh cultural groups. The member for Wales, Jenkin Alban Davies, suggested to the senior officers in the Authority that they should seriously consider establishing a Welsh Advisory Committee, along the lines of the ITA's Scottish Committee. In a memorandum to Robert Fraser, the ITA's Director-General, his deputy, Bernard Sendall, noted that Alban Davies 'seems to think that there will be a political need for an I.T.A. Welsh Committee'.[6] However, as noted in chapter 3, the ITA did not establish a Welsh Committee until 1963, when it was recommended that it did so following the Pilkington Committee's report. The reluctance to establish such a committee was based on the fact that the only 'Welsh' company at the time was TWW, and a Welsh Committee had been established within the company to safeguard the interests of the country.

From this point onwards, there was constant pressure on the ITA to act in respect of the television service in Wales. In July 1958, TWW met with representatives of national Welsh bodies at the Pontcanna studios. The representatives included Wyn Griffiths and Sir John Cecil-Williams from the Cymmrodorion, T. I. Ellis from Undeb Cymru Fydd, R. E. Griffiths from Urdd Gobaith Cymru and Sir Thomas Parry-Williams of the National Eisteddfod Council. From TWW, Huw T. Edwards, one of the company's directors, also spoke at length. Following discussions, three main points emerged: a clear desire on the part of the groups for a single television service for Wales in both languages; the need to release Granada of any responsibility to provide Welsh programmes, as it was not contractually obliged to do so; and concern about the 'conspiracy' to divide Wales up into separate parts by allowing TWW to broadcast to the south and Granada to the north.[7] It is interesting to note that the ITA's representative witnessed 'a good deal of muddled thinking' during the meeting.[8] As a result of this meeting, Mark Chapman-Walker, Managing Director of TWW, sent a report to Fraser. In his reply, Fraser noted his desire to see a company operate in west Wales which, he noted, would be an all-Welsh service area.[9]

It is clear that the BBC in Wales, and its Controller Alun Oldfield-Davies in particular, recognised the particular linguistic and cultural problems of broadcasting in a dual region (Wales and the west of England). On 7 July 1958, Oldfield-Davies sent a memo to the BBC's Deputy Director of Television noting that any opt-out or ex-network programming for Wales resulted in partial coverage of the country only, as the opt-outs could only be transmitted from Wenvoe and Blaenplwyf. BBC viewers in central and north Wales were served by the Sutton Coldfield and Holme Moss transmitters respectively, both serving predominantly English viewing areas. The solution, according to Oldfield-Davies, would be the allocation of frequencies in Band III in order to provide a regular bilingual service for the whole country, effectively providing a separate service. The urgency of the situation was underlined:

> There is growing agitation in Wales that this be done ... It is of supreme importance to Wales that it should have a regular television service which it can regard its own however limited in hours ... It would seem the natural obligation of a public service corporation to meet the legitimate national needs of Wales, and it is to be devoutly hoped that the Corporation will do so.[10]

The message from Oldfield-Davies to London was clear – if the BBC failed to answer the calls for a separate television service, the competition would. As John Davies notes, 'he used the spur of commercial television, urging that for the BBC to be upstaged by an upstart would be to undermine its role as the national service'.[11] The view from London, however, was that as little money as possible should be diverted into competition with ITV, which, it was felt, would not be able to provide Welsh programmes for any considerable length of time, due to commercial pressures.

At a meeting of the Joint Television Committee on 22 August 1958, it was resolved to contact TWW to ascertain whether or not the ITV company was willing to cooperate with the BBC on developing a Welsh television service and to share, if possible, both a frequency and a mast with the BBC.[12] If the request reached TWW, it was not recorded in the minutes of the company's Welsh Committee of 8 September 1958, although the company noted that Wales was not commercially viable as an entity on its own, albeit the special needs of Wales within the dual region were a high priority.[13]

Towards the end of 1958, issues relating to Welsh television were taking up an increasing amount of ITA time. On 8 September, Fraser wrote to Sendall in what could be interpreted as an agitated tone. He suggested preparing a paper for the Authority on the 'problems of the Welsh language and this sporadic propaganda for a unified Welsh television programme, whatever that may mean'.[14] The technical impossibilities were also worrying Fraser. He noted that providing a Welsh station similar to that in Scotland would not be possible. 'I can see that it is a bit of bad luck for Wales that they are caught in this technical net, as Scotland is not', he wrote. However, he did muse on the idea of trying to get a channel for north Wales in Band III, and hinted that the Post Office might allow it. This is the first indication that a breakthrough might have been possible.[15]

At the end of 1958, the ITA was given an opportunity to comment on a draft memorandum from the General Post Office (GPO) and Office for Welsh Affairs, which was to be submitted to the Postmaster General and the Minister for Welsh Affairs.[16] The memorandum was drafted as a result of representations from various Welsh groups and, although it did not make any specific recommendations, it summarised the situation with regard to both BBC and ITA provision in Wales. Fraser responded to the GPO development in characteristic fashion. He stated that the very *raison d'être* of Independent Television, based as it was on a regional structure, 'would give the Welsh the substance of their desires'.[17] In elaborating on this point, he underlined the fact that regional companies were to be owned and controlled by inhabitants of the region, 'so that the programmes may respond to precisely the same kind of regional aspiration as moves the Welsh, and with which the Authority has a broad sympathy'.[18] What followed was a swipe at what Fraser considered to have been Welsh inactivity at the time of the first licence invitation in 1956. After the ITA had decided to locate the transmitter on Welsh soil, and had insisted that the headquarters of the region's company be in Cardiff, '[t]he way was therefore wide open for the appointment of a Welsh programme company. Unfortunately, the Welsh did not move, and in consequence there was appointed a company not owned and controlled by the Welsh.'[19] Fraser then offered a solution, based on utilising channels in Band III in the west and north of Wales. There followed another swipe:

> Of course, all this depends on the assumption that the present agitation comes from something deep and strong enough to express itself in the formation of a programme company ready to accept the responsibility. If no Welsh programme company comes forward, we cannot appoint one. If the Welsh are interested only in a subsidised B.B.C.-type service that does not have to earn its own living, then of course, we cannot help.[20]

Although Fraser may have been losing patience with the Welsh situation, the ITA's Chairman, Sir Ivone Kirkpatrick, showed a more sympathetic view. In an undated handwritten note to Fraser, he stated, 'I really sympathise with the Welsh desire to get away from having to serve an English clientele and to be put on the same footing as Scotland and Ulster.'[21] Also, in a response to a letter sent to him by Sir Ifan ab Owen Edwards, he stated that he sympathised with Edwards's view that Wales should be regarded as a unit in broadcasting terms. 'A geographical accident has enabled us to provide a Scottish and an Ulster station. If we could do the same of Wales, I should be more than pleased.'[22]

In January 1959 Plaid Cymru's Organiser, J. E. Jones, wrote to all local authorities in Wales on behalf of the party's Executive Committee, requesting their cooperation 'in a matter of urgent importance' for Wales.[23] Plaid called upon local authorities to urge the government to release television channels for use in a television service for Wales, but the letter did not make clear who would be responsible for such a service. The letter stated that as there were no Welsh-language programmes broadcast after 5 p.m., when most working people were free to watch them, 'the effect upon Welsh life of this most potent technique, when added to that of the cinema, radio and press, may be disastrous'.[24] In a meeting of the

Plaid Cymru Executive Committee at Aberystwyth on 3–4 April 1959, it was reported that fifty-six out of the seventy-three councils that had been contacted by the party had pledged their support for a television service for Wales.[25] As a result, the Plaid Executive passed a resolution to ask Undeb Cymru Fydd to organise a national conference on the topic. As Ifan Evans notes, Undeb Cymru Fydd was seen in political circles as a more moderate political force, compared with Plaid Cymru, and for this reason it was felt that the Union was more likely than Plaid to be able to harness support throughout Wales.[26]

The National Conference on Television met in the City Hall, Cardiff, on 18 September 1959 and was convened by the Lord Mayor of Cardiff, Alderman Helena Evans. There were representatives present from eighty-two local authorities and twenty-four organisations, together with observers from the BBC, TWW, the ITA, the Ministry of Education, the Council for Wales and Monmouthshire and the Welsh Office of the Ministry of Housing and Local Government.[27] The purpose of the conference, as outlined by the Lord Mayor, was to discuss the fact that Welsh-language and Welsh-interest programmes were in a minority on television, to focus 'informed and responsible opinion' in Wales on the desirability of securing a television service for Wales and to consider making representations to various authorities to this end.[28] Helena Evans called for Wales and its leaders to be united, as this would be the only way to convince those in authority of the justice of the claim. The Conference was seen by those present as a way of building upon what had already been achieved through the deputations of the University of Wales Television Committee and the Welsh Parliamentary Party to government Ministers. Cennydd Traherne (Lord Lieutenant of Glamorgan and a member of Undeb Cymru Fydd) was appointed as the Conference Chair, and T. I. Ellis (Secretary of Undeb Cymru Fydd) was appointed Secretary to the Conference. The opening speech was delivered by Jac L. Williams, who, according to Ifan Evans, 'spoke predictably, using well-rehearsed arguments'.[29] Williams pointed out that all attendees agreed that Wales should be treated as a unit for political and cultural purposes. He drew attention to the fact that Scotland and Northern Ireland were regarded as units by the BBC, and that the reasons given for the difference in status in Wales – technical difficulties and fears over a shortage of programme material – were redundant. Television was, according to Williams, 'a great power that could affect the heart and soul of a nation . . . without a television service that reflected its own cultural pattern, [it] had little chance of survival'.[30] He also paid tribute to the BBC for the way in which the Welsh Home Service had 'added to the cultural life of Wales,' and hoped that this would develop even further when Wales had a television service of her own.[31] Dr Haydn Williams, Director of Education for Flintshire and Chairman of the Council of the National Eisteddfod, spoke next. Whilst he paid tribute to the BBC, TWW and Granada, he also stated that partial coverage of Wales by the BBC and ITV was inadequate and could not contribute to the preservation of Welsh culture. The sole purpose of establishing a separate television service for Wales, according to Williams, was the preservation of the language and culture of the nation. He refuted the arguments put forward by the government and Post Office that technical problems were to blame for the lack of a Welsh service, and called for an independent television service for Wales, 'enabling Welsh language programmes to be put out at peak periods'.[32]

The debate, once opened to the floor, elicited a number of interesting responses. Trevor L. Williams from Wrexham urged the conference not to overstress what he called the 'Welsh-speaking side', for fear of alienating non-Welsh speakers.[33] This point was echoed by the Bishop of Llandâf, who underlined the importance of a service to non-Welsh speakers. He considered it essential that they should be aware of the historical and cultural background of the country to which they belonged, and believed this could be done only through a separate television service for Wales.[34] Gwynfor Evans, President of Plaid Cymru, argued that the decision over who should be responsible for operating a Welsh television service should be taken at a later date, and that the key issue was getting the appropriate channels to offer the service, at whatever cost.[35] The actor Clifford Evans agreed with Gwynfor Evans over the urgency of the issue and announced that the case for a separate television service for Wales had the unanimous support of actors, artists and writers of Wales.[36]

In closing the conference, Cennydd Traherne proposed a motion which was seconded by the chairman of Aberdare Urban District Council. It was resolved unanimously:

> That this Conference, composed of representatives of Local Authorities, voluntary bodies and other organisations in Wales, is of the opinion that the only way to secure an improved Television Service for Wales is by treating Wales as an entity for further Television Services and by releasing the necessary channels; it desires to bring before the Minister

for Welsh Affairs and the Postmaster General this resolution with a request that it be given the most serious consideration, and also to bring to their notice the lack of Television Services in certain parts of Wales; it authorises the Chairman of the Conference (Major C. G. Traherne, Lord Lieutenant of Glamorgan), the Secretary (Mr T. I. Ellis, Aberystwyth), with the Lord Mayor of Cardiff (Alderman Mrs Helena Evans) and the two opening speakers (Dr Jac L. Williams and Dr B. Haydn Williams) to act on behalf of the Conference in accordance with the terms thereof.[37]

The group identified in the resolution adopted the title of 'Continuation Committee'. What is apparent is that there was a lack of consensus in the resolution, which charged the Continuation Committee with pressing for a television service for Wales. The lack of a clear definition stating the preferred broadcaster or the preferred type of service left the way open for members of the Continuation Committee to investigate all avenues open to them. The resolution allowed them the flexibility to press both the BBC and the ITA (which they did, as will be shown), and so the committee worked within the framework of ambiguity constructed by the conference's resolution.

The Continuation Committee met for the first time in Cardiff on 13 November 1959. It was noted that Undeb Cymru Fydd would bear the costs of administering the committee for the time being, but that Cennydd Traherne would press local authorities for contributions. During this meeting Haydn Williams made a proposal that effectively signalled the beginning of what was eventually to become WWN. Noting that the BBC operated in the restricted Band I (and therefore could not provide an all-Wales service on the more widely available Band III), he stated that there *were* channels available for an independent Welsh programme company under the ITA's plans in Band III.[38] Williams also suggested that such a company could invite applications from shareholders, and that the controlling authority might include members of Welsh voluntary associations and the University of Wales. The Continuation Committee met for the second time on 11 December 1959, and by the time of the meeting, Haydn Williams had prepared a technical memorandum which detailed the channels required to provide a full service for Wales.[39] The memorandum argued that only one extra channel in Band III was required (Channel 13) to complete a Welsh network. Williams proposed that the St Hilary transmitter should transmit on Channel 8 (Horizontal) to avoid the Channel 8 (Vertical) from Lichfield, which covered the English Midlands, but which also reached parts of central Wales. A Pembrokeshire mast would pick up these signals and transmit them to the Cardigan Bay area on Channel 11. A mast on the Llŷn peninsula would take this signal and retransmit it to the east on Channel 10 (Horizontal, so as to avoid the Emley Moor transmission from Yorkshire), and this signal in turn would be transmitted to the north-east (Flint and Denbigh) area on Channel 13, on a hitherto unauthorised mast.[40] Central to the memorandum's message was that out of the thirty-five hours of programming broadcast per week, fifteen hours should be in the Welsh language at peak times, with the remainder being both English-language Welsh-interest programmes and programming from the ITV network.

The memorandum is a key document in tracing the development of WWN and locating its provenance. It stated that it was not the function of the Continuation Committee to 'take sides' as to the nature of the authority or company that would eventually undertake responsibility for the television service, should one be approved, and so, in this respect, the committee was working within the parameters of the resolution passed by the first conference. Yet, it made it clear that the committee had a duty to indicate the ways in which the service could be implemented without delay, and therefore it had to take cognisance of the present political situation with regard to the allocation of channels between the BBC and the ITA.[41] Therefore, based on the research undertaken by Haydn Williams (which was conveyed in his technical memorandum), the committee stated that:

> the most practicable way of immediately implementing this claim would be to establish a Welsh Television Programme Company under the Independent Television Authority to operate the channel sequences as already outlined . . . [T]he impetus behind this movement is not of a commercial character. It has been brought into being by a wide spread national feeling amongst all sections of the population, particularly the Welsh-speaking section, by all recognised cultural organisations and by the local authorities in the Principality, that this potent instrument of spreading entertainment and culture should be harnessed to the present day widespread movement to preserve the language and culture of Wales. Such a company should not, therefore, be established purely for the purpose if commercial gain.[42]

Three key issues emerge from the memorandum based on Haydn Williams's technical report. Firstly, the fact that it was conceivable to provide fifteen hours of Welsh language programming per week. Given that even the large network companies such as Associated-Rediffusion were producing twelve and a half hours a week of English-language programmes, the figure was likely to be beyond the means of a Welsh ITV company destined to operate in a sparsely populated rural area, where advertising revenue would be scarce.[43] Secondly, the suggestion that these programmes would be shown during peak hours. It could be argued that this demonstrated a lack of awareness of the political economy of commercial television, as Welsh-language programming at peak hours would fail to attract the large advertising revenues essential for a commercial company to succeed. It might also 'deprive' the viewing population of popular network programming. Thirdly, Haydn Williams emphasised the non-commercial nature of the company, whilst at the same time arguing that a television service of this kind could only operate within the ITV framework. Evans has argued that, 'the motive was so uncommercial as to be philanthropic, or the memorandum displays a startling ignorance of the realities of independent television broadcasting in 1960'.[44] It could be argued that Williams did not (mistakenly, perhaps) see the primary concern of the company as being commercial, but as being cultural. The aim was to redistribute profits in a restricted way, giving a minimal dividend to shareholders and ploughing most of the profits into programming. This, in Williams's view, would be of cultural benefit to Wales.

On 7 January 1960, the Continuation Committee met with Robert Fraser at the ITA. Following the meeting, Traherne noted that the ITA had been sympathetic to the ideas contained in Haydn Williams's memorandum and that they would consider offering a Welsh licence if the channels were made available by the Postmaster General.[45] In a memorandum to the ITA's Deputy Director-General (copied to Alban Davies, Lyn Evans and the ITA Chairman, Sir Ivone Kirkpatrick) dated 11 January 1960, Robert Fraser referred to 'a new situation' which had arisen in west Wales, bringing with it the possibility of appointing an ITV company in the area, which had hitherto been regarded as 'a colony, or colonial belt, of St. Hilary'.[46] It is clear from the memorandum that Fraser was aware of the cultural politics of Wales:

> [I]t should perhaps be noted that there are two political factors which could affect the final technical decisions. Firstly if the area is to be self-governing, it must have a capital, and the natural cultural capital would seem to be Aberystwyth, where the programme company would have its

headquarters. I suppose Caernarfon would be the second choice, and Pembroke hardly acceptable. Another interesting possibility would be Cardiff as the capital, with the programmes being sent out to the western transmitters.[47]

Furthermore, Fraser noted that the possibility of appointing an independent company had arisen from the progress that had taken place in the campaign for Welsh television. 'The leaders of this movement', he wrote, 'are now agreed that the preferred institutional form would be a non-profit-making but self-supporting programme company within the framework of ITA.'[48] What is clear from Fraser's ITA memorandum is that the Continuation Committee had created an impression:

> We could not, of course, enter into any commitment to extend their area into South Wales if we are given Channel 13 when the problem of the remaining half of Band III is resolved, but plainly, if they were a fully representative Welsh group, *they would not be unfavourably placed.*[49]

In a letter dated 11 January 1960, Sir Robert Fraser pointed out to the Continuation Committee that the only area likely to be covered by a transmitter was the west of Wales, although there was a possibility that the Flint-Denbigh area might be reached by another transmitter at a later date.[50] Crucially, Fraser at this point also warned the committee that he was doubtful that a company could reach satisfactory viewing figures or coverage with only two stations. He also asked the committee's opinion on the issue of the location of the headquarters and studio, suggesting Aberystwyth as a possible site.[51] Traherne replied on 13 January, pointing out that the Continuation Committee was not a prospective ITV company, and that Aberystwyth would be the preferred location for the new company's headquarters and studio.[52] Indeed, in a letter to Jac L. Williams on 18 January, T. I. Ellis noted that Lyn Evans, the ITA's Officer for Wales, and the Estates Officer from the ITA were due to visit Aberystwyth, which implies (though it is not explicitly stated) that Aberystwyth was being considered as a possible site for the company's base.[53]

On 22 January, the Continuation Committee met with Hugh Carleton Greene, the new Director-General of the BBC. The fact that the meeting took place suggests that the committee had not decided wholeheartedly on the ITA option, but was still investigating all possibilities with regard to a television service for Wales. Greene outlined the BBC's plan to use the

Wenvoe transmitter to split the Wales and west of England television services, although this would depend on the use of Channel 13 in Band III, to be authorised by the Postmaster General. The BBC had been pressing the government for some time for an uncommitted channel in Band III, so that transmissions for south Wales and those for the west of England could be separated. In an undated document (though probably published during 1960–1 at the time of the Pilkington Committee evidence-gathering), the BBC quoted from a speech by its Director-General, who stated that the plan to split Wales from England had begun in 1952, but that the 1954 Television Act – 'for which we were not responsible' – had scuppered the plan.[54] The revised plan, which was being mooted from the early 1960s onwards, rested on a six-station/transmitter plan for Wales: one in Blaenplwyf near Aberystwyth (which was already in existence), a transmitter in each of Llandrindod, Pembroke and Caernarfon (all of which were approved in principle, with only Llandrindod built), a second station at Wenvoe and one in Llangollen.[55] It was the Wenvoe transmitter that was the pivot of the BBC's plan; this would allow the separation of transmissions between Wales and the West.

By 22 June 1960, Robert Fraser was convinced of the need to go ahead with appointing an ITV company in west Wales:

> I think we must take it absolutely for granted that we must appoint an independent company for West Wales if there is any prospect that a group of people will appear who are ready to accept the responsibility. In fact, it is a wonderful opportunity for Independent Television to be the first to provide the Welsh with a programme company of their own, even on a limited scale.[56]

Fraser also suggested that the company's headquarters might be in Cardiff, noting that he could see only advantages in a move of this kind, as locating the studios in one of the smaller towns would not permit the production of Welsh programmes 'in a continuous way'.[57] The first reference by the Independent Television Authority to the proposed new licence area was made on 26 July 1960, when Alban Davies requested that the press notice giving the ITA's plans for the new area be made available as soon as possible. There would be a delay, however, as the plan required the Postmaster General's approval, and so the minutes noted that the notice was unlikely to be released until September 1960.[58]

The major step forward came on 4 August 1960 during the National Eisteddfod of Wales in Cardiff, when Sir Robert Fraser, together with Jenkin Alban Davies, announced that the Authority was to advertise for a television company to broadcast to the west and north of Wales.[59] It was anticipated that the company would start transmitting in late 1962 or early 1963 from transmitters in Preseli and Arfon, and from Flintshire in due course. The licence would complete the ITV network. Despite the fact that the Post Office would need some time to provide a link from the company's proposed headquarters and studios in Cardiff to the Pembroke transmitter, despite the reservations held by Fraser, and despite the fact that the Postmaster General had yet to finally approve the three-station plan, the announcement was made at that particular point in time due to what Sendall referred to as 'the manifest eagerness of pressure groups in Wales'.[60] It is also important to recognise that the ITA already had Channels 8 (which was used in Preseli) and 10 (Arfon) at their disposal; however, the use of Channel 13 in north-east Wales would require the Postmaster General's authority.

On 29 September, Williams, Traherne and Ellis (on behalf of the Continuation Committee) met with the Postmaster General, the Minister for Welsh Affairs and the Minister of State for Welsh Affairs in London. At this meeting, the committee were led to believe that the Flint-Denbigh transmitter would be operational eventually. Following the meeting, according to Sendall, Williams contacted the ITA, noting that the Postmaster General had shown a good deal of interest in the ITA plan for television in the west of Wales.[61] On 7 October, Robert Fraser wrote to Alan Wolstencroft at the GPO, stating that the Authority had given 'further thought to the shape of Independent Television in Wales'. The letter began by stating that the ITA was disappointed not to have been able to have appointed a mainly Welsh company in 1958, and that '[i]f a Welsh or mainly Welsh company had come forward, I think we would not all now be facing the current and understandable agitation'.[62]

Wales Television Association

On the same day as the Continuation Committee met with the ITA in London on 7 January 1960, the *Western Mail* ran a story which announced that a group of prominent Welshmen were planning to form a commercial television company.[63] The story was based on an article in the Welsh-language weekly newspaper, *Y Faner*. According to *Y Faner*, a group of Welshmen – who could not be named – were adamant that the venture would be backed by advertisers and that sufficient finance would be available. With this backing, the aim would be to broadcast four hours per day of Welsh-language programming, in addition to the English-language programmes that would be bought in. Furthermore, a 'leading member of the group' (nobody was named) stated that there were no technical difficulties standing in the way of the provision of an excellent service, but that the only problem was the need to obtain a channel on which to broadcast.[64]

In a 'Meeting of Sponsors' held in Cardiff on 12 September 1960 the aims of that company were made clear:

> [T]he prime purpose of the company would be presented to the public and those in authority as a desire on behalf of the Promoters to contribute towards the safeguarding of the language and culture of Wales through this potent instrument of culture and entertainment.[65]

Those present had been invited to attend by Haydn Williams. They were Cennydd Traherne (Lord-Lieutenant of Glamorgan), Lady Olwen Carey Evans (the daughter of the former Liberal Prime Minister David Lloyd George), Moses Griffith (a former Plaid Cymru Treasurer), the landowner Islwyn Davies, Colonel J. F. Williams-Wynne (Lord-Lieutenant of Meirionydd), T. I. Ellis, Llewellyn Heycock, Dr William Thomas, Gwynfor Evans, Sir T. H. Parry-Williams (former Professor of Welsh at Aberystwyth) and the Trades Union Leader Tom Jones. Others were invited, but sent their apologies for absence: the businessman Kenneth Davies, Sir David Hughes Parry (President of the University College of Wales Aberystwyth), Principal Thomas Parry (Aberystwyth), the actor Emlyn Williams, David Vaughan (Executive Director of Barclays Bank) and Emrys Roberts (the former Liberal MP).

As a preamble to the business of the meeting, Williams outlined the background to the current situation, noting the deputations from the University of Wales Television Committee and Continuation Committee to government Ministers and the ITA. He noted that the ITA had announced a contract area which embodied part of the Continuation Committee's scheme, in that transmitters would be located at Preseli and at Arfon, and that the committee (of which Williams, Ellis and Traherne were members) would press the Postmaster General to release Channel 13 in the north-east, so as to allow a Flint-Denbigh transmitter.[66] Williams also informed the meeting that this was the beginning of a process that he believed would lead to a separate television service for Wales, and that those present had been called together with the aim of forming a company to apply for the west Wales licence area. The company, he noted, could hope for estimated advertising revenue of £600,000, and, whilst acknowledging that TWW might apply for the licence, he also noted that there would be 'substantial reasons' (not noted in the minutes) why a company represented by those present would 'command more sympathetic consideration from the ITA'.[67]

By the time the company met again as a board of the Welsh Television Association, on 3 February 1961, key members of the company had already aired doubts about the validity of the financial plans. On 11 November 1960, David Vaughan, the south Wales Regional Director of Barclays Bank and member of the company board, wrote to Alban Davies:

> I have advised the Syndicate that whilst I am in entire sympathy with the cultural aims which are so keenly and properly desired by yourself, and are shared by the Members of the Syndicate, I do not believe these aims will be served unless we go forward as primarily a commercial enterprise.[68]

Likewise, Emrys Roberts, another board member, felt that it was wrong to sell the proposition to the people of Wales as an 'easy salvation for the Welsh language' plus easy profits. The commercial imperative should, in Roberts's opinion, be given a higher priority, due to the nature of commercial television. There was a need to balance commercial viability with originating the greatest possible number of programmes for Wales.[69] Alban Davies was also concerned about the financial viability of the company. On 24 January, he wrote to Emrys Roberts noting his worries about Haydn Williams's estimates for advertising revenue: 'To me he appears to have gone off at a tangent ... Please do not lose patience with him. People of your experience must carry this through.' The letter ended with a statement arguing that this was the only way forward for television in Wales.[70] There was therefore apprehension (at an early stage in the history of the Wales Television Association) about Williams's abilities as a financial manager, which was to arise again later in the year and throughout the period of WWN. The letter from Alban Davies also demonstrated the fact that there was considerable support and a desire for the venture to succeed.[71] The precarious nature of the venture was highlighted when David Vaughan and Emrys Roberts met with the group's advertising agent, Everett Jones, on 16 March 1961. In his notes from the meeting Roberts recorded that if the Postmaster General 'succumbed' (as he put it) to the BBC's demands for the Band III channel and failed to give the third transmitter in Flintshire to the ITA, then the whole project would be in jeopardy. From the commercial point of view, the north-east audience was seen to be a crucial factor in the success or otherwise of the company. As Roberts deduced from the meeting, 'Western Wales, including the Lleyn Peninsular [sic], is of little sales value in the National'. Roberts demonstrated a sound awareness of the commercial nature of the venture of which he was part. If peak times were to be devoted entirely to Welsh-language programmes, the areas would witness a decline in the number of sets staying switched on to the channel, and therefore there would be a resistance from the national advertisers to placing Welsh programmes at peak hours (that is, after 7 p.m.).[72]

This point of view was supported by Everett Jones in letters to Roberts and Vaughan. Writing to Roberts on 23 March 1961, he insisted that Welsh programmes should finish before 7 p.m., given that this would constitute the start of the 'peak' period, when people would be most likely to be settling down, in a rural and semi-rural area such as west and north Wales. He cited the BBC's popular early evening programmes – the news, regional news and weather – as running from 6 p.m. to 6.20 p.m., and the *Tonight* programme, which started at 6 p.m. In Jones's opinion, the 6.20–6.50 p.m. slot would be 'quite adequate' for Welsh programming.[73] This, of course, was contrary to what the company wanted to hear and to what had been announced in the *Western Mail* and *Y Faner* articles on 7 January 1960. Jones stressed the point further in a letter to David Vaughan on 27 March: 'I would insist that there can be no attempt to mount a Welsh programme between 7 and 10.30pm.'[74]

On 7 April 1961, the ITA issued a press notice 'inviting applications from persons interested in acting as programme contractors for stations in West and North Wales'.[75] The notice referred to the erection of three transmitters which would serve a combined population of around 640,000, of whom some 360,000 would be 'new' ITV viewers (the remainder already receiving ITV from TWW or Granada/ABC). The total population in the area, including 'fringe areas', would be one million. The notice made it clear that the ITA would go ahead on the basis of two transmitters (Preseli and Arfon) if it did not receive the Postmaster General's permission for the third transmitter in Flint-Denbigh. It was also clear from the notice that there was to be a requirement for Welsh-language and Welsh-interest programming at 'good evening hours'.[76]

At the same time the ITA issued guidelines for prospective companies, noting that it had hoped to advertise before this time but, 'in the absence of complete certainty about the technical arrangements which it would be able to adopt, this has not been possible'.[77] The Authority also gave a warning:

> The Authority is conscious of the fact that the combined West and North Wales area is, in terms of population covered, small and likely to be only marginally profitable for any independent company which is appointed to operate there. The Authority will, therefore, need to be fully convinced both as to financial stability of applicant groups and as to their ability to provide programmes of high quality, including a certain number of programmes of Welsh interest and in the Welsh language during the evening hours.[78]

The fee to be paid to the ITA for rental would be £72,000, and this was based on the figure of a 636,000 population (which included those viewers in 'overlap' areas). The ITA also acknowledged that locally originated programming would be modest during the first year, but it stated the requirement to broadcast the regular Welsh-language programmes of TWW and Granada at 'good viewing hours', as well as a Welsh-language bulletin of not less than five minutes per day. There would also have to be not less than one hour per week of other Welsh-language programmes.[79]

The full meeting of the Association on 12 April 1961 was presented with an annual expenditure estimated at £400,000 by Haydn Williams, and an estimated advertising revenue of £580,000, on the assumption of one hour of Welsh-language programmes a day.[80] The board accepted that the company would have to retransmit Welsh-language programming from TWW and Granada in order to keep costs down. Not all accepted these figures – surprisingly perhaps, David Vaughan, Treasurer of the Association, made public the concerns he had expressed in private to Roberts and Alban Davies. In the meeting, he asked that expenditure should be kept to £300,000 per annum, since '[t]he people of Wales will forgive anything except the loss of their money'.[81] In a notebook kept at the time, Roberts reflected a similar concern for those who had invested money in the company:

We must primarily safeguard our revenues because we are trustees for some hundreds of ordinary Welsh people who have entrusted us with their savings as an investment . . . West and North Wales – sparsely populated, largely claimed to intents and purposes by existing contractors. Areas of high cost distribution with comparatively few large chain shops and stores. Almost a speculative venture.[82]

Nevertheless, the Association decided to go ahead with an application for the ITA's west and north Wales licence area.[83]

On 15 May 1961, the Wales Television Association submitted its application to the ITA, with the proposed company title 'Wales Television Limited/Cwmni Teledu Cymru'.[84] The policy statement noted that the group had been brought into existence as a result of the demand for a Welsh television service, 'which would enable such a potent and influential instrument of education, culture and entertainment to contribute materially and effectively to the maintenance of the language and culture of the people'.[85] One hour of Welsh programming would be shown between 6 p.m. and 10.30 p.m., mostly in the Welsh language but also in English, though of special interest to Wales. The application noted that following Haydn Williams's letter of appeal to around 800 people in April 1961, approximately £210,000 had been raised from some 500 people, the names of whom were printed in the application. A study of the names reveals that all parts of Wales are 'covered', but that the predominance was, as would be expected, in the west and north of Wales. Many of those named were Plaid Cymru supporters (including Huw T. Edwards, who joined Plaid Cymru from the Labour Party in 1959, and Saunders Lewis), but they encompassed a wide range of political and cultural backgrounds. The one thing all shareholders had in common was their desire to see the venture succeed.[86]

Four groups were interviewed by the ITA on 30 May: Television Wales Norwest, led by Lord Tenby, Gwilym Lloyd George; the Wales Television Association, led by Haydn Williams and Cennydd Traherne; Cambrian (North and West Wales) Television, under the leadership of the Marquess of Bute; and Cambrian Television, led by Lord Ogmore. Prior to the interviews, Jenkin Alban Davies had been given the opportunity to comment on all four applications. Of Cambrian Television he said that apart from three members, the board was 'of little consequence in the life of Wales'. His comments on Cambrian (North and West Wales) Television were slightly more positive, although he noted that '[t]his company is largely the [Marquess of Bute's] own creation and is controlled by his friends in the Cardiff area who are men of high repute and of little importance in the life of Wales generally'. Television Wales Norwest, wrote Davies, was the formation of Wyndham Lewis, 'who has a reputation in South Wales of having a shrewd business mind'. Other notable members of the board were Myfanwy Howells (a producer with TWW) and Raymond Edwards, Principal of the Cardiff College of Music and Drama. Nevertheless, 'there are few Members of the Board who are national figures or who have been concerned with the cultural or social life of Wales nationally'. Alban Davies raised concerns about where the control of the company would lie, given the high number of local newspapers and cinema interests who were shareholders. His comments on the Wales Television Association began with a revealing comment on the group's chairman: 'Dr B. Haydn Williams is regarded in Wales with very mixed feelings. Certainly conceded to be an enthusiast but has created a large number of enemies and is reputed to be tactless.' He also painted a critical picture of the Wales Television Association Board:

> Colonel Cennydd Traherne is held in high esteem but I would not regard him as an able business man. The Board contains many national figures but appears to me to be slightly overweighted with educationalists and lacks people with experience in the Arts and entertainment . . . All political parties are represented and the leading laymen of all the religious bodies. . .[87]

The first round of interviews took place during the morning of 30 May. In introducing the Wales Television Association, Haydn Williams 'said that it had come into being as a direct result of the desire of Wales to have a television service of its own'. The ITA, in all cases, reiterated the point that the authorisation for the third transmitter had yet to come, and Haydn Williams confirmed that his group were prepared to operate with only two stations.[88] However, in a letter to Emrys Roberts on 31 May, Everett Jones warned him of the dangers of operating with only two transmitters: advertisers would see the areas as being less attractive and, whilst the area could be economically sound, there would be less growth and therefore less promise of Welsh-content programming.[89] On 6 June 1961, the licence was awarded to the Wales Television Association (WTA).

After almost two years of activity on the part of the Continuation Committee, on the afternoon of 7 July 1961, the second National

Conference on Television, again called by Undeb Cymru Fydd, was held in the City Hall, Cardiff.[90] With the Lord Mayor of Cardiff in the chair, T. I. Ellis made the opening remarks and reported on the first National Conference, including the resolution, which was read out. Traherne, as chair of the Continuation Committee reported on the work of the committee, which had included six meetings and five interviews with government Ministers and broadcasting bodies. By this time, three members of the Continuation Committee – Haydn Williams, Cennydd Traherne and T. I. Ellis – were also members of the Wales Television Association, the company formed to apply for the ITV licence in west and north Wales. No doubt in an attempt to deflect criticism from some quarters (particularly those who were favourably disposed towards a BBC-based television service for Wales), Traherne declared:

> It is here stated that the three members of the Continuation Committee who are also members of the Wales Television Association, the successful applicants to the ITA's advertisement, acted on their own initiative in joining the Association. The Association did not grow out of the Continuation Committee.[91]

Although he admitted that there existed no mandate from the committee to form such an association, he felt, nevertheless, that it was 'in the interests of the Conference' that an association be formed which was capable of accepting the ITA's plan, and which was generally 'in sympathy' with the conference's resolution. Traherne ended by asking that the Continuation Committee be dissolved and alternative arrangements made to continue the work of the conference.[92]

Haydn Williams told the conference that the Continuation Committee had approached the ITA because of the Authority's intention to expand into west Wales. Had they expanded the TWW service (as Williams suggested they were planning to do), it would have created an impossible situation in which to create an all-Wales service in the existing Band III channels. The Continuation Committee therefore suggested a modified plan, whereby the ITA would 'start afresh', with a view to establishing, as far as was practicable, a Welsh television service on a commercial basis.[93] The BBC had been approached by the committee but, due to the limitations of Band I, it was decided not to press this option further. 'So', Williams stated, 'taking all this into consideration, we thought the best thing to do was to urge I.T.A. not to go on with their original intention, but to start afresh. We were successful in persuading them to do this'.[94]

The first voice of objection noted in the minutes of the conference was that of T. Haydn Thomas, a member of the Broadcasting Council for Wales. He reminded the conference that every speaker at the 1959 conference had reiterated the need for Wales to be considered a cultural and political unit, and that the structures that existed in 1959 did not support that ideal. Now, he argued, there were signs that the country would be even more fractured: '[T]he main resolution . . . has been submerged. It did ask to treat Wales as an entity etc. Nothing has been done in that direction.' Thomas, as might be expected, argued the case for the BBC to provide an all-Wales service, because '[t]he BBC serves the public and is not a commercial body'.[95] Haydn Williams responded vehemently, arguing that, given that Pilkington was in the process of reviewing the whole British broadcasting system, 'better half a loaf than no bread at all'. The ultimate goal of a full Welsh service could continue to be pursued, but for the time being a Welsh service for a million people was surely cause for celebration.[96]

Traherne, in a more moderate and measured contribution, admitted that the Continuation Committee had not been able to get what the first conference had asked for; nevertheless, the new company was, he argued, a step forward. He put forward a resolution that:

> This Conference, while acknowledging the increase in Television facilities for Wales which the new Independent Television Company Wales Television (Teledu Cymru) will be providing from autumn 1962 from two or possibly three I.T.A. transmitters in Wales, considers there is still much to be done to obtain fulfilment of the Conference's wishes as expressed in the resolution of 18th September 1959.
>
> It wishes the aims and objects of the Conference as stated in that Resolution, and confirmed at this meeting, to be pressed and maintained. It acknowledges and appreciates the work that has been done by the Continuation Committee, whose services have now terminated with the holding of this Conference.
>
> It requests the New Wales Union (Undeb Cymru Fydd) . . . to undertake to pursue the aims and objects of the Conference and to be prepared to call another Conference at some future date if, in its opinion, the situation of Television in Wales demands it.[97]

The first part of the resolution, which called for further representations to be made to ensure a television service for Wales, was unanimously adopted. There was some objection to the second part of the resolution (recommending that Undeb Cymru Fydd be given the task of continuing the work of the Continuation Committee) from Haydn Thomas, who proposed an amendment that a new Continuation Committee be formed. The amendment was rejected by a large majority, and the resolution was carried by the same large majority.

The two National Television Conferences, therefore, drew together a wide variety of groups within Welsh society who were focused on a common goal – a television service for Wales. The conferences, driven by Plaid Cymru and Undeb Cymru Fydd, also mobilised support for such a venture. However, during the first conference, there emerged a clear lack of consensus as to the means of achieving that goal which led to the voices of discontent during the second conference. It could be argued that the unstable foundations set during this period did nothing to ensure a secure and firm start for WWN.

Wales Television (as it now was) met in Cardiff on 20 June 1961. The key announcement at this meeting was that the Postmaster General had expressed a willingness to give the ITA the go-ahead for the company to transmit from a third transmitter, to be built in the Flint-Denbigh area.[98] The requirement from the Post Office, however, was that 50 per cent of the programming had to be originated from within the company. Fraser succeeded in negotiating this down with the Postmaster General to ten hours originated programming per week and, in addition, agreed to reduce the annual rental fee for the transmitters from £200,000 to £50,000. This meant that the ITA was subsidising the company to the tune of £150,000 per annum.[99] However, the conditions placed upon Wales Television were still onerous: the company would need to broadcast at least ten hours per week of Welsh-language and Welsh-interest programmes. This 'burden' was placed on the company by the Post Office in order to justify the building of a new transmitter in an area where programmes were already received from Winter Hill (albeit not in the Welsh language). Yet the ITA, privately at least, saw things differently. Sendall, for example, wrote that '[The Postmaster General] and his officials had, by their unreasonable demands, done all they could to put the infant company's chances of survival in jeopardy.'[100] However, it is also important to bear in mind the deliberations and recommendations of the

Pilkington Committee in this context, which clearly influenced the government's decision about the transmitter and the amount of originated programming. The conditions also raised doubts in the minds of some of the Wales Television board members. The minutes of the meeting on 20 June record that '[g]rave doubts were expressed by some members as to whether we could accept the concession and still be a commercial success'.[101] The board, however, decided to continue with the venture, despite these reservations.

The meeting also witnessed the first public rift in the board, when David Vaughan announced that he would, and could, not continue with Haydn Williams in the chair. Following a period of shock (as minuted), Sir David Hughes Parry proposed a vote of confidence in Williams, which was seconded by Llew Heycock and supported by all present, apart from Vaughan. On 26 June, Vaughan wrote to Emrys Roberts informing him that he refused to serve under the chairmanship of Williams. Neither did he feel able to work with a group 'with obvious links with a Party whose political activities are deplored in a good many areas'.[102] It was clear to Vaughan that the main pressure to ensure that the venture succeeded was coming from Plaid Cymru, despite the fact of all-party coverage on the board. By the time Wales Television next met, on 7 July, Vaughan had resigned.

By now, the TWW directors were also becoming alarmed at some of the Association's plans. On 10 August 1961, Sir Ifan ab Owen Edwards wrote to fellow TWW director Huw T. Edwards stating that the appointment of Haydn Williams's company was a turning-point in Welsh television. Sir Ifan was clearly angry at Williams's suggestion in the Wales Television Association application that the new company would, eventually, be locating a mast in the TWW area. What irked him most was the aggressive tone of Williams's rhetoric, although he found comfort in the knowledge that the new company could not survive without the help of TWW in terms of programming. What he wanted to see was a more cooperative spirit between the two companies: 'WTV + TWW versus BBC' was the way forward to secure improved Welsh programming, according to Sir Ifan. Before this could happen, Williams would have to adopt a position of compromise and cooperation. He asked Huw T. Edwards to help persuade Haydn Williams to do this, as he knew that Edwards had influence over him.

> Churchill was a first-rate bull-dog, but he failed during peace time. The time for attacking in Welsh television is over; Haydn fought brilliantly

and secured a victory. Yet like Churchill, <u>if he does not co-operate</u> now that the campaign has been won, <u>he will have to go</u>.'[103]

Some of Sir Ifan's points were reiterated by Huw T. Edwards in a *Western Mail* article on 12 August. Whilst TWW would give the Wales Television Association every assistance possible, 'we shall not', stated Edwards, 'yield one inch of our territory, nor, however, shall we encroach on the territory of any other company'.[104]

Matters did not improve for Wales Television when, in January 1962, an inflammatory pamphlet, *Teledu Mamon* ('Mammon's Television') was published by Radical Publications of Carmarthen.[105] The pamphlet can be read as a critique of commercialism in general. In this sense, it follows in the tradition of other publications, by groups such as the National Television Campaign and the Labour Party, during the years leading up to the introduction of commercial television in 1955.[106] The author highlighted what he saw as the inherent incompatibility of commercialism with the survival of the Welsh language and culture. This sentiment is an important theme which runs through this period – that of a general dissatisfaction with commercial television per se. Gwynfor Evans and J. E. Jones of Plaid Cymru, for example, argued in a 1958 pamphlet that 'no commercial concern is likely to entertain the idea of providing an adequate service for Wales on a commercial basis', and yet both were to become involved in the establishment of WWN later.[107] *Teledu Mamon*'s argument was that by its very nature, commercial television was at the mercy of the London-based advertisers. This would dictate the timing of programmes and that Welsh programming, which had been promised at good viewing hours, would again be shunted into the inconvenient off-peak hours.

> The fact that there are a good number of Welsh people who have invested in this company will not impress the advertisers. They have only one measure – the size of the audience. This is the foundation of their ungodly profits over the last few years.'[108]

The Welsh-language weekly newspaper, *Y Cymro*, sprang to the defence of those under attack – including WWN directors Haydn Williams and Gwynfor Evans – in *Teledu Mamon*. Under the pseudonym 'Blaen Troed',[109] and under a bold front-page heading 'Mamon – a'r Saint' ('Mammon – and the Saints'), the writer condemned the author for undermining the work of the television company in attempting to provide a worthwhile and necessary television service for Wales. At the end of the article, 'Blaen Troed' listed the board of directors, in order to highlight the 'good Welsh roots' of those involved in the venture (and to highlight the point, no doubt, that WWN was run *by* Welsh people *for* Welsh people). Eric Thomas was listed as a publisher, but what the article failed to note was that Thomas was, in fact, the publisher of *Y Cymro*.[110] Little surprise, therefore, that the paper supported the aims of the company.

Pilkington

The period between 1960 and 1962 was one in which Pilkington dominated discussion over television provision, not only in Wales, but in the whole of the UK. The 'spectre' of the committee hung over much decision-making on the part of the Postmaster General and, in the Welsh context, the Minister of Welsh Affairs. In all, eleven organisations submitted written evidence (including TWW, Urdd Gobaith Cymru, Undeb Cymru Fydd, Plaid Cymru and the Welsh Parliamentary Group), in addition to memoranda submitted by the BBC and the ITA which related specifically to Wales. The majority of the written submissions presented to the committee raised concerns over the impact of television on the Welsh language, culture and 'way of life'. They presented a united front, in terms of supporting the principle that Wales should get its own distinctive television service – a view summarised by the final paragraph of the submission by Urdd Gobaith Cymru:

> It is surely obvious that the one and only solution is to treat Wales as an entity, to divorce her from other regions and to give her the respect a nation deserves. This means a separate television service adequately covering the entire country, providing programmes of all kinds in both Welsh and English at convenient viewing times.[111]

As in the case of its memorandum to the Beveridge Committee in 1949, Plaid Cymru underlined the importance of the Welsh language in the definition of nationhood, noting that 'the key to our national life has at all times been the Welsh language.'[112] In a section lamenting the decline of the language, the party argued:

> One of the most decisive causes of decline in Wales has been the vast growth of new media of mass-communication, which, although they reach every corner of Wales, are aimed specifically at meeting the needs of the numerically much greater English public.[113]

Plaid also premised its arguments on the basis of a concept or – as is noted in the submission – 'fact' of nationhood, 'a distinct cultural and historical unit having its own distinctive character'.[114] The Undeb Cymru Fydd written submission included the words: 'We claim fair treatment for a minority: we claim also fair treatment for a nation which has through the centuries survived storms and struggles from within and without.'[115] During the oral evidence session, the Undeb Cymru Fydd Secretary, T. I. Ellis, rebuked Sir Harry Pilkington at one stage, when the Chairman referred to Wales as an important minority: 'You say a minority, Sir; we say a nation.'[116] The Urdd Gobaith Cymru memorandum focused on the perceived effects of English-language television on the young people of Wales. 'The present state of television in Wales', it stated, 'is fast undermining our efforts and rapidly undoing all that we have achieved since 1922 to get the youth of Wales to cherish their language and culture.' Whilst slightly idealist in tone – there was a suggestion in the fifth paragraph that children and young people lived their lives *completely* through the medium of Welsh and that television would change this – the submission is again passionate in its cultural defence of what it sees as the rights of a nation.[117]

Many of the divisions and debates which had been prevalent throughout the 1950s in Welsh broadcasting politics, crystallised in *Teledu Mamon*, were still there on the eve of the company's launch. Yet, just as in the period from 1949 to 1959 there had been consensus on the diagnoses but no agreement on means, so this was true in the period from 1960 to 1962. The Pilkington Committee and the government had therefore to negotiate their way through a situation where action was demanded, but controversy surrounded action when it was taken. From the evidence available, it would appear that the government appeared to be willing to move forward with the demands made by the Welsh groups via Pilkington, albeit in a slightly compromised way. The key demand was that a 'separate' television service for Wales should be provided, and this was conceded when the BBC was given the necessary channels to provide a service to the whole of Wales, starting in 1964. The government's decision to provide the BBC with Channel 13 in Band III from Wenvoe is in line with the received picture of the outcome of Pilkington, that is, that it was predisposed to the BBC from the outset.[118]

The first edition of TWW's programme journal, *Television Weekly*, published in January 1958.

7.0 NEW AIRS AND FACES

A weekly variety show featuring
WYN CALVIN
introducing
young professional artistes in the world of entertainment who are making their television début—
including
RIC RICHARDS
BERYL CORNISH
THE ROLLING STONES
MAUREEN EVANS
RON CLARK
This week's New Air is
"PATTERN ON THE PAVEMENT"
composed by **RONNIE HILL**
Choreography by Peter Darrell
Designed by John Hickson
Produced and directed by
Jeff Inman

TWW's talent show, *New Airs and Faces*, gave new artistes – including a group called 'The Rolling Stones' – a chance to perform for the first time. The programme was transmitted during the TWW's first week, on Thursday 16 January 1958 (*Television Weekly*, 10 January 1958).

"*Diffyg cwsg, 'rwy'n ofni—gweld gormod o raglenni Cymraeg.*"

'Lack of sleep, I'm afraid – watching too many Welsh programmes.' Hywel Harries, the cartoonist, reflecting the fact that Welsh-language programmes were often broadcast late at night, out of peak viewing hours (from *Blodau'r Ffair* (Summer 1961), p. 66, courtesy of Mrs Cassie Harries and Urdd Gobaith Cymru).

TELEDU MAMON

gan

SODLAU PRYSUR

" *Ni fu gennyf lawer o gewc ar deledu masnachol y Mamon diwyllianol hwnnw!* "

—*Sodlau Segur.*

A Ddarlleno, ystyried

CYHOEDDIADAU RADICAL
SGWAR NEUADD Y DREF
CAERFYRDDIN

Pris 1/-

Teledu Mamon, the inflammatory pamphlet published by Radical Publications of Carmarthen which castigated commercial television and members of the Welsh Television Association (January 1962).

"*Tro'n ol i'r B.B.C., da ti!*"

41

'Turn back to the B.B.C., for goodness sake!' The cartoonist Hywel Harries's take on the perceived crude and vulgar nature of ITV (from Blodau'r Ffair (Christmas 1963), p. 41; courtesy of Mrs Cassie Harries and Urdd Gobaith Cymru).

"*Anyway, we no longer have to keep up this awful 'Indeed to goodness, look you, bach' to all and sundry.*"

Punch's view of TWW's loss of its licence (28 June 1967). Reproduced with permission of Punch Ltd, *www.punch.co.uk*.

Bruce Forsyth, Stanley Baker and Harry Secombe rehearsing for Harlech Television's opening night (courtesy of ITV Broadcasting Ltd).

A helicopter taking off from the Harlech studios in Pontcanna, Cardiff. Note the temporary sign of the new company and the faint markings on the wall where the 'TWW' sign once stood (courtesy of ITV Broadcasting Ltd).

'Blodyn Tatws', from HTV's popular 1970s children's programme in Welsh, *Miri Mawr* (courtesy of ITV Broadcasting Ltd).

6

Wales (West and North) Television, 1962–1963: Operation, Programming and Demise

Introduction

This chapter considers the operation of WWN by looking at three areas: staffing, finance and technical issues. These three have a major role in explaining the demise of the company in 1963. The penultimate section looks at WWN programming, noting in particular the debates around the scheduling of Welsh-language programmes, and the concluding part of this chapter seeks to provide reasons for the failure of the company. The reasons for the demise and financial collapse of the company in 1963 were complex and raise a number of issues about the relationship between ITV, the government, the BBC and the Post Office at this time.

Wales (West and North) Television/Teledu Cymru

WWN went on the air for the first time on 14 September 1962. The programmes were carried by the Preseli transmitter alone, as the other transmitters in Arfon (formerly the Llŷn transmitter) and Moel-y-Parc (the Flint-Denbigh transmitter) were not ready.[1] After speeches by the Lord Mayor of Cardiff, Haydn Williams and Sir Ivone Kirkpatrick (the ITA Chairman), Kirkpatrick pressed the master control button to begin the transmissions.[2] Writing in the first edition of the television-programme listings journal, *Teledu Cymru*, Haydn Williams stated that:

> The aim of *Teledu Cymru* is to introduce on your screen the rich heritage and entertainment which exists in Wales. We will try to offer patronage to the Welsh language, but we will also have to offer programmes which will be of interest to those of us who do not speak Welsh . . . I hope that the programmes will be interesting and edifying to the people of Wales, and that they will be a way of uniting north and south by allowing one to better understand the other.[3]

The *Western Mail* gave the company a cautious welcome. Its editorial of 14 September posed the question, 'A quiet start – and then?' It noted the company's rather inauspicious beginning but stated that the output would increase as time went on and the other transmitters were opened. The paper quoted Iorwerth Thomas, the Labour MP for Rhondda East: 'This is the little mouse that creeps out of the Welsh mountain of oratory and emotion that erupted at the All-Wales conference.'[4] The editorial ended by juxtaposing what it saw as two ends of the spectrum, namely Welsh culture and entertainment. The difficult task facing WWN, it argued, was to create a satisfactory balance of the two: 'We are still speculating on how much of this network's output would be cultural and Welsh and how much entertainment?'[5] However, from the outset, the company was plagued with problems relating to its directors and staff, finances and technical issues.

Directors and staffing

The executives and senior staff appointed to run WWN on a day-to-day basis were an experienced team. The General Manager, Nathan Hughes, was formerly an employee of Associated-Rediffusion and TWW, who had focused on the technical and engineering aspect of television. Havard Gregory was appointed as Senior Producer, having worked with the BBC as announcer and producer. Other key production staff included John Roberts Williams as News Editor, who had been editor of *Y Cymro* since 1945, and the American Ernest G. Byrne, who had previously worked for Telefis Eireann.

The first signs of a strained relationship between management and directors emerged during the first meeting of the executive committee of WWN, on 12 October 1962. Nathan Hughes had been appointed General Manager of WWN in early September 1961, and the evidence suggests that he was, at times, defiant in the face of board decisions with which he did not concur. Certain directors, such as Thomas Parry and Emrys Roberts, clearly felt that he overstepped the mark on a number of occasions. One such case was discussed on 12 October 1962, when Hughes was reminded that network programme policy was the responsibility of the board, and that only they should decide on the type of network programme to be transmitted. Hughes retorted by arguing that changes very often had to be made at the last minute and that referral was not always possible.[6] Although this may appear to have been a minor disagreement, it was symptomatic of the antagonism that was to resurface over the following twelve months.[7] The relationship between Hughes and the directors deteriorated further at the end of January 1963. On 21 January, a memorandum was sent from the budgetary and staffing committee to the board of directors. The third item in the memorandum was based on Nathan Hughes's report on 'Management and Control Policy'. This report effectively castigated the WWN directors for interfering with the day-to-day running of the company and for asking questions of, or giving direct instructions to, individual members of staff. He also referred to the matter of direct correspondence between staff and directors as 'quite unnecessary'.[8] When T. I. Ellis met with Thomas Parry the day after the memorandum had been circulated, he noted in his diary that Parry was not happy at all with the way in which the company was being run.[9] Indeed, on 23 January, Parry circulated a memorandum to all board members and informed them of his resentment at the 'piece of impertinence' on the part of Nathan Hughes. He also called for a full enquiry into the relationship between Nathan Hughes and other members of staff.[10]

Concerns about Nathan Hughes's actions surfaced again in March 1963. On 19 March, T. I. Ellis met with Thomas Parry, who, Ellis noted in his diary, was uneasy about WWN, blaming Hughes for being 'at the root of the evil'.[11] Emrys Roberts's concerns over staff morale surfaced again in March 1963. On 27 March he wrote to Haydn Williams, copying the letter to fellow directors Thomas Parry, David Hughes Parry, Eric Thomas and Philip Williams. In it he voiced his concern over the weakness of the WWN administration. According to Roberts, the administration was responsible for the lack of financial control. He asserted that the cause of the bad staff relations within the company, together with the failure to adhere to board rulings, was Nathan Hughes, the General Manager.[12] The deteriorating relationship between the General Manager and the Board of Directors was a barrier to the effective operation of the company. It soured the working atmosphere and created tensions which were not conducive to a positive working environment. The directors who were vociferous in their opposition to Hughes were angry at his working methods, his perceived lack of tact and diplomacy with staff, his lack of control over the budgetary system and extravagant spending.[13] T. I. Ellis described him as 'out of control' and Thomas Parry once referred to Hughes as a 'megalomaniac'.[14] At the same time, it could be argued that Hughes was one of the more pragmatic members of staff and that he realised that the running of the company had to be grounded in economic and commercial reality. He succeeded in reaching the quota of ten hours of originated material per week by January 1963, and he was aware of the financial pressure under which the company operated. The company was, after all, a business.[15]

The WWN directors (who appear to have adopted what could be termed a 'hands-on approach' in relation to programming and finance) were, on the whole, busy establishment figures who had commitments in a number of areas of Welsh cultural, educational and political life. It was therefore inevitable that difficulties would arise in attempting to bring the whole board together, because of the other demands that were made on the directors' time. On a number of occasions, for example, Haydn Williams as chairman was late or absent, due to commitments to Flintshire Education Authority.[16] On other occasions, executive committee and board meetings were cancelled or changed at the last minute, with no particular reason given.[17] The cancellations and poor attendance levels did nothing to help the overall planning and strategy of the company. Clearly, by the summer of 1963, the directors of the now-depleted WWN were becoming weary and disenchanted. In his diary on 30 July, T. I. Ellis wrote that he had decided not to travel to Cardiff for the board meeting the following day, because, 'I have been very faithful over the months and I am beginning to tire of the whole thing by now'.[18] The directors met on 31 July 1963, with nine absences. It was to be Haydn Williams's final meeting. He resigned from the board at the meeting, but further recriminations were to come. Thomas Parry met T. I. Ellis in Aberystwyth on 1 August and informed him that he would like to see Haydn Williams ousted from his position as Chair of the National Eisteddfod Council. Again, on 20 August, Parry informed Ellis that, in his opinion, Williams and Nathan Hughes were primarily responsible for the failure of the company.[19] The board meeting on 13 September 1963 was attended by only nine of the directors. The aim was to start drawing things to a close. As T. I. Ellis noted in his diary in a resigned way, '[t]he story is sad, but there we are'.[20]

Financial issues

At the meeting of the board of directors on 12 October 1962, it was reported that the Television Audience Measurement (TAM) service had estimated that 46,000 homes were receiving the WWN signal from the Preseli transmitter.[21] When the directors next met, on 10 November,

Gwynfor Evans proposed that a fourth transmitter (in addition to the ones at Preseli, Arfon and Moel-y-Parc) be erected in Montgomeryshire, so as to increase the set count. The directors agreed to put this proposal into abeyance for the time being (although no reason was given), although it may have demonstrated a certain amount of confidence on behalf of the board that they should already be thinking in terms of a fourth station.[22] However, it could also suggest that Evans was concerned at the likely slow growth in the overall set-count, and that his suggestion, in the eyes of the board, complicated an already complex situation. The implications of an increased set-count was one of the main items for discussion at the board meeting on 23 November. The Sales Director, Philip Thomas, estimated that a count of 100,000 with three transmitters and an average TAM rating of 45 would result in a net income of £400,000.[23]

At a meeting of the Independent Television Authority on 18 December 1962, the financial situation of WWN was a topic of discussion, the outcome of which was an agreement on the part of the ITA to a moratorium on the balance of the rental due for the first year of the company's operation.[24] The WWN board meeting on 21 December 1962 received a report from the Chairman, Haydn Williams, which predicted a set count of 124,000 by the time the Moel-y-Parc transmitter began transmitting. At the same meeting, concerns were raised as to the late hours at which Welsh-language programmes were broadcast. This practice was defended by Williams and Nathan Hughes, on the grounds that the company had to transmit network programmes which attracted high TAM ratings, as these resulted in large advertising revenues.[25]

On a more positive note, the Moel-y-Parc transmitter, covering the Flint-Denbigh region, began transmitting on 28 January, and this was welcomed in the first meeting of the ITA's Advisory Committee for Wales, on 1 February 1963.[26] Yet, despite the addition of a third transmitter, the financial situation of WWN grew worse. On 25 February, Nathan Hughes wrote to all directors, alerting them to his concern that the quantity of original programming being produced was in excess of the company's facilities and resources. The meeting of the board of directors on 1 March underlined this fact. Pre-air losses were confirmed as being £160,000, and the set count had only reached 83,000.[27] On 7 March, the WWN directors met with the ITA. The annual rate of loss was estimated at £100,000, and Fraser raised the key question as to whether or not the ITA was right to expect the company to become a viable proposition, even with three transmitters.[28] A two-day directors' meeting on 28 and 29 March called for reductions in expenditure, noting that whilst the weekly expenditure in March 1963 was £8,000, income was only £6,500.[29]

Meeting on 3 May 1963, the ITA's Advisory Committee for Wales noted a chronic lack of income for WWN, which was hampering the effective running of the company. The key issue for the Authority was the need to ensure the conversion of sets and to ensure that relay companies carried WWN programmes.[30] By the time of the meeting of the full Authority on 9 May, however, it became apparent that there was no possibility of WWN continuing as a viable programme company. The idea was raised of TWW transmitting its programmes from WWN's three transmitters, and this was put to a meeting between a group of WWN directors (Haydn Williams, Emrys Roberts, Cennydd Traherne, Eric Thomas and P. O. Williams) and ITA senior officers on 14 May 1963.[31] At a meeting of the board of directors in Shrewsbury on 17 May 1963, the unanimous decision was taken that all original programme production would cease to be forthwith.

Technical issues

The technical problems which dogged the company were threefold: those that related to the transmitters, those that related to the relay companies and those that related to the television sets. Due to the terrain of south Wales, which created reception problems, relay companies provided television to a number of areas. Several of these companies refused to carry the programmes of WWN, one of these being in the Neath and Port Talbot area, which was on the border between WWN and TWW territory. Gaining access to these households was paramount if WWN were to increase their set count in the overlap areas and eventually to compete with TWW in Glamorgan and Monmouthshire, as Haydn Williams had hoped. During the first meeting of the ITA's Advisory Committee for Wales, on 1 February 1963, Jenkin Alban Davies drew attention to the situation and noted that the relay company in question (which was not named in the minutes) was relaying Westward Television programmes to the area. Lyn Evans, the committee's secretary, expressed concern, as Neath and Port Talbot were well outside Westward's area, and stated that the company had a 'moral obligation' to 'pipe' WWN's programmes instead of those of the West Country broadcaster.[32]

The matter was still on the agenda of the Welsh Advisory Committee at its meeting in July 1963. Lyn Evans had prepared a report on relay television which painted a negative picture of the companies. The report noted that when Teledu Cymru was launched, certain companies in the Cardigan, Lampeter and Llandovery areas replaced TWW with WWN and drew an adverse response from the audience, members of which called for TWW to be reinstated (as noted in chapter 3). The Rediffusion Company in the Swansea Valley was recorded as having said that they had no intention of supplying WWN programmes. The reasons given by the relay companies for not piping WWN programmes related to the audience. A Post Office engineer is quoted in the report as saying that the WWN service had been rejected by viewers – including Welsh speakers – for a number of reasons, which included the perception that WWN had not lived up to the promises it had made; that too many old films were transmitted; that the majority of Welsh-language programmes were TWW repeats and were on late, at 10.30 p.m. or 10.45 p.m.; that the production values were seen as 'amateurish'.[33] In summarising the situation, Evans stated that, from the evidence available to him, 'it is clear that WWN have a continuingly difficult task in building up their set count in South West Wales'. He continued by noting that the situation could be improved if the major relay companies – Red Dragon and Piped Television (Wales) – could be persuaded to change affiliation. Again, Evans referred to a 'moral obligation' to provide WWN programmes, but he acknowledged that as commercial companies they provided what the customers wanted, which was TWW and Westward.[34]

The final technical issue related to the fact that anybody wishing to receive WWN programmes had to purchase a new set or convert an existing set. This proved to be a barrier for many and, according to Nathan Hughes, resulted in consistently low set-counts for the company.[35] As a result, potential income was lost.

Programming

Bernard Sendall wrote of the opening night of WWN that, '[t]o the professional eye the first week's programmes were not unpromising'. It opened with a musical arrangement of the Welsh National Anthem over shots of various locations in Wales.[36] However, what Sendall failed to mention was the fact that the film was initially projected back-to-front and that it had to be stopped and started again.[37] The remainder of the opening night's fare was a balance of originated programming and popular programmes taken from the network:[38]

5.30 p.m.	*Croeso* – welcome and introduction to the personalities to be seen on WWN, from Cardiff by Welsh actor, Clifford Evans (WWN)
5.55 p.m.	ITN News broadcast from WWN studios in Cardiff (ITN)
6.06 p.m.	*Newyddion a'r Tywydd* (News and Weather, in Welsh) (WWN)
6.16 p.m.	*Cip ar Chwarae* – a Welsh-language sports programme looking over the weekend's sport (WWN)
6.24 p.m.	*Impact* – first in a series of fortnightly English-language discussion programmes. Iorwerth Thomas MP (Rhondda East) and Dr Gareth Evans (University College, Swansea) discussed the impact of television on Wales. The programme was chaired by the poet and novelist T. Glynne Davies. He was also the producer and later became part of the company's news team. (WWN)
6.42 p.m.	News of Wales and Weather (WWN)
6.56 p.m.	*Moment for Melody* (WWN)
7.00 p.m.	*Take Your Pick* (Associated-Rediffusion, entertainment)
7.30 p.m.	*Emergency – Ward 10* (ATV, drama)
8.00 p.m.	*Desilu Mystery Theatre* (Associated-Rediffusion, drama)
8.55 p.m.	*Animaland* (cartoon)
9.00 p.m.	ITN News
9.15 p.m.	*Probation Officer* (ATV, drama)
10.10 p.m.	Melody and Rhythm (ATV, music programme)
10.40 p.m.	*Crwydro'r Alban* – the dramatist Emyr Edwards on a journey through the Celtic countries, this week in Scotland (TWW)
11.18 p.m.	*Markham* – starring Ray Milland (an imported programme, though billed as a 'Teledu Cymru Presentation')
11.48 p.m.	Closedown

Teledu Cymru and *Wales Television* were the Welsh-language and English-language versions of the company's television-listings paper, which were produced weekly. Both editions were published by Woodalls in the Caxton Press in Oswestry, the same publishing firm that published *Y Cymro*, the editor of which, Eric Thomas, was a member of the board of WWN and became its Managing Director in May 1963, after the resignation of Haydn Williams. Following the dispute with TWW and the ITA over the use of the 'Wales Television' title, the paper's banner was the words 'TELEDU CYMRU' in upper-case in large white print on a red background, with a smaller font, lower-case 'Gorllewin a Gogledd' ('West and North') just above the banner. The edition published in time for the August 1962 National Eisteddfod in Llanelli included the company's official title, 'Wales (West and North) Television Limited', together with the red dragon logo. However, only the logo (minus the wording) remained from the first edition 'proper' onwards. Until the 18–24 November edition, the paper covered only the Channel 8 (Preseli) transmitter area, adding 'Channel 10' (that is, the Arfon area) to the paper's front cover in late November 1962. It is interesting to note, however, that the special edition published to coincide with the Eisteddfod showed a map of Wales with the Preseli (Pembrokeshire), Arfon (Caernarfon) and Moel-y-Parc (Flint-Denbigh) transmitters, although only the Preseli transmitter was operational at the time of the company's first broadcast in September 1962. It was known at the time that the Flint-Denbigh transmitter would not be ready until late 1962 at the earliest. It is also significant that even in English-language material in the paper, the reference is to 'Teledu Cymru' and not 'Wales (West and North) Television' or 'WWN'. The branding is clear from the outset; this was to be television for Wales as a whole, although the reality was that it covered a smaller area of the country than WWN had.

During the early weeks of the company the journal received a number of letters from members of the public. The letters were invariably concerned with the timing of Welsh programmes. One such letter was written by Saunders Davies of Fishguard, who called for Welsh programmes to be transmitted between 7 p.m. and 10 p.m. in order that farmers in west Wales (who comprised a sizeable proportion of the audience) could see the programmes after they returned from milking. At the same time, Davies wished WWN 'every luck to expand the boundaries of your vision and be a true tool to save our language and culture'.[39] Another, Lynn Davies from Carmarthen, also asked why the programmes were transmitted at a late hour, but at the same time and, no doubt, crystallising the views of many viewers, thanked the company 'for what we do get in Welsh'.[40] A writer from Aberystwyth, L. Jones, came to WWN's defence in October. Jones stated that he was fed up with the critics, who expected WWN to 'perform miracles', and reminded readers that the company had began to transmit under the disadvantage of having only the Preseli transmitter at its disposal.[41] What is noticeable is that, after this point, more letters do not materialise, which may suggest a lack of interest or of the motivation to write to express views. Even in the months of crisis, when the paper put out a weekly request for letters, not a single one was published (which suggests that no letters were received).

WWN's programming policy can be split into two distinct periods: that prior to January 1963, and that after the first week of January 1963. From 14 September 1962 until the end of the year, Welsh-language and Welsh-interest programmes were transmitted between 6.06 p.m. and 7 p.m. and from 10.30 p.m./10.45 p.m. until 11 p.m./11.15 p.m. on weekdays. Only occasionally were Welsh-language or Welsh-interest programmes broadcast at the weekend. It can be seen from this that although such programmes were broadcast during 'good' evening hours (between 6 p.m. and 7 p.m.), the programmes broadcast later were considered to be on the periphery of the schedule. In general, the programmes during the early evening period tended to be those originating from WWN, whilst the late programmes were those from TWW (such as the magazine programme *Amser Te* or the quiz show *Taro Deg*). It should also be noted that the government's regulations allowed for a total average of around eight hours of broadcasting per day.

During the first period (September to December 1962), WWN originated approximately four and a half hours of its own programming per week, with approximately three hours per week coming from TWW. The remainder came from the network companies, such as Associated-Rediffusion, ATV and Granada.[42] During the last week of November 1962, WWN announced that it would be increasing its original output and transmitting around ten hours per week of Welsh-language and Welsh-interest programmes from January 1963 onwards, which was heralded by the company as 'quite an achievement and a challenge'. At the same time, it reassured its viewers that they would not be missing out on the popular network programmes, such as *Coronation Street* or *Emergency – Ward 10*, thereby underlining the popularity of such programmes amongst the WWN audience.[43] By extending the early evening hours from 6.06 p.m. to 7.30 p.m., WWN was able to boast that it offered Welsh-language or Welsh-interest programming during the peak time period (7 p.m.–7.30 p.m.). It also offered viewers the chance to watch programming from Wales on a Sunday. For example, on Sunday 6 January 1963, viewers could watch *Myfyr a Mawl* (a religious programme) from

5 p.m.–5.30 p.m. and TWW's *Amser Te* between 5.30 p.m. and 6.05 p.m. The monthly networked Land of Song (a TWW production) was transmitted from 6.15 p.m.–6.55 p.m., and at 10.35 p.m. a programme on Welsh museums, *Trysorau Cymru* (another TWW production) was broadcast.[44]

As a result of the increased broadcasting hours, and the opening of the Moel-y-Parc transmitter, WWN maintained an average of ten hours fifty-one minutes of Welsh-language or Welsh-interest programmes per week (the balance between the two languages averaging out as being 50:50), thereby fulfilling the requirements as set out by the Postmaster General.[45] There was, therefore, a concerted effort on the part of the company to reach its target, albeit with the help of programming from TWW.

WWN's strengths in Welsh-language programmes were in the factual area. TWW had pioneered television quiz shows and these were retransmitted to the WWN area. WWN soon developed a strong news output and drew on the expertise of John Roberts Williams and the ex-BBC journalist T. Glynne Davies. The company was also a pioneer in this area, and the team headed by Williams provided peak-time Welsh-language television news for the first time ever. One reason for the strength of the service was the fact that Williams had been editor of *Y Cymro* for sixteen years before joining WWN, and had built up an impressive base of contacts. The news team also depended on stringers to report from various parts of the area, who were willing to contribute to the venture for very little money.[46] Sport was also seen as an important part of the output, and *Cip ar Chwarae* and its English-language counterpart, *Welsh Spotlight*, featured regularly in the schedule.

The more general Welsh programming tended to focus on the history, politics and literary traditions of Wales, an example being *Golwg ar Gymru*, produced by Havard Gregory, the company's senior producer. Other programmes, such as *Pawb a'i Bethau*, were presented by John Roberts Williams and profiled Welsh 'characters'. Although no footage exists of this programme, the billing suggests that its aim was to capture a way of life that was rapidly changing or disappearing, which was important, given the nature of WWN itself and its cultural aim.[47]

At the same time, concerns about the location of Welsh-language programming in the schedule were prevalent and were discussed in the board meeting on 21 December 1962. It was minuted that '[m]embers of the Board were perturbed at the late hour in which Welsh language programmes were being transmitted'.[48] Haydn Williams and Nathan Hughes defended the schedule, pointing out that locating such programmes was very difficult, 'in view of the necessity of the company to transmit Network programmes which commanded a very high TAM rating'.[49] Already, the realities of commercial television were hitting home, and the meeting signalled a turning-point in the fortunes of the company.

The issue was raised again on New Year's Day 1963, when Nathan Hughes presented a memorandum entitled 'Local Origination and TWW Programmes' to the company's Programme Committee. He outlined the company's policy on transmitting Welsh and Welsh-interest programming during the period 6 p.m. to 7 p.m., and drew attention to the fact that most of the WWN-originated programmes were of a magazine style because the company had no formal agreement with the artists' union and could not, therefore, produce music programmes. Hughes also highlighted the fact that light entertainment programmes, such as *Disc-a-Gogo* and *Taro Deg*, were already being supplied by TWW. Hughes's suggestion was for the company to consider presenting Welsh-language programmes in the 7 p.m. to 7.30 p.m. slot on certain weeknights. Whilst acknowledging that this would be a risk in commercial terms, he argued that WWN and the ITA could be exposed to serious criticism, should no attempt be made to transmit Welsh-language programmes between 7 p.m. to 10.30 p.m. He ended by arguing that it was essential that a policy decision be made as soon as possible on the notion of transmitting such programmes between those times.[50] The company had already taken the decision to broadcast a Welsh-language programme between 7 p.m. and 7.30 p.m., and had announced its decision at the end of November 1962 in the programme journal.

Criticism of WWN's Welsh-language programming also became an issue, following the announcement of the cessation of original production. On 23 May 1963, the radio and television critic of *Baner ac Amserau Cymru* reported on the motion passed at the Undeb Cymru Fydd Women's Conference criticising WWN programmes. The lack of Welsh-language programming was noted as being disappointing: 'We were promised more than was possible to achieve.'[51] Nevertheless, the critic's own view, having watched almost all the company's output, was that 'the standard is generally very satisfactory considering that the company does not possess the enormous resources of the corporation and the English companies'.[52] The paucity of Welsh-language material was also highlighted in a sardonic comment from 'Iolo' (Aneirin Talfan Davies) in the *Western Mail* on 25 May 1963, when he wrote that 'the literary output last year was as scarce as Welsh language programmes on WWN'.[53]

What is striking, from an examination of the programme listings, is that WWN did not produce any original drama. The main reason for this was the prohibitive cost of producing drama, and, as John Roberts Williams confessed, Welsh-language television drama would not necessarily attract the advertising revenue desperately needed by the company.[54]

The financial implications of programming were underlined in a memorandum from Nathan Hughes to the Programme Committee on 21 January 1963. Referring to the committee's decision to transmit a special forty-five-minute St David's Day programme on 1 March, Hughes noted that this would require opting out of the ITV network's *Take Your Pick*, which, it was argued, would be 'unwise'.[55] What Hughes suggested was a half-hour programme in the usual *Heno* slot between 6.15 p.m. and 6.45 p.m., as there was no suitable later place in the schedule. Although this was not totally satisfactory, Hughes was pragmatic enough to note that this was the 'only way of presenting [a] St David's Day programme within the budget'.[56]

A further memorandum from Hughes to the Programme Committee was sent on 25 February 1963. Hughes again asked the committee to consider in more detail the hours of local origination. He felt that the company was producing a quantity of programmes far in excess of the facilities that were at the production staff's disposal, and as a result the quality of the programming was declining. He also criticised programme staff for engaging 'outsiders' to produce and present programmes, calling it the 'wrong way of doing television'.[57] Hughes flagged up a key concern of his, namely that the present programme pattern (in particular the timing of the Welsh-language programming) was uneconomic. The strong opposition from the BBC, TWW and Granada was resulting in poor ratings. It was also at this point that Hughes raised the issue of cutting back on locally originated programmes.[58]

The final originated programme (in a magazine style) was transmitted live on 31 May 1963 from the television studios in Western Avenue, Cardiff. Accompanying part of the final news bulletin was the musical lament of a dying harpist ('Dafydd y Garreg Wen' (David of the White Rock)), over shots of the studio staff preparing to end production.

The most symbolic shot was that of the traffic barrier at the entrance to the studio grounds being lowered.[59]

Conclusions

The origins of WWN can be traced back to the period of the Beveridge Committee (1949–51). An understanding of the divisions and lack of consensus at the time of the Beveridge submissions ultimately led to the unstable foundations on which WWN was founded. The lack of unity amongst Welsh political and cultural groups in the early 1950s on issues such as public and commercial broadcasting, the role of broadcasting in Welsh society, and whether or not to advocate a separate broadcasting corporation for Wales, continued into the early 1960s. Tracing WWN's roots back to Beveridge provides a clearer framework for understanding the reasons for its failure. Had there been more consensus on the way forward amongst these groups, then the WWN initiative would perhaps not have been the chosen route, or, if it had been, it might have received more financial and managerial resources from those pressing for a Welsh television service.

The period between 1956 and 1959 raises a number of issues which are a key to understanding the history of WWN. It is clear from the cultural, political and educational groups and institutions that engaged in broadcasting politics in the late 1950s that the shared assumption was that television was an influential medium. The main line of argument was that, in order for the Welsh language and culture to survive, a television service for Wales would be a prerequisite. Whilst this common assumption was held by the groups, at the same time there was a distinct lack of clarity over the best way forward, and a number of different voices and opinions were put to the broadcasting authorities and the government. The main division amongst the groups concerned the nature of the service – commercial or public. At the same time, both the ITA and the government came under increasing pressure to act to move towards a Welsh television service, not only from the aforementioned groups, but, in the case of the government, from the BBC. The Corporation was keenly aware of the nature of the competition from commercial television, and during the period embarked upon an effort to secure its own service for Wales.

The WWN initiative stemmed from the widespread view that the media influenced cultural life and, as such, needed to be harnessed to a nationalist agenda. The lack of consensus over what the agenda should be – public service, commercial, Welsh, English – led to a situation by 1959 (the first National Television Conference) in which there were no unified proposals coming from Wales. The advent of commercial television in Wales in 1956, together with the fact that the BBC's television coverage of Wales was only partial, provided a platform for political intervention. From 1956 onwards, the level of activity amongst political and cultural pressure-groups increased, and the roles of the ITA and the government became increasingly prominent. At this point, the complexity of Welsh politics meshed with the changing nature of television in Wales and engaged with Westminster politics. Added to this were a BBC under increasing pressure from ITV and a growth in the institutional rivalry between the two broadcasters. The environment from which the WWN initiative emerged was one which fused Welsh politics with Westminster politics.

One of the issues which may help to explain the demise was the cultural basis of the company. The board lacked the requisite business and financial acumen required for any television company operating within the commercial sector. Added to this, the evidence shows that the organisation and management of the company was poorly executed, particularly in the area of finance. At the same time, however, the geographical (overlap areas) and technical complexities (transmitter delays and the demands for Channel 13 in Band III) created a situation which made the day-to-day operation difficult. The growing institutional rivalry between the BBC and the ITA was bound up with the technical issues, as both broadcasters demanded Channel 13 in Band III to provide a service for Wales. This debate, taking place as it did in the shadow of Pilkington, exacerbated delays, which in turn created financial difficulties for WWN. The timing of the project is also a crucial factor in assessing the company's history. The willingness of the ITA to advertise the contract and of the Wales Television Association to apply for it were badly timed. Haydn Williams and the Wales Television Association were seeking a speedy solution to a problem that had been in existence for a number of years, and the ITA was keen to appear in a good light to both Pilkington and the government. Had both parties waited until after the Pilkington Report, the venture might have been more fruitful.

The history of the demise of the company was not merely a heroic failure against all the odds, neither can it be explained by gross incompetence on the part of the directors (especially Haydn Williams) driven by nationalistic zeal.[60] The notion of 'blame' is not one which adequately explains the reasons for the failure of WWN; rather, a complex interweaving of events, circumstances and personalities led to the formation and failure of a television company which was founded on clear ideological principles. The context in which WWN emerged and operated was one characterised by internal and external divisions, financial difficulties and lack of internal financial control, external criticism, technical problems and shifting government policy. Arguably, those involved in the company were operating within a climate over which they had little control, especially as the timing of the establishment of WWN, coinciding as it did with Pilkington's review of broadcasting, was unfortunate. Indeed, the Pilkington Committee overshadowed much of the deliberation and decision-making in the early years of the 1960s, at a time when demands were being made on the government from the Continuation Committee, the ITA and the BBC. The timing of the emergence of WWN resulted in delayed decision-making and compromise from a government which not only had to balance the demands which were being made on it, but also had to avoid pre-empting the Pilkington Committee's recommendations.

Criticisms could be made of the key players in the history of the company. The ITA clearly played a pivotal role in the formation of what was to become Teledu Cymru. The evidence demonstrates willingness on the part of the Authority to ensure that a Welsh television service was in place in the west and north Wales, one which would be responsive to Welsh needs and which would satisfy the demands of the various groups and organisations in Wales. It was also a service that the Authority hoped might expand to cover the whole of Wales, controlled within, and with capital investment from, Wales (unlike TWW). This willingness is exemplified in the ITA's plan to move ahead on the basis of two stations, whilst awaiting the Postmaster General's approval for the Flint-Denbigh station. At the same time, however, it is clear that the Authority was aware of the lack of consensus of opinion as to the best and quickest way to achieve the goal of a separate Welsh service. The ITA used the National Television Conference and the Continuation Committee as a proxy for Welsh opinion, to register the level of 'official' Welsh support for independent television. The ITA was in a stronger position than the BBC, to offer something to the Continuation Committee, and was able to deliver in a relatively short space of time. In addition, the ITA was clearly conscious of the need to act so as to match any moves which would allow the BBC to create an all-Wales service.

The ITA could also be criticised for not properly scrutinising the company, once it had been established. The government should have responded by intervening in a more active way, particularly after Pilkington, to remedy the situation in Wales. Clearly, the lack of commercial expertise and of financial management amongst the WWN directors lays some responsibility on their shoulders. In this sense, there was no one person or organisation entirely at fault. The failure of the company came about as a result of a combination of factors which worked to produce a difficult environment, in which a commercial television company, founded as it was on clear ideological goals, found it impossible to operate. On 27 January 1964, TWW formally took over WWN and a new episode in the history of independent television in Wales began.

7

Television Wales and the West, 1964–1968: Operation and Programming

Introduction

This chapter considers the company's second contract period, between 1964 and 1968. During this time TWW provided a service for the whole of Wales in addition to the west of England, following the demise of WWN. The period, however, signalled the beginning of the end for the ITV contractor. Increasing criticism from the ITA on a range of issues primarily concerned with programming dogged the company, and in 1967 the company lost its licence to a rival consortium, led by Lord Harlech. The chapter begins with a chronological narrative of the period and then moves on to a consideration of the programmes produced by TWW between 1964 and 1968. Critical issues arising from the period will be discussed in the next chapter.

Overview: 1964–1968

By the time the operational takeover of WWN took place on 27 January 1964, TWW was in a strong position. The company had gained international recognition the previous year when the documentary film *Dylan Thomas* won an 'Oscar' award for Best Short Documentary. The film, directed by Jack Howells and produced by TWW, was a lyrical portrait of the life of the author and poet, and starred Richard Burton as the narrator. The acclaim which came in the wake of the award, together with the renewal of the licence which came at the end of 1963, the 'saving' of WWN and the favourable financial settlement with WWN shareholders stood the company in good stead for the years ahead.[1] At the end of January, Lyn Evans, the ITA's Officer for Wales and the West, wrote to John Baxter, TWW's Managing Director, noting the new contractual obligations from the new contract period of July 1964 onwards. A total of eleven hours of originated programming would be required, but, given that a separate channel for south Wales would not be available until the end of 1964, there would be a 'progressive development' towards the full complement of hours.[2] The letter also outlined the ITA's plans for the mix of programmes, which included a clear reference to drama productions. In a rather pointed comment, Evans noted that:

> [The ITA Committee for Wales] have on several occasions drawn attention to the absence of drama productions in the Welsh language on independent television. They feel that there is plenty of talent among Welsh people in this field and that some effort ought to be made to exploit it.[3]

The issue of drama production (or, rather, the lack of it) was to dominate much of the dialogue between TWW and the ITA's Welsh Committee during this period and will be discussed in the next chapter.

Also by the end of January, TWW's Production Panel was discussing plans to enable the company to meet the new programming requirements. Interestingly, Lord Derby underlined the importance of the west of England to the company; he stated that after the new licence period had started (post-30 July), the ITA would recognise 'Wales and the West' as an entity in its own right, and urged the panel and the company not to highlight differences between the two parts of the franchise.[4] The reason for Derby's statement is not entirely clear, but it could be explained by two factors. Firstly, the Postmaster General had granted permission which ultimately led to a Welsh (and Welsh-language) service for the whole of Wales, which would be transmitted on Channel 7 in south Wales from the St Hilary transmitter, thus leaving Channel 10 free for a service to the West Country and a general English-language 'bridging service' for south Wales and the west of England. Given that Channel 10 would be free of all Welsh material, Derby was aware of the potential split, both in TWW and amongst the audience, and wanted to ensure the continued unity of the company. Secondly, Derby would have been aware that the licence, which ran from August 1964, would expire in July 1968 and that a new licence-renewal process would soon be initiated. He would not have wished to enter the renewal process with a seemingly divided company and audience and this would explain his insistence that it was not in TWW's best interest to perpetuate the notion of separate sub-regions within one ITV region. Alternatively, Derby's attitude also have betrayed a sense of detachment from the desire of many on both sides of the Bristol Channel to see the 'marriage' between Wales and the West nullified.

In June 1964, TWW began to make moves to augment the Welsh board with representatives from west and north Wales, as requested by the ITA following the takeover of WWN. It was agreed to approach the Archdruid of Wales, the Revd Albert Evans Jones (Cynan), Ivor Kelly, a mining training instructor with the National Coal Board, and Glyn Davies, a former High Sheriff of Cardiganshire and Managing Director of E. T. Davies (Aberarth) Ltd Builders.[5] All three agreed, and a formal announcement of the appointments was made at the Llangollen International Eisteddfod on 9 July.[6] Cynan and Ivor Kelly attended their first board meeting on 10 September 1964, and Glyn Davies attended his first meeting on 29 October.

TWW's first contract period came to an end at the end of July 1964. Although a strike across ITV by members of the technicians' union, the ACTT, threatened to disrupt programmes at the beginning of the month (including elaborate plans for outside broadcasts from the Llangollen International Eisteddfod), the dispute was settled before the Eisteddfod began and the contract period ended on a high (which included significant bonuses in the pay packets of staff). As the television critic of the *Western Mail* noted, 'the BBC may excel at Wimbledon – but when it comes to Llangollen, you have to hand it to TWW'.[7] The second contract period started with a change of chairman for the ITA's Committee for Wales. Dr Jenkin Alban Davies retired, after having served two terms, and was replaced by Rhondda-born Sir Ben Bowen Thomas, a former Permanent Secretary to the Welsh Department of the Ministry of Education and President of the University College of Wales, Aberystwyth.[8] For TWW, in the meantime, it was 'business as usual'. The National Eisteddfod of Wales visited Swansea and the company went to great lengths to associate itself with the festival. In addition to presenting the Eisteddfod chair, TWW produced 30,000 copies of a four-page *Teledu* ('Television') supplement, arranged closed-circuit English-language commentary for non-Welsh-speaking visitors, provided a special viewing tent for 300 people and arranged the first ever eve-of-Eisteddfod Church in Wales service, for transmission on 2 August.[9] Writing to John Baxter on 24 August, Huw T. Edwards commented on the excellent coverage of the Eisteddfod and said that as a result the company's standing in Wales was 'higher than it has ever been before'.[10] Edwards's further comment to Baxter that his 'guiding hand' would prevent the company from 'developing into small cliques' is interesting. Although the board minutes do not suggest any major discontent, Edwards had noted his concern in the June 1964 meeting of the Welsh board that all English-language productions were being produced in Bristol and all Welsh ones in Cardiff, and that the split was divisive.[11] Clearly, there were concerns (aired by Edwards, by Derby and by Wyn Roberts – see later in this chapter) that the company was in danger of splitting and that this could affect the licence bid in 1967.

October 1964 was dominated by the General Election and the Olympic Games, and TWW covered both. Lyn Evans, in his monthly report to the ITA's Director General, noted that two of the four gold medallists at the Olympics – Lynn Davies and Mary Rand – came from the TWW region, and that this had provided the opportunity for the company to produce topical inserts for news programmes.[12] The remainder of the year was spent preparing for the launch of Channel 7 from St Hilary, which would provide an all-Wales service to 90 per cent of the population for the first time.[13] The company also continued working on the extension to the Pontcanna studios, which would enhance production output.

Preparations for the new service continued into January 1965 and trade test transmissions began on 20 January. The company did, however, suffer a setback at the beginning of 1965 when Jack Hylton, one of the founder directors of TWW, died, on 29 January. Described by Lyn Evans as 'a good protagonist of the Welsh cause', Hylton was seen as a steadying influence in TWW. Such was his standing in the world of television and entertainment that a televised tribute show was transmitted on 30 May 1965 from the Theatre Royal in Drury Lane, London. Hylton's death prompted Lyn Evans to suggest that an additional Welshman be added to the board of TWW, as the majority of TWW's viewers were now in Wales.[14] As a result, Lord Brecon (who had been one of the founder directors of TWW and had served as Minister of State for Welsh Affairs between 1958 and 1964) was appointed to the board.

On 15 February 1965, TWW launched its new service for Wales, Teledu Cymru, on Channel 7 (St Hilary), Channel 8 (Preseli), Channel 10 (Arfon) and Channel 11 (Moel-y-Parc). Programming began with speeches from James Griffiths, the Secretary of State for Wales and Labour MP for Llanelli, Goronwy Roberts, Labour MP for Caernarfon and Minister of State for Wales, Sir Ben Bowen Thomas, and Sir Grismond Philipps, as chairman of TWW's Welsh board. At the same time, the

TWW Channel 10 service from St Hilary became the general television service for the west of England and south Wales, with no Welsh-interest or Welsh-language programming. The signal from St Hilary reached most of south Wales, but relied on the Rediffusion relay company to carry the signal to the south Wales valleys. The irony was that the signal could be received perfectly in Swindon.[15] The headline in the *Guardian* referred to a 'Great day for Wales – and West', stating that the new service would be a 'happy release for the West of England half of TWW's 3½ million viewers, for whom the Welsh-language programmes can hardly have been enthralling entertainment over the past seven years'.[16] By the end of the year, the audience for the Teledu Cymru service in south Wales had grown much more rapidly than had been expected by the ITA.[17] However, the company encountered problems with certain relay companies, who were unwilling to carry the new service in the south. In late February TWW executives met with the General Manager of Rediffusion South Wales, who was taking a decision whether or not to take the Channel 7 service to that company's 80,000 subscribers, as there were only four channels available for the five services that were available in south Wales: BBC1 (Channel 5), BBC Wales (Channel 13), TWW General Service (Channel 10), TWW's Teledu Cymru Service (Channel 7) and BBC2 (from September 1965). The consensus was that the BBC1 service on Channel 5 would have to be dropped, as the BBC Wales service was offering a high proportion of 'local' content.[18] The situation was not resolved by May 1965, as the TWW Welsh board minutes record that some relay companies were reluctant to carry Channel 7 for fear of displacing the fledgling BBC2 service, which was proving to be popular in south Wales.[19] In general, however, the new broadcasting landscape in Wales satisfied those who had long campaigned for an all-Wales television service. The creation of BBC Wales in February 1964 and the launching of the Teledu Cymru service a year later meant that twenty-two hours of television a week of English-language and Welsh-language programming was now possible. As a *Times* feature stated in March 1965:

> For a while all television in Wales was bedevilled by a repetition of the unnatural forced marriage with the West of England which the sound broadcasters had once perpetrated in a romantic attempt to recreate on the air the mythical realm of Arthur. The alliance has now been happily dissolved both by the B.B.C. and by T.W.W.[20]

Despite having a separate service for Wales, TWW was still keenly aware of the competition from the BBC. In a memorandum to John Baxter and Bryan Michie, the company's Programme Controller, Wyn Roberts, underlined the intense competition faced by TWW in south Wales. Faced with three BBC alternatives – BBC1, BBC Wales and BBC West – it was, he wrote, 'imperative we remain on top'. In particular, Roberts drew attention to the *Here Today* programme, which had hitherto acted as a 'bridging' programme for south Wales and the west of England. Since the launch of the separate Channel 7 and Channel 10 services, the programme had been strongly associated with the West Country, although it was still broadcast on the general Channel 10 service, and Welsh viewers were tending to turn to the BBC's *Wales Today* programme. The logical way forward was to offer completely separate Welsh and English services, as the BBC did, with no general service to link Wales and the West. This, however, was not feasible for, a commercial television company, for as Roberts argued:

> The separatism of Wales and the West must be minimised as much as possible. There is too much separatism at present. I have stressed again and again the importance of the 1½ million Welsh viewers of Channel 10 who are not interested in Teledu Cymru as it stands. There is a great danger that they will be driven into the arms of the BBC Welsh Service . . . [21]

At the annual meeting of TWW on 1 May, a dividend of 107 per cent for shareholders was approved, and a total income of £4.2 million was noted for the previous year.[22] Yet the ITA appeared to be impressed not so much by the financial success of the company as by the amount of locally originated production. In his monthly report to the Director-General in June 1965, Lyn Evans sought to explain this success, but could not find a satisfactory answer. One suggestion was that the power centre was 'firmly entrenched' in Sloane Square in London, distant from the production bases at Cardiff and Bristol, and therefore both centres were able to get on with responding to local needs with minimal interference.[23] At the same time, the ITA did have qualms about some aspects of TWW's programme schedule (see chapter 8).

If the ITA was impressed by the company's local production output, one person who certainly was not impressed was the author and novelist Caradog Prichard. Writing in the *Western Mail* on 2 August 1965, he attacked TWW for its 'undesirable intrusion' at the Llangollen

International Eisteddfod and suggested that the company be barred from the National Eisteddfod:

> The growing flamboyance with which this English-run company intrudes on the festival year after year cannot but have an alienising and vulgarising influence on the Eisteddfod as we wish to know it... The broadcasting requirements of the National Eisteddfod are adequately met by the various Welsh departments on the BBC. The intrusion of TWW is commercial in the guise of a benevolent but alien patronage.

He ended by urging the Eisteddfod organisers to stick to humble ideals and 'cast out the vulgarisers'.[24] The Eisteddfod Council responded by defending TWW, and Huw T. Edwards retorted in a letter to the newspaper on 6 August, asking whether or not Caradog Prichard had complained when TWW rescued WWN and its shareholders from a complete financial loss.[25]

By the end of 1965 prospects were bright for TWW; the average share of the audience had moved upwards, in comparison with other regional ITV companies, and 80 per cent of Welsh homes were able to receive the new Teledu Cymru service. The company had opened its extended studio in Bristol in October, and in December, parts of the extension to the Pontcanna studios were opened. Share prices were also up, with the 2s. 6d. shares being quoted at a record 30s.- by the end of the year.[26] In addition, TWW were pioneering colour television, and in this sense were well ahead of any other regional ITV company (or, indeed, the BBC). In December 1965, the company invested in a complete colour television unit – two colour cameras, monitor sets and ancillary equipment – for staff training in Cardiff and Bristol, and by June 1966, TWW was challenging the Postmaster General, Tony Benn, to give the go-ahead for a colour television service.[27] Speaking at the Bath and West showground, Frank Brown, the company's Publicity Director, stated that TWW could offer a colour service immediately and forecast that once BBC2 began to broadcast in colour from 1967, viewers would want to see all channels in colour.[28] The issue was raised again on 20 October, when Sir Ben Bowen Thomas opened the £250,000 extension to the Pontcanna studios of TWW. Lord Derby reiterated that the company was ready to offer a colour service on the 405-line system, which could be viewed by the majority of people.[29]

If 20 October 1966 was a day of celebration at Pontcanna, the following day could not have been more different. On the morning of Friday 21 October 1966, part of the village of Aberfan, near Merthyr Tydfil, including the primary school, was buried under waste from a nearby coal tip. In all, 144 people were killed, including 111 schoolchildren, an event aptly described by John Davies as 'the most heart-rending tragedy in the history of modern Wales'.[30] Wyn Roberts described the event: 'The monstrous tip, swollen with water, had tumbled like a black avalanche onto the school shortly after prayers. A desperate, frantic search began for survivors and the world's media descended upon us.'[31] The first local news flash went out at 11.45 a.m., followed by an ITN news flash from London five minutes later. Filmed reports from the site of the disaster began to arrive at Pontcanna and an outside broadcast unit was sent to Aberfan. News was fed into local and national news programmes throughout the day and the more film that became available, the greater was the realisation of the horror of the tragedy. One of the most controversial moments came when TWW broadcast a programme at 6.50 p.m. on 23 October which contained a moving interview with a child who had lost her friends. Despite around seventy phone calls of complaint, the company stood by its decision to transmit the programme, which went out on the ITV network. In an internal company report on TWW's involvement with the Aberfan tragedy, Wyn Roberts wrote that he 'did not meet a single person employed in television, either on the scene of the disaster or in the studio, who was not very much affected by what had happened'.[32] Forty years later, Roberts recalled that the 'mental strain and anguish were devastating'.[33]

With licence renewal on the horizon, the ITA began to explore the possibility of establishing Wales as a programme contract area completely separate from the west of England. Initial investigations showed that, in engineering terms, a split was feasible. The Authority considered a number of factors in its deliberations, including: concern that there was still a lack of sufficient Welsh influence in the top management of the company; that apart from 'patriotic and sentimental aspirations', the major benefit of having a separate Welsh service would be an ability to increase the amount of Welsh and Welsh-language programming; that a Welsh company with an estimated income of £3.4 million (pre-levy) would be a little smaller than Tyne-Tees and a little larger than Anglia; and that the loss of revenue from the English 'part' of the existing licence could threaten any further development of a separate Welsh service. Ultimately, the Director-General concluded that 'the indisputably desirable treatment of Wales as a separate television area is blocked, as it always has been, by a complex of financial and technical factors', and that the Authority had done all that it could 'by creating the Welsh service as something separate from the old Channel 10 service'.[34] These arguments were reiterated in a memorandum from the ITA's Director-General, Robert Fraser, to Lord Hill, the Authority's Chairman, in November 1966. The memorandum was prompted by a parliamentary motion calling on the ITA to split Wales from the west of England for the next licence period. The motion had been proposed by Gwynfor Evans, the Plaid Cymru MP for Carmarthen, and had received the backing of a number of Welsh MPs, among them the Labour MP for Cardiganshire, Elystan Morgan.[35] Furthermore, Fraser noted that Channel 7 was now proving to be a 'flop' in south Wales, as Channel 10 and the BBC's Channel 5 attracted audiences 'because they don't have unintelligible Welsh-language programmes'.[36] Clearly persuaded by Fraser's arguments, Lord Hill, on behalf of the ITA, announced in December 1966 that the Wales and West contract area would remain intact. Perhaps understandably, the press in the Bristol area were not impressed, the *Bristol Evening Post* commenting that 'if the same company obtains the contract to provide programmes from next July, they will not be so prone to pander to the allegedly low taste of the people they serve in the thickly populated areas of South Wales'.[37]

On 15 February 1967, TWW won five of the eight awards at the *Western Mail* and *South Wales Echo* Television and Radio Awards for 1966. The company won awards for the best television production and the best television documentary (*The Growing People*, a film about Russia), the best television performers, in both English and Welsh (Gwyn Thomas and Eirwen Davies, presenter of *Y Dydd*, respectively) and the award for the best entertainment programme (*Share My Music*, featuring the opera singer Gwyneth Jones).[38] It was a positive start to the year, and when the call went out from the ITA in February for applications for programme contractors in all fifteen ITV regions, TWW could justify considering itself worthy of contract renewal for a third period. The closing date for applications was 15 April 1967, by which time two applications had been received: one from TWW, the other from a group calling itself the Harlech Consortium.[39] Both companies were invited for interview at the

ITA on 19 May, and on 10 June 1967, W. A. C. Collingwood, the Secretary of the ITA, sent a letter to George Bailes, the TWW company secretary, informing him that the contract for the period from 30 July 1968 had been awarded to the Harlech Consortium.[40] TWW continued to produce and broadcast its programmes, but agreed with Harlech that a handover would take place before the start of the new contract period. On 3 March 1968, TWW broadcast its final programme, in two parts, entitled *All Good Things* and *Come to an End*. The first part took the form of a finale, which included many of the stars and presenters of TWW over the years. These included Bernard Braden, Eric Morecambe and Ernie Wise (whom Bryan Michie, TWW's Programme Controller, had 'discovered'), Stan Stennett, Wyn Calvin, Danny Blanchflower, Ivor Emmanuel and Stanley Unwin. The second part featured a personal reminiscence by the poet Sir John Betjeman, bidding farewell to what he (and others) called 'Tele Wele Wales'. The final poignant shot was that of Betjeman leaving through a door marked 'Exit'.

Programming

The period between 1964 and 1968 saw TWW increase its average weekly production by 112 minutes:

1964–5	11 hours 4 minutes[41]
1965–6	11 hours 47 minutes[42]
1966–7	12 hours 24 minutes[43]
1967–8	12 hours 56 minutes[44]

TWW had the highest regional production of all ITV regions (apart from the major network companies, Associated-Rediffusion, ABC, ATV and Granada). Not only did this demonstrate a commitment to the region, but it also reflected the complex dual nature of the area, in that programmes had to be provided for different audiences, both geographically and linguistically.

As in the previous contract period, viewers in Wales and the west of England were provided with programmes emanating from the network companies, and these filled over 80 per cent of the schedule. The remaining programmes were the usual mix of news, light entertainment, documentary and sport. Notable absences were drama, schools programmes and adult education, an issue that often brought TWW and the ITA into conflict (as will be seen in the next chapter). The seventh issue of volume 7 of *Television Weekly* was published in February 1965 as the first all-Wales edition. TWW was now transmitting on Channels 8, 10 and 11 to the west and north of Wales, and maintained the 'Teledu Cymru' brand for the area. As a result, specific programmes for the 'sub-region' could be transmitted, particularly those in the Welsh language. A regular pattern of locally originated programming was soon established, whereby the day's news in Welsh would be broadcast at 4.20 p.m. followed by a Welsh-language general interest or quiz programme (shown on the general network in south Wales on Channel 10 and later on the Teledu Cymru network). *TWW Reports* would follow at 6.13 or 6.15 p.m. and then an English-language programme, such as *Here Today* (topical discussion) or *Think of a Word* (quiz). Surrounding these programmes were those from the ITV network. The following nightly viewing schedule from *Television Weekly* for 19 February 1965 provides an idea of the mix of TWW and ITV network programming during this period.

Friday 19 February 1965
TWW General Service (Channel 10 for south Wales)

11.15 Schools
2.25 Closedown
4.35 *Crossroads*
5.00 *Ollie and Fred's Five O'Clock Club*
5.25 *Stingray*
5.55 News
6.05 *TWW Reports* [TWW]
6.13 *Here Today* [TWW]
6.30 *Ready, Steady, Go!*
7.00 *Take Your Pick*
7.30 *Emergency – Ward 10*
8.00 *Bonanza*
8.55 News
9.10 *The Villains*
10.05 *Cinema*
10.35 News, followed by *In the News* [TWW]
11.20 *Crusader in Europe*
11.40 *Summing Up* [TWW]
Weather and Close

TWW Teledu Cymru Service (Channels 7, 8, 10, 11 for various parts of Wales) as General Service, apart from:

5.25	*Teli Ho!* [TWW]	
5.30	*Cylchgrawn Natur* [TWW]	
6.05	*Y Dydd* [TWW]	
6.25	*All Our Yesterdays*	
6.50	*TWW Reports* [TWW]	
10.05	*Pobl a Phethau* [TWW]	

What is clear, therefore, is that an evening's viewing on TWW comprised Welsh and ITV network programming. Little English-language programming for Wales was shown.

In June 1964, TWW began what was to become a long-running and popular Welsh-language quiz show, *Sion a Sian*, hosted by Dewi Richards.[45] Married couples were asked questions about each other and could win varying sums of money, depending on the accuracy of the answers. Such was the popularity of the show that the company eventually produced an English version, *Mr and Mrs*, which went on to become a hit on the ITV network. Welsh-language music programmes, such as *Discs-a-Gogo* and *Land of Song*, were, by this time, becoming somewhat 'tired'. Increasingly, *Discs-a-Gogo* faced competition from the BBC's *Top of the Pops*,[46] and in July 1964, the final *Land of Song* was broadcast. If some Welsh formats were tired, others were creating the headlines. On 24 April, the *Daily Telegraph* reported that TWW was to dub an episode of the 'Western' television series *Pony Express* into Welsh.[47] The experiment was broadcast on the south Wales and west of England and the Teledu Cymru transmitters on Whit Monday 1964. Norah Isaac, a member of the ITA's Welsh Committee and drama lecturer at Trinity College, Carmarthen, congratulated the company on the programme, and other members suggested that the experiment might be extended to 'whodunnits' and science fiction stories.[48]

On 1 September 1964, the company launched *Y Dydd*, a daily news programme in Welsh. The programme heralded a new approach in news reporting in the Welsh language, as English-language news bulletins were no longer merely translated (which had been a concern of the ITA Welsh Committee earlier in the year).[49] *Y Dydd* went on to win critical acclaim and gained a substantial following amongst Welsh-speaking viewers. In April 1965, for example, *Y Cymro*, the Welsh-language weekly newspaper, compared *Y Dydd* with the BBC's *Heddiw*. The former, it suggested was akin to a tabloid newspaper, whilst the latter resembled a magazine. The key difference, argued the paper, was that *Y Dydd* was always topical and relevant, factors that, for a viewer, the paper concluded, were important.[50] The end of 1964 and beginning of 1965 saw a slight internal concern about TWW's fortunes as a result of the impact of the levy, new union agreements (including a 14.5 per cent pay deal), studio extension work and a ban on cigarette advertising.[51] The company's Production Panel was warned by the main board that there was no certainty that the revenue position, which had hitherto been very healthy, could be maintained. As the minutes noted: 'In these circumstances, it is unlikely that the company will look with favour on programme projects additional to those required by the licence, which do not either promote the company's profits or do not pay for themselves by sale outside the TWW area.' Moreover, in relation to regional programming on the ITV network, the panel noted that it 'would not rush in with offers but would watch the position carefully and take advantage of opportunities as they presented themselves'.[52] Clearly, the company was aware of the tensions between regional provision and network exposure and was placing a greater emphasis on the former, at the expense of the latter.

English-language programming was varied, although regular non-news programmes focusing on Wales were fewer in number than Welsh-language equivalents (see chapter 8). *TWW Reports* continued to be the main news programme in the region, and when the Teledu Cymru service began, in February 1965, the company produced a separate *TWW Report on Wales* each weekday evening for the Welsh audience. *Police 5*, a forerunner of today's *Crimewatch*, was one of TWW's most popular programmes on the Channel 10 general service. Indeed, Bristol Police even attributed the decline in car theft in the region to the programme.[53] Documentary production continued to be a strong feature of TWW's output, and on St David's Day 1965 the company broadcast a documentary (produced and directed by Jack Howells) on the life of Aneurin Bevan. *Nye!* The documentary was broadcast on the ITV network in July that year. TWW was also involved in collaborating on programming with other regional companies. In November 1965, for example, work was being undertaken on producing an arts magazine programme with Border Television, Scottish Television, Grampian and Ulster, and in April 1967, plans were afoot for a joint venture between TWW and Scottish Television in the field of children's programmes.[54]

January 1966 saw TWW in pioneering mode once again as it launched a series of programmes in association with Swansea College of Higher Education and University College, Swansea. *Croeso Christine* ('Welcome Christine') was a series for Welsh-language learners and was first broadcast on 27 January 1966.[55] The series was the brainchild of Wyn Roberts, who got the idea from a similar programme teaching French through the use of television. The 'Christine' of the series, Christine Godwin from Cardiff, was a non-Welsh-speaking props buyer with TWW who kindly volunteered her services. In an inspired move, Frank Brown, TWW's Publicity Director, published a pamphlet to accompany the series, which sold 10,000 copies at 3s. 6d. each.[56] The reaction in Wales was positive, particularly in the Welsh-language press, as one might expect.[57] On 8 September 1966, TWW undertook its largest outside broadcast operation when the Severn Bridge was opened by the Queen. Fifty production staff and eight cameras were deployed to cover the event, and Brian Connell and Havard Gregory provided the commentary for the programme, which was networked to Rediffusion, Scottish Television, Southern, Westward and Grampian. As well as edited highlights and inserts into ITN news bulletins, two documentaries were produced by TWW.[58]

There were a number of other programmes produced in English and Welsh, most of which no longer survive in the archive. *Movie Magazine* and its offspring *Junior Movie Magazine* were devoted to discussing the latest film releases. *Clwb y Llenor* ('The Poets' Club') was a literary magazine programme hosted by Professor Idris Foster of Oxford University. *Am y Gorau* was an inter-collegiate quiz programme, whilst *Claim to Fame* was an English version of TWW's successful panel game *Pwy Fase'n Meddwl*. *Tregampau* was another successful quiz, in which towns competed against each other. The overall tone of the programme output of TWW during this period, in both Welsh and English, was populist. Perhaps this is best exemplified by the policy of the main board of TWW, following the news of the loss of the licence to the Harlech Consortium, when it decreed that 'the first three months of 1968 should be well loaded with entertainment programmes'. These included six shows starring Ivor Emmanuel (the irrepressible host of *Land of Song*) and another series of *Mr and Mrs*.[59] From time to time, the company's populist outlook on its programming came into conflict with the outlook of the ITA. In response to increased criticism of the nature of TWW's output (see chapter 8 for more information), Bryan Michie noted that he thought that the ITA were placing too great an emphasis on educational programmes, at the expense of the company's ratings. This clash of ideals went to the heart of the ITV venture, which was, as established in 1955, an advertising-funded, ratings-driven yet public service broadcaster. It is an issue to which I will return in the concluding chapter.

Coverage, reception and transmitters

When TWW took over the WWN licence area in January 1964, one of the first tasks facing the company was the need to persuade viewers in north Wales to retune their sets away from the Granada signal at the Winter Hill transmitter.[60] In addition, the BBC had made gains as far as viewers were concerned, particularly during the latter months of WWN. As Frank Brown, TWW Publicity Director, admitted to the *Western Mail* in April 1964, 'TWW is now faced with the difficult task of rebuilding public interest and loyalty to ITV in North and West Wales.'[61] The Welsh Board decided to monitor Granada programmes to see if coverage, particularly in news and topical programmes, of north Wales was 'excessive', and to inform the ITA if that was the case.[62] At the end of the year, TWW organised a tour of west and north Wales by its outside broadcast unit, as part of a public relations drive 'to capture viewers in areas where Granada is still firmly entrenched'.[63] The problem had not abated by March the following year, and the TWW Welsh board minutes reflect concern that Granada was still popular in parts of north Wales.[64] The reason given by viewers was that they were concerned about losing the best network programmes by opting for the Teledu Cymru service, and so a 'concerted plan of action' was agreed upon, but no further details were given.[65]

Not only did TWW have to woo viewers from Granada and the BBC, but parts of Wales were still faced with poor reception of ITV programmes or, indeed, were unable to receive any ITA signal. The Welsh board of TWW noted in June 1964 that viewers in north-east Wales served by the Moel-y-Parc transmitter were experiencing constant reception problems, sometimes which may have been caused partly by the transmitter's proximity to the Winter Hill transmitter.[66] It also meant, of course, that efforts to build up the TWW viewer base in the area were hampered. At the same board meeting, Sir Ifan ab Owen Edwards stated that many parts of mid and north Wales had no ITV coverage or transmitter within reach, and urged the board and the company to lobby the ITA to move faster with a satellite transmitter plan to provide a signal to hitherto uncovered parts of Wales.[67] The matter of satellite transmitters was raised in the House of Commons in July 1964, when Emlyn Hooson, the Liberal MP for Montgomery, asked the Postmaster General, Reginald Bevins, why the ITA had delayed erecting satellite stations in parts of rural Wales to enable a wider audience for ITV. Bevins replied that the matter was one for the ITA and not for his department.[68]

Pressure mounted in September 1964, when the Welsh board of TWW estimated that 22 per cent of Band III households (that is those that could technically receive an ITV signal) or 105,600 homes were unable to receive TWW. There were an additional 46,200 Band III households who suffered from poor reception. It was resolved to put pressure on the Post Office and the ITA to secure additional transmitters and to undertake a strong conversion campaign (although this was clearly dependent on the availability of transmitters).[69] Huw T. Edwards was concerned that the BBC would get a clear advantage over ITV, as it was embarking on an extensive satellite transmitter programme, in spite of uncertainties over the future of the 405-line service. Sir Ifan ab Owen Edwards wanted to put the whole matter to Sir Ben Bowen Thomas, Welsh Member of the ITA, as he was, in Edwards's eyes, 'sympathetic towards TWW and its desire to extend and improve its coverage of Wales'.[70]

The Welsh board raised the matter again in January 1965, when it referred to the lack of progress in relation to the ITA memorandum to the Pilkington Committee in April 1961, which had outlined the Authority's plan to erect 'a large number of small satellite stations in Welshpool, Bala, Brecon/Hay, Abergavenny and Llandrindod Wells/Builth Wells'.[71] In April 1965, fifty delegates, primarily from rural councils, attended a conference at Llandrindod Wells, mid Wales, to discuss poor or non-existent television reception in the area. The ITA's Officer for Wales and the West, Lyn Evans, was invited to attend and recorded that the conference passed unanimously a resolution calling on the ITA to improve reception in mid Wales. As Evans reported to the ITA's Director-General, 'I was as non-committal as possible but felt able to say that the prospects looked a little brighter and there was some hope of a service being provided in the not too distant future.'[72] By June, the ITA had announced that three transmitters would be built in Wales over a three-year period and that it was awaiting approval from the Postmaster General for their erection in mid Wales.[73]

Meanwhile, meetings between the ITA in Wales and TWW regarding reception problems continued into 1965. In June, the company made known to Sir Ben Bowen Thomas and Lyn Evans that the priority areas for the improvement of reception by building VHF transmitters were the Swansea and Neath valleys, the east Carmarthenshire valleys and the Llanelli area. Furthermore, key Welsh-speaking areas, such as Blaenau Ffestiniog, Bala and Corwen in north Wales, could not receive a TWW signal at all and therefore were noted as high-priority areas.[74]

By October 1965, the ITA had in place a two-stage plan for the erection of transmitters. The first stage (to be completed within three years) included stations at Blaenau Ffestiniog, Llandrindod Wells, Abergavenny, Llandovery, Bala and Brecon. The second stage would see transmitters at Machynlleth, Newtown, Welshpool, Llanidloes and Dolgellau. TWW's Welsh board remained sceptical, however, and noted that the plan was unlikely to be implemented in full, given 'superior claims' of more populous areas of Britain and a general restraint on capital expenditure at the ITA.[75] The scepticism may have been well placed, as the ITA was fully aware of the problems of securing a signal to the remoter, predominantly Welsh-speaking areas of rural Wales. The only way of ensuring a good picture, given the geographical location of the areas of non-reception, would be to erect transmitters in the immediate vicinity, but this was discounted on economic grounds. Although the first stage of the ITA's plan would go some way to easing the problem, Lyn Evans readily admitted to Sir Robert Fraser that '[it] would not, I'm afraid, solve it completely'.[76] Eventually, permission was forthcoming from the Postmaster General, and on 11 March 1966 it was confirmed that the transmitters noted in the first stage of the plan would be built over three years.[77] The transmitter for the Bala area would be ready in time for the 1967 National Eisteddfod, which was to be held in the town, thus allaying the concerns of the festival's local organising committee that ITV programmes would not be available for local viewers.[78]

In summary, TWW's attempts at securing an audience in north Wales were impeded by the nature of the overlap area, where Granada's signal and adherence to the Manchester-based broadcaster was strongest. This meant that TWW had to embark on an exercise to persuade viewers to switch loyalties. In addition, pockets of poor reception or non-reception existed in mid, west and north Wales and, although not exclusively, many of these areas were predominantly Welsh-speaking. Viewers would write directly to TWW to complain of poor or non-reception without fully understanding the complexities of transmission and without fully realising that transmitter matters lay in the hands of the ITA and, ultimately, the Postmaster General. What is important to note in this context is the attitude of the ITA. Given the uncertainty of technical developments in relation to 625-line high-definition television and the move away from the 405-line system, and in the light of the future move from VHF to UHF, the response of the Authority to questions and demands from TWW was similar to that in the pre-Pilkington days: a 'wait and see' attitude which did little to appease the concerns of the company.

8

Television Wales and the West: The End of the Road

Introduction

The second contract period, between 1964 and 1968, was one of mixed fortunes for TWW. Profits remained high, locally originated programmes remained popular and there was a certain viewer loyalty to the company within the area. TWW were seen as 'saviours' in 1964 for rescuing the doomed WWN. Yet, by the middle of June 1967, the company had lost its licence as an ITV contractor. There is no *one* reason to explain the loss, but this chapter will consider a number of critical issues which contributed to the company's downfall.

Increasing criticism from the ITA

One of the main characteristics of the second contract period was increased criticism from the ITA, primarily via its Welsh Committee and Regional Officer. This coincided with the appointment of Lord Hill as ITA Chairman and a shift at the Authority towards a more interventionist stance.[1] In September 1964, Lyn Evans noted a slippage of 'serious programmes' into the late evening, and the following month, the company was chastised for dropping *University Challenge* in favour of an American comedy, *No Time for Sergeants*.[2] Much of the criticism tended to focus on individual programmes. For example, in January 1965, the Welsh Committee criticised *Y Dydd* for being 'too crowded' and *Discs-a-Gogo* for deterioration in quality. It also noted that there was room for improvement in Welsh pronunciation by continuity announcers, as the programme *O Gwmpas y Tŷ* ('Around the House') often sounded like 'Oh Compass Sooty'!.[3] Other negative comments drew attention to the perception that the TWW schedules of programming were not changing and that the locally originated programmes had what Lyn Evans called a 'sameness' about them.[4]

Programmes on contemporary issues
Another common complaint that arose more than once was a concern over the lack of regular programmes on contemporary political, social and economic issues. Lyn Evans raised the matter with TWW programme planners in December 1965,[5] and in September 1966, Gwilym Prys Davies, a member of the ITA's Welsh Committee, presented a memorandum to the committee criticising TWW for failing to reflect contemporary Welsh life. 'What one requires for a Welsh television service', he wrote, 'is a service deeply concerned in the lives, problems and aspirations of its Welsh audience that plays its part as an active agent in the life of Wales. It appears that TWW does not accept this as being its role.' Berating the company for perpetuating a nostalgic image of Wales, Davies asked: 'Is it beyond the means of the Company [sic] to produce a serial documentary in the form of an imaginative penetration into the lives of a Welsh family in the valleys in rural Wales of 1966?' The memorandum ended with a plea for TWW to take a more proactive stance in Wales, not one which merely presented news and entertainment to the viewers.[6] Davies reiterated his call in December 1966, by stating that TWW should do more to help the viewers understand the changing political, social and economic life of Wales. These included the dawn of the computer age, the impact of the creation of the Welsh Office, the Welsh Economic Plan and the influence of America.[7] When Wyn Roberts attended the committee in January 1967 to discuss TWW's programme plans for 1967, Gwilym Prys Davies took the opportunity again of accusing the company of focusing on 'the lighter type of programme', at the expense of programmes which investigated contemporary socio-economic issues in urban and industrial areas.[8] Davies's criticisms continued in June that year, when he suggested that suitable topics for programmes might include the government's White Paper on the Welsh language, the reform of local government in Wales or the Severnside development project.[9] It would appear that Davies was eventually placated in early 1968 when, following discussions with the new programme contractor, Harlech, 'he was re assured by the company's fresh approach to ... their clearly expressed intention to reflect the culture of Wales in its present urbanised form and to portray the life of contemporary Wales'.[10]

Some of the criticism could be justified. The slippage of 'serious' programming is borne out by a study of *Television Weekly*.[11] Yet it must be remembered that TWW was a commercial television company with a need to maximise viewing figures and, de facto, advertising revenue. Programmes that would attract a larger audience (in particular at peak viewing times) would therefore take priority over those which would yield a smaller audience. Such was the nature of commercial television, and such was the conflict between public service and commercial necessity. What is interesting about Davies's interventions, in relation to programmes on contemporary issues, is that his comments reflect the fact that Wales was changing considerably at this time in political, economic and social terms.[12] His suggestions about possible topics for programmes reflected his own interests, particularly as a Labour Party candidate for the Carmarthen seat won by Gwynfor Evans for Plaid Cymru in July 1966. As a committed devolutionist and patriot, Davies was determined that TWW should be active in what he saw as its public service duty by reflecting a changing Welsh society.[13] His accusation that the programming, particularly in the Welsh language, was biased towards a nostalgic, rural-based 'Welsh way of life' is justified to a degree, based on a study of *Television Weekly* in the 1964–8 period. Programmes such as *Chwedlau Cymru* ('Legends of Wales') and *Y Caban Pren* ('The Log Cabin'), both broadcast in September 1964, focused on historical myths and legends, in the case of the former, and, in that of the latter, traditional Welsh musical idioms.[14] The programme *Ffiesta* was based around folk dancing and singing, whilst quiz shows such as *Hogi'r Meddwl* ('Sharpening the Mind') questioned participants on Welsh history and literature.[15] It is important to note, of course, that *Y Dydd* did report on contemporary issues in the Welsh language but this was within a news context. What Davies was calling for was a more in-depth awareness, treatment and representation of contemporary Wales within general programmes and documentaries on screen.

Programmes for schools and adult education

Other areas of programming which were criticised by the ITA were schools and adult educational programmes, English-language programmes about Wales and drama productions. In September 1964, the ITA's Welsh Committee expressed dissatisfaction with the lack of adult education programmes in TWW's schedules. Sir Ben Bowen Thomas, the committee's new chairman, stated that he hoped that the company would 'pay special regard' to education programmes, not surprisingly, perhaps, as he was a former Permanent Secretary at the Ministry of Education's

Welsh Department.[16] Further criticisms of the lack of adult education programmes were made in November 1964 and August 1965. Attempts were also made by the ITA Welsh Committee to encourage TWW to produce programmes for schools (in both Welsh and English). In January 1965, the committee heard from the ITA's Education Officer, Joseph Weltman, that smaller ITV companies such as Border, Scottish and Grampian were producing schools programmes, often in conjunction with local colleges and universities. The committee therefore asked TWW to take the lead from these companies and to liaise with BBC Wales to ensure that there would be no duplication in provision.[17] By October 1965, TWW had agreed with the ITA to produce a series for schools in English, although there were only 400 television sets in Welsh schools.[18] However, Wyn Roberts remained sceptical of such a move. In a letter to Sir Ifan ab Owen Edwards in October he noted that with only 400 sets in schools, and with an average of 30 children watching each set, the 12,000 audience would be far fewer than the average daily audience for *Y Dydd* (at around 100,000 viewers). Roberts also conceded that Sir Ben Bowen Thomas would now be satisfied with the decision to produce the programmes. The pressure from the ITA to produce more programmes was clearly becoming an issue for the company as Roberts ended his letter by noting that the ITA would not increase the amount of concession in the levy to meet the cost of increasing local output. Roberts urged Edwards to oppose the stance but warned that attacks on the company and on individuals might follow.[19]

English-language Welsh interest programmes

As seen in chapter 3, TWW directors such as Huw T. Edwards were aware of the need to cater for non-Welsh-speaking viewers in Wales, and yet specific Welsh-interest programming in English beyond the news was still a weakness of the company in 1965.[20] In April that year, the ITA Welsh Committee acknowledged that TWW had, until recently, focused on establishing the Teledu Cymru, service but that it would now expect progress to be made with regard to an expansion of English-language Welsh-interest provision.[21] At the same time, Lyn Evans wished to see a programme similar to *Here Today* – which had taken a west-of-England stance since the launch of the Teledu Cymru service in February 1965 – for Wales.[22] In July, ITA members 'expressed the view that there was room for improvement in the quality and balance of TWW's output, more particularly in the English language'.[23] Later that year, Trevor Vaughan, a member of the ITA Welsh Committee from Newport, in south Wales, stressed what he called 'the need to rouse and maintain the interest of Welshmen who did not speak the language'.[24] The criticisms continued in 1966, and in January that year, the committee complained of a lack of English-language programming on Welsh affairs: 'It was felt that there was no dearth of material for such a programme.' This general concern with TWW's programming was crystallised by an article in the *Times* in March 1965:

> English language programmes from the Cardiff studios of TWW seem so far to lack a sense of direction. Apart from the musical clichés of the *Land of Song*, there is little evidence of any attempt to effect a creative contribution in English to Wales as a distinctive community, still less to project the Welsh image on to the Independent Television network. No drama, little serious music and few feature programmes – though it must be said that when features are attempted, as in Jack Howells' St. David's Day portrait of Nye Bevan they can be notable events.[25]

Drama productions

The most constant criticism from the ITA, however, related to the lack of original drama productions. At its first meeting of 1964, the ITA's Welsh Committee underlined the importance of 'regular drama and serial plays' in the Welsh-language output of TWW.[26] This was further stressed in a letter from Lyn Evans, the ITA's Regional Officer, to John Baxter, TWW's Managing Director:

> My committee have on several occasions drawn attention to the absence of drama productions in the Welsh language on independent television. They feel that there is plenty of talent among Welsh people in this field and that some effort ought to be made to exploit it.[27]

Nevertheless, when the programme proposals for the post-August 1964 period were scrutinised by the ITA in March that year, the absence of drama was noted, despite the satisfactory nature of the proposals overall. It was suggested that TWW might liaise with the Arts Council and the BBC with a view to supporting a Welsh drama company.[28] A meeting took place between Roger Webster of the Arts Council in Wales and Alfred Francis, the Vice Chairman of TWW, but there is little evidence to suggest that the discussions were fruitful. By July 1964, the ITA had requested that TWW should be required to produce 'four dramatic productions a year' and that these should be a mix of Welsh-language and English-language Welsh-interest productions.[29] However, the TWW Welsh board responded by stating that no new drama could be produced until a new studio and production facilities had been completed at Pontcanna.[30] The ITA's concern was growing, and in his monthly report to the Director-General, Lyn Evans emphasised the need for a drama department and drama productions in Welsh at TWW. 'I have conveyed the [Welsh Committee]'s views to TWW', he noted,

> but the reaction so far leads me to think that some pressure may be required before anything is done. The company keeps saying it is an expensive business to produce drama; with profits running at the rate of £2 millions [sic] a year this sounds a trifle hollow; they really cannot plead poverty.[31]

There was still no sign of any plans for Welsh-language drama by September 1964, although in October, TWW's Welsh board discussed the possibility of producing 'a few' short plays. Cynan suggested a Welsh translation of Chekov's *The Bear* and he, Rhydwen Williams, Wyn Roberts and Dorothy Williams, all from TWW's Welsh Department, would examine the issue further.[32]

The pressure continued in January 1965, but TWW's Welsh board were cautious, agreeing on three issues: that all programmes needed to have a popular appeal; that production of programmes for a 'minority within a minority' was not part of the company's policy (a reference to 'quality drama' possibly); and that the planned St David's Day drama, *Dwywaith yn Blentyn* ('Twice a Child'), by R. G. Berry, would act as a test case before any further commitment to drama production.[33] It is clear from a study of the minutes of the Welsh board of TWW that the company was aware of the issue of Welsh-language drama. In July 1965, the board noted the difficulty in finding Welsh dramas and plays for production. Translation of plays from other languages was not considered a long-term option, as the company wanted to stimulate original work. As a way forward, the board agreed to ask three prominent Welsh writers, Islwyn Ffowc Elis, Eic Davies and W. S. Jones (Wil Sam), to submit ideas.[34] As a further incentive to writers, the board agreed to a competition with a prize for the best half-hour Welsh-language television drama.[35]

The ITA's concern over drama was compounded by the advances being made by the BBC in the field with its 'ambitious . . . schedule'.[36] By the end of the year, matters progressed, as three plays were submitted by J. R. Evans, Wil Sam and Gwenlyn Parry.[37] On 18 December 1965, TWW transmitted a translation of *The Bear*, which was well received by the ITA. In addition, the company also produced a Welsh-language pantomime based on Cinderella, *Sinderela*, which was described by Lyn Evans as being 'a pleasant enough pantomime with a nice blend of traditional and modern songs'.[38] The positive notes were not to last, and by September 1966, the ITA had cause for concern once again. Lyn Evans reported to the ITA Director-General that the BBC had ambitious plans for its English-and Welsh-language drama output, including a full-length drama in English and Welsh, a Welsh-language six-part drama series and a regional play for the BBC network. In total, thirty drama programmes were to be produced. Although Evans accepted TWW's arguments regarding studio facilities and a lack of suitable material to a degree, his concern, in light of the plans of BBC Wales, was clear.[39] Yet despite the ITA's concern, and TWW's awareness of it, the company still turned down drama proposals. For example, on 6 October 1966, TWW's Production Panel rejected a proposal for a drama entitled *Lily of the Valley* on the grounds that there was 'no demand for full scale plays as part of the company's licence requirement at present'. Good plays, it was suggested, should be sent directly to the ITV network.[40]

Loss of the licence

The ITA advertisement inviting applications for the fifteen ITV contract areas was published on 28 February 1967. Between two hundred and three hundred groups had originally applied for information, but only thirty six applications from different groups were actually received by the 15 April deadline.[41] Two applications were received for the Wales and West contract area: one from TWW, the other from a group calling itself the Harlech Consortium. The rival application was dismissed by TWW's Welsh board. In its meeting on 20 April, it was noted that:

> Members of the Board did not attribute undue importance to the application of the rival Consortium headed by Lord Harlech. Sir Ifan stated that the Consortium was not backed by popular sentiment or by significant political groups in Wales. Its power appeared to be derived from the West Country.[42]

This sentiment was based on a mix of complacency and a belief that TWW could, and would, stand on its record of service to Wales. It was also based on a belief that the speed with which the rival application had been put together would count against the consortium.[43] Bernard Sendall, writing about TWW's application for the licence for the next contract period, suggested that there was 'no evidence that the Chairman and directors of TWW entertained any doubts that they would be considered . . . fully qualified to remain programme contractor for the ITV region in Wales and the West'.[44]

The Harlech Consortium Application

Contrary to Sir Ifan ab Owen Edwards's belief, the Harlech Consortium did not have a power-base in the West Country alone. It was a hybrid group, formed by the joining of two groups; one based in Wales, the other in Bristol. The latter had been formed some years earlier with a view to applying for a commercial radio station licence, had the government gone ahead with an idea which was being mooted at the time. The Welsh group had been formed somewhat hastily by the journalist and broadcaster John Morgan and Wynford Vaughan Thomas, an experienced broadcaster, both of whom had been working for the BBC.[45] As a Free Communications Group publication in 1969 put it: 'Not only can an outfit fixing to set up a commercial radio station . . . bed down comfortably with the community-caring brethren from across the channel, but cash and culture march companionably hand in hand.'[46] The list of twenty four directors of the Harlech Consortium application made for impressive reading. They included Lord Harlech, the former UK ambassador to the US, Deputy Leader of the Conservative Opposition in the House of Lords and President of the British Board of Film Censors (Chairman); Stanley Baker, the Welsh-born film actor; Sir Frederic Bennett, Conservative MP for Torquay but from Aberangell in Meirionydd; Geraint Evans, the opera singer; Richard Burton, the internationally renowned actor; Alun Talfan Davies QC; Alun Llywelyn-Williams, a former member of the ITA's Welsh Committee; John Morgan; Wynford Vaughan Thomas; Walter Hawkins, Chairman and Managing Director of the *Bristol Evening News*; and William Poeton, Director of the Bristol Art Centre.[47]

The consortium's application was eloquent and well written, despite the speed at which it had been put together.[48] As the *Sunday Times* noted, if there were any deficiencies in the application they 'were supplemented by fine phraseology in the bid document'.[49] The consortium intended to have its head office in Cardiff and the board would meet in Cardiff or Bristol six or eight times a year, with an executive board meeting in Cardiff, Bristol or London on a more regular basis. 'The programme parts of the Harlech application', wrote Sendall, 'held great appeal for the Authority . . . They were extremely well-written and displayed a particularly thoughtful approach to regional television.'[50] Interestingly, the consortium put forward a thesis (upon which much of the application was based) which argued that the growth of mass-media communication had resulted in a greater need for regionalism and a heightened sense of regional identity: 'Instead of the spectre of an Orwellian state in which people increasingly come to resemble each other, there is emerging in Britain a sharper sense of regional feeling.'[51] Statements such as 'The consortium was formed with the conviction that regional independent television should be administered and financially controlled from the locality it serves . . .'[52] ensured that the ITA, with what Sendall calls its 'persistent public commitment to regionalism', took note of and warmed to what was being stated in the application.[53]

The TWW application

TWW's application was succinct and to the point. It highlighted what the company saw as its first-class relationship with the ITA, although evidence in the period after 1964, as noted in this chapter, suggests otherwise. The application also underlined the particular problems of the licence area, including the bilingual nature of the region, but noted at the same time that 'Welsh is regarded as the living language of living people and not as an academic exercise'. TWW also emphasised the concept of 'Severnside', explaining that the region had undergone rapid social and technological expansion in recent years and how the company bridged the two parts of the region. A statement by Lord Derby, reproduced from the company's 1966 Annual Report, underlined this idea:

> Too much today is talked about Welsh interest or West of England interest programmes – the truth of the matter is that if we were forced to be too parochial instead of regional we should only succeed in annoying our Welsh viewers or our West of England viewers and fail in our obligations to the viewers in our area as a whole. We know that if we

produce local programmes which are of general interest they will please viewers on both sides of the Severn.[54]

This statement could, of course, be read in a different way. There is a suggestion, perhaps, that the requirement for local programming, as defined under Section 3(1)(e) of the 1954 Television Act – a provision that programme contractors should offer a suitable amount of programming designed to appeal specifically to those people served by the station – was being flouted in favour of general interest programmes.

On 16 May, Wyn Roberts wrote to TWW's joint Managing Director, John Baxter, pre-empting some questions that might come from the Authority during the interview. One of the key concerns was the fact that the company's finances were, in effect, controlled from London and Lancashire in the form of its main shareholders, with only a quarter of TWW's shareholders residing within the contract area. Roberts wondered whether or not the source of finance really mattered, arguing that the main shareholders took a personal interest in the company. The second point raised by Roberts related to representation on the board. Only seven of the sixteen board members lived within the TWW area, although others had close connections with the area. The existence of the Welsh and West local boards was noted as a positive point, in terms of links with the region.[55] Finally, Roberts suggested that the ITA might wish to probe the relationship between Cardiff, Bristol and the general management and sales operations of the company, which were based in London.[56] All three points were raised at the interview.

The interviews

The interviews to determine the ITV contractor for the Wales and West area after July 1968 were held on 19 May 1967 at ITA headquarters in London. TWW was interviewed first, at 2 p.m. The meeting was chaired by the ITA Chairman, Lord Hill; other Authority members present were Professor Hugh Hunt, Mary Adams, Sir Owen Saunders, Sir Patrick Hamilton, Lady Plummer, Sir Ben Bowen Thomas, Macfarlane Gray, Lady Burton, Sir Vincent Tewson, Lady Sharp, David Gilliland and Sir Sydney Caine. Lord Derby led the TWW deputation and was accompanied by Managing Director John Baxter, programme executives Wyn Roberts and Dorothy Williams, and directors Stephen James, Huw T. Edwards and Mark Chapman-Walker. The transcript of the interview reflects the relatively hostile nature of the forty-minute session. The key areas on which the TWW representatives were interrogated were drama programming, the relationship with viewers, the nature of the licence area and the location of senior staff. Hugh Hunt (unsurprisingly, perhaps, as Professor of Drama at Manchester University) probed TWW on its lack of drama production. Derby explained that other companies 'made drama one of their main things' and that TWW had produced three plays with the Bristol Old Vic, all of which had been turned down by the network. Dorothy Williams interjected, stating that four plays in the Welsh language had been produced, to which Hunt replied pointedly, 'In how many years? Ten.'[57] Williams explained the absence of drama by citing a dearth of Welsh playwrights and, professional actors and a lack of Welsh theatre. However, Hunt pursued his line of questioning until Wyn Roberts explained that the company did not feel that there was 'a great deal of point in producing plays for local consumption only. We do not think that they would be of an acceptable standard even as local programmes'.[58] The relationship with viewers was queried when Lord Derby explained that the preferred method of eliciting audience responses to programmes was not TAM, but viewer letters. In explaining the reasons for this to Sir Sydney Caine, Derby argued that '[TAM] is only dealing with a hundred and fifty homes in our area, whereas we are getting five hundred letters a week', to which Caine retorted: 'People who write letters are not typical members of the public.'[59]

The nature of the contract area was a theme which ran throughout the interview. Sir Ben Bowen Thomas suggested to Lord Derby that his comments in TWW's 1966 Annual Report (quoted above) could indicate that he considered the region to be 'a bit of a nuisance' and that he wished to pull out of regional responsibility. Derby denied this. Later in the interview, Lady Sharp referred to the region as 'extraordinarily awkward' and asked for the TWW representatives' comments. They had a clear message:

> Lord Derby: I do not think we feel that. We feel that the [Severn Bridge] has linked it to a great extent. We find that the Welshmen are coming to shop more in Bristol, and we hope that the West of England people are going to the Welsh resorts for their holidays. We believe it is an area.
> Lady Sharp: North Wales and all?
> Dr Edwards: Oh, yes.

Lady Sharp: Dr Edwards, you did not use to think that Wales and the West of England were one.

Dr Edwards: I am a bit older now, and wiser I hope.[60]

Lord Hill and Sir Patrick Hamilton both questioned Lord Derby on the nature of the TWW board and on the fact that six of the company's senior staff lived and worked outside the area (in London and the south-east of England). Derby attempted to defend this, and argued that the Programme Controller, Bryan Michie (who was notably absent from the interview), had to live and work in London in order to liaise with the networking companies. The interview ended abruptly with a curt 'thank you very much' from Lord Hill. The TWW representatives did not do themselves any favours at the interview. As Sendall noted, they seemed 'ill-prepared and confused, at times even self-contradictory. They appear not to have foreseen the possibly decisive importance of the interview, nor to have anticipated the likely course of the interrogation.'[61]

The interview with the Harlech Consortium took place at 3.20 p.m. From the transcript it is clear that the overall tone of the meeting was less hostile than that of TWW's interview. Throughout the session, the spirit of regionalism was highlighted time and time again. As in the case of TWW, the matter of the nature of the region was raised by the ITA. Referring to the nature of the consortium, a mix of Welsh and West interests, Lord Harlech declared that 'the marriage . . . is extremely amicable', and Wynford Vaughan Thomas reassured the Authority that 'as we are determined to be locally based we had to conquer twelve centuries of resistance before joining, but now we are very firmly joined'.[62] Later in the interview, Vaughan Thomas admitted that satisfying viewers on both sides of the Bristol Channel was not going to be easy: 'We are a region of split personality', he said, 'The bridge is there, but mentally we are still on both sides of the Severn Sea.' Another line of questioning focused on the involvement of stars such as Richard Burton – the 'all-star policy', as Hugh Hunt called it.[63] There was some scepticism amongst members of the Authority, but John Morgan, who had secured the support of Burton, his wife, Elizabeth Taylor, Stanley Baker and Harry Secombe, was adamant that they would become fully involved as directors of the company and would play an active part in the programme schedule. As Sendall noted: 'A Welsh TV station seemed to offer a welcome means for the expression of their cultural patriotism.'[64]

The interview ended with a clear statement from Lord Harlech, who argued that:

> In the cultural and in the communications field we should do everything possible to foster and encourage regional feeling. It is with this very much in mind that we feel the programmes we would put out should reflect the life of the area. It is because of this that we feel the ownership and control of the enterprise should spring from the area, and finally we think full use should be made of the talent which is available in the area. It is because we have felt that there have been deficiencies in all these fields that has been the main cause of our coming forward as a consortium.[65]

Such was the confidence of the consortium that Harlech ended by addressing Lord Hill directly: 'I can say our group is deadly earnest about this application. If we do not succeed we very much doubt that any group in the future will feel it worth while to seek a franchise in the West and Wales.'[66] As Bernard Sendall remarked: 'The Harlech delegation . . . were more impressively convincing than the TWW spokesmen . . . the concluding statement by Lord Harlech was the finest piece of spoken prose heard at any of the thirty-six ITA interviews.'[67] Lord Hill wrote in his memoirs:

> When the TWW representatives departed, I had no reason to suppose that they would not gain the contract. But when the Harlech interview was over it was clear that . . . we had to concentrate our minds on the basic question of which applicant would be more likely to produce the better broadcasting in the area. Where lay the greater talent, the fuller potential for the next six years? TWW did not need to be bad to lose; Harlech had to hold out the prospects of something substantially better to win. That it did hold out that prospect was the general view of the members of the Authority, Harlech got the contract.[68]

The contract was offered to Harlech with three conditions: that the Harlech group would have to purchase the studios in Cardiff and Bristol (if TWW were willing to sell them); that TWW would be offered 40 per cent of non-voting shares in the new company; and that priority would be given to TWW staff when recruiting for the new company.

Reaction to the ITA's decision

Although the applicants received notification of the outcome of the interviews on 10 June, the story did not feature in the press until 12 June, a day after the ITA had held a press conference to announce its decisions. In the north of England, Telefusion Yorkshire Limited (which later changed to Yorkshire Television) was offered a new contract area covering Yorkshire. ATV was offered the seven-day operation in the Midlands, while in London Rediffusion lost the weekday contract to Thames Television and London Weekend Television took over the period from 6 p.m. on Friday until Sunday. Roy Thomson's Scottish Television held the contract for central Scotland, albeit in a slightly reconfigured form. The remainder of the ITV network remained the same.[69] The decision to oust TWW was summed up by a headline in the *Times* on 12 June: 'TWW's defeat is the main surprise of ITA's new deal.'[70] The *Western Mail*'s leader called the decision a 'bombshell',[71] whilst the *Daily Express* accused the ITA of 'acting hastily and brusquely towards one small company'.[72] The *Financial Times* said that Lord Hill had 'shaken the commercial television world to its foundations', and that TWW had been the 'biggest sufferer'[73]. The *Daily Telegraph* was impressed by what the paper saw as the local roots of the Harlech consortium, but at the same time thought it strange that TWW had had no intimation beforehand that its licence would be withdrawn: 'Surely, when a man is to be hanged, he should at least have the right to know the reasons for the sentence?'[74]

At the same time, there were those who were pleased to see TWW go. James Brock from Somerset, writing in the *Western Daily Press* in April 1967, hoped that TWW would lose its licence. Describing it as 'the most philistine and least enterprising company in the whole network', he stated that he could not recall a single play from the TWW studio and that, of the eighty-nine hours of viewing for that week, fewer than six hours originated from the company.[75] In a letter to the *South Wales Echo* on 21 June, G. Roberts from Cardiff wrote that:

> In comparison with other regions, the TWW area has suffered poor programmes for too long ... The standard of the announcing has been amateurish generally. Programmes like Claim to Fame and Mrs and Mrs, the latter at peak viewing time are an insult to the intelligence of the viewers ... If [Lord Derby] had watched the programmes transmitted by his own station he would know why his charter has been terminated.[76]

Others were concerned, not so much at losing TWW, but at the perceived Welsh bias of the new contractor. Robert Cooke, the Conservative MP for Bristol West, questioned the commitment of the Harlech Consortium to the west of England during a House of Commons debate on the 1964 Television Act:

> I believe that the Harlech Consortium did not want to have to take on Bristol, and one of the reasons it got the contract was because it was prepared to give more emphasis to the Welsh content of programmes... I hope that the Welsh will get a splendid television service, but I do not see why they should get it at the expense of a link with Bristol which is not wanted by all true West Country men.[77]

The *Guardian* quoted Ronald Nethercott, West Country regional secretary of the Transport and General Workers' Union, who had written to Lord Harlech asking that Bristol and the south-west be given the service and representation it deserved.[78] Others suggested giving Wales its own ITV contractor and allowing Westward to serve the Bristol area,[79] or even allowing a new consortium to cater for the West Country based on the argument that 'the Severn Bridge may join Wales and the West physically but it by no means joins them psychologically and their interests are different'.[80] In a letter to the *Times* on 23 June, Lord Harlech sought to reassure ITV viewers in the West Country that their needs would be catered for, noting also that 'the Consortium is made up equally of representatives from Wales and the West and the necessary finance is being raised in equal parts from the two areas'.[81]

Meanwhile, Lord Derby had written to all TWW shareholders on 16 June 1967. The letter, which was also released to the press, noted that Derby had received that news of the loss of the licence 'with the deepest sense of concern' on behalf of the shareholders. Derby's frustration revolved around key issues, upon which he elaborated in his letter. TWW, he stated, had not received any warning from the ITA that the licence might be in danger, either during the tenure of the licence or during the interview. He also stated that he had not been told in detail why or how TWW had failed to hold on to the contract, apart from having been told in a short meeting with Lord Hill (which had come to an abrupt end) that the company was too 'London-based'.[82] Hill responded on 19 June, copying the letter to the press. In it he explained that when a contract ended there was no presumption that it would be offered to the existing contractor, a fact that Derby himself had acknowledged at the time of the 1963–4 contract renewal. Hill accepted that, to a degree, the procedure for licence renewal was based on performance for an existing company and promise for a new one but, he added, 'if a promise is never to be preferred to performance, then every television company will go on for ever'.[83] Two other points were made: that the ITA had judged Harlech's claim to be the better of the two, and that the meeting had not been brought to an abrupt halt by Hill. The letter ended with an unambiguous statement:

> It is no pleasure for the Authority to be parting in due course from a company with which it has worked for ten years. It would be easier in so many ways to leave things alone. But that is not what the Television Act says we should do. However adequate it programmes, a company always lives with the risk that it will encounter a better competitor. In the nature of things, it may not happen often. This time it did.[84]

Derby, however, continued to berate Hill and the ITA. In a letter to Hill on 20 June, he referred to the ITA's decision as 'capricious' and argued that 'nobody has imposed any obligation on you to unseat a satisfactory Contractor without a word of warning after previous reassurance that you were happy with their work'.[85] On 23 June, Emrys Roberts, a former WWN (and now TWW) shareholder, wrote to Derby, informing him that he was fearful of the line being taken by the company. He argued that the animosity with Hill was not helpful and that it would be more fruitful to concentrate on the security of staff and protection of shareholders.[86] On the same day, Wyn Roberts wrote to Lord Derby suggesting that TWW should re-examine the fronts on which the company was fighting. He suggested a number of points of action, including a sticker campaign to get what he called the 'half dormant public feeling' on the side of the company. Roberts also suggested beginning the move from London, so as to respond to one of the Authority's basic objections. He also thought that those who had benefited from TWW's £100,000-worth of donations over the years should be contacted to gain their support.[87] One cannot help but feel that such gestures were a case of 'too little too late'.

It is worth noting that very little discussion was recorded in the minutes of TWW's Welsh board regarding the loss of the licence. A brief two sentences is all that is minuted on 7 July 1967, with a further reference on 14 July to the fact that no more donations would be made to outside bodies.[88] The ITA's Welsh Committee paid little attention to the loss of the licence, although there was a lengthy discussion over the expediency of celebrating the tenth anniversary of ITV in Wales without the participation of the programme company itself.[89]

The ITA's decision regarding TWW led to the matter being raised in the House of Commons. During a debate on the 1964 Television Act, the Labour Postmaster General, Edward Short, defended the ITA, stating that the Authority had allowed TWW shareholders to acquire 40 per cent of non-voting shares in the new company and suggesting that Lord Hill, the ITA's Chairman, had hinted at preferential allocation for those who were set to lose most.[90]

Why did TWW lose the licence to Harlech?[91]

The decision to revoke TWW's licence and award it to the Harlech Consortium aroused a good deal of controversy and was one of the shock decisions in the 1967 licence round as has already been seen. Two of the key questions are how did this happen, and why? There is no one simple answer. To try to understand the ITA's decision it is worth considering the three key players: TWW, the ITA and the Harlech Consortium.

TWW had a problem, in that its head office was in Sloane Square in London. There were clear advantages to this, in terms of liaising with the ITA and network companies, which also had London offices; in addition, the sales staff were near the heart of the advertising industry. There was also an advantage, in that a 'neutral' head office would ensure that neither Cardiff nor Bristol would see themselves as being superior to the other, which, in an awkward dual region, was a major consideration. The problem was that out of ten senior staff, six worked from London, three from Wales and one from the West Country. In his assessment of ITV's early years, Peter Black wrote that Bryan Michie and John Baxter had both been tipped off by colleagues from other ITV companies that the situation was not satisfactory. Yet 'though the board had accepted the likelihood of being asked to move to Cardiff they decided, fatally, to wait until they were asked'.[92] When faced with the Harlech Consortium's arguments over regionalism and regional roots, TWW looked weak. None of the major shareholders – the *Liverpool Daily Post*, the *News of the World*, Lord Derby, Jack Hylton, the Imperial Tobacco Company – had local roots. Moreover, of the seventeen UK-based directors on the company's main board, ten did not live in, or have any obvious connections with, the region. However, a letter in the *Western Mail* questioned whether or not the ITA was being consistent in its decision-making. Wyndham Lewis asked why the ITA had not revoked the licence from Granada and pointed out that 'the Bernsteins can in no way be identified with Manchester having operated from London since the inception of the company, and the same goes for a number of other companies'.[93]

TWW did not submit a highly polished application and did not perform well in the interview, compared with the rival Harlech Consortium. Indeed, the company may well have approached both with a sense of complacency. The company relied too much on its record, but failed to see that the record itself was not without fault. As has been shown, increasing criticism from the ITA highlighted perceived deficiencies in the programme schedules, in particular in terms of the lack of drama productions, schools and adult education programmes, English-language Welsh-interest programmes and programmes which focused on contemporary Welsh issues. Neither did TWW appear to appreciate the fact that the interview was forward-looking, in the sense that the ITA were looking for the best company to serve the region in the next contract period. It was not an interview which would reward loyal service. Lord Derby claimed on a number of occasions that TWW had not received any indication of the ITA's dissatisfaction with the service being provided or that the licence was under threat. It is difficult to believe that he was unaware of the criticisms levelled at the company, particularly from 1964 onwards. Implicit in the concern of the Authority, in terms of the weakness of certain areas of programme provision, was a level of dissatisfaction. Added to this were the underlying tensions that existed between TWW and the ITA, discussed in chapters 3 and 4, which did not make for the most positive working relationship.

One of the key issues to bear in mind from the perspective of the ITA was that, for a considerable time, the Authority had wanted to see a Welsh company serve the region. As discussed in earlier chapters, the ITA would have been happy to see WWN as the contractor for the whole of Wales, had it not failed. The Authority was obliged to renew TWW's contract in 1964, the company having come to the rescue of WWN. In 1967, however, faced with a dynamic, forward-looking company with clear Welsh roots, a Welshman as Chairman and capital from within the region (unlike TWW), there existed an opportunity to appoint what the ITA regarded as a truly regional contractor. Given the nature of the relationship between TWW and the ITA, this may have been the opportunity for which the Authority had been waiting for some time.[94] Indeed, the ITA was keen to signal a complete change within the Wales and West region. As Lord Hill told David Meredith, HTV's Head of Press and Public Relations in Wales, in 1975: 'We not only had to get rid of Lord Derby, but we had to get rid of a whole strata of society as well. It was very fortunate that Harlech made a success of it or it would have been very awkward for us.'[95]

In her study of the fall of TWW, Elain Dafydd suggests that the ITA was influenced by the recommendations of the Pilkington Committee on Broadcasting, which published its report in 1962.[96] In addition to noting Pilkington's arguments regarding the trivial nature of much of ITV's output, it is possible that the Authority was aware of the description of the ITA's authority over the ITV companies as 'illusory and negligible'.[97] They will also have taken on board the Pilkington Committee's conclusion that, despite appearances, the regional or local service was non-existent and that many programmes were merely local in origin rather than in appeal.[98] Michael Darlow also argued that Pilkington was an important factor in explaining the decisions that were made by the ITA in June 1967:

> Following the drubbing it had received at the hands of the Pilkington Committee, in selecting the new contractors the ITA had seen itself as being as much on trial as those competing for the franchises. The Authority had wanted not only to exercise its power but to have been seen to exercise it.[99]

Given the Authority's concerns over TWW's programming, and the desire to improve the image of the ITA, this factor may go some way to explaining the decision taken by the ITA. The ITA may also have been influenced by a group of Welsh Labour MPs who were critical of TWW's record. Led by Ness Edwards, the former Postmaster General and MP for Caerphilly, they met with the ITA on a number of occasions, criticising, amongst other things, TWW's lack of success in breaking through on to the UK network.[100] It is also conceivable that the Authority was impressed with what the *Guardian* referred to as 'the galaxy of stage and screen talent' backing the Harlech bid. Amongst the stars was the opera singer Geraint Evans, who, the paper discovered, was fully booked until 1970 and would therefore not be available to undertake work for Harlech. The article ended:

Experience, alas, shows that starry artistic names have scant time for regular TV. Sir Laurence Olivier . . . is a substantial shareholder in Ulster Television. Back on opening night in 1959 he appeared on the opening show and delivered the epilogue. Since then, he's been notable only for total absence.[101]

Finally, a major reason for the revoking of TWW's licence was the strength of the Harlech application and interview. The application succeeded in targeting all of TWW's weak points, particularly when the consortium was required to discuss programme plans. The consortium had strong roots in the region, created as it was from the merger of one Welsh and one West of England group. The application and subsequent interview appealed to the ITA's sense of regionalism, which had been heightened in the aftermath of the Pilkington Committee's report. The BBC also recognised this strength. In a meeting of the Broadcasting Council for Wales on 16 June 1967, Professor Glanmor Williams, the Chairman, warned that the appointment of the Harlech Consortium meant 'stiffer competition than ever before for the BBC in Wales', particularly in the fields of drama and news and current affairs.[102] It is also important to take into account the political, social and economic context. During this time, the south Wales and Bristol areas were developing in industrial and economic terms, to the extent that the notion of 'Severnside' had been created. Politically, it was a time of change for Wales, the first nationalist MP, Gwynfor Evans, having been returned to Westminster in 1966. The Harlech Consortium reflected this new dynamism in its vigour, enthusiasm and approach to programming in the region. Its application reflected a desire in its programme plans to engage with contemporary changes in modern Wales, something which TWW programming appeared not to do.

Interestingly, Alun Llywelyn-Williams resigned from the ITA's Welsh Committee just two days before the deadline for applications on 15 April 1967 and was a member of the Harlech deputation at the interview on 19 May. As a member of the Welsh Committee he would have been privy to the criticisms made of TWW's programme performance and would have been in a strong position to aid Harlech in its bid. Wyn Roberts raised this issue in a memorandum to Lord Goodman, TWW's solicitor, on 13 June 1967. He noted that Wynford Vaughan Thomas had been quoted in the *Western Mail* as saying that the Harlech Consortium had received a lot of help from Alun Llywelyn-Williams.[103] In addition, Llywelyn-

Williams and Sir Ben Bowen Thomas, the ITA's Welsh member, were neighbours in Bangor; as David Meredith notes: 'They understood each other's train of thought and respected each other's opinions.' Meredith also suggests that another member of the Harlech Consortium, Eric Thomas, played an important role in Harlech's success. It was Thomas, at the behest of the ITA, who had steered WWN through its most difficult period, following the resignation of Haydn Williams (see chapter 6).[104]

Conclusion

On 13 July 1967, TWW and the Harlech Consortium met to discuss the purchase of studios. A further meeting was held the following day, this time to discuss whether or not TWW would take up the 40 per cent of non-voting shares in the new company.[105] On 7 August, TWW turned down the offer of a 40 per cent stake in the Harlech Consortium, partly on the grounds that there was no guarantee that the licence would be renewed at the end of the six-year term and that investment in such a venture would be unwise.[106] By November 1967, however, Harlech Television (as it was now known) and TWW had agreed on a £1.6 m. deal for the sale of the Cardiff and Bristol studios.[107] Later that month Tony Gorard, Harlech's Managing Director, Wynford Vaughan Thomas and Aled Vaughan, the Welsh Programme Controller, met with the ITA's Welsh Committee for the first time in Cardiff.[108]

Meanwhile, TWW's Welsh board continued to meet. In October 1967 it noted that the morale of staff had been maintained throughout the crisis and Bryan Michie, the Programme Controller, reported that the work and enthusiasm of the programme staff had not diminished, despite the obvious distress over the loss of the licence.[109] The Welsh board met for the final time on 15 February 1968, three years exactly after the launch of the Teledu Cymru service. Stanley Leach, the company's Sales Director, expressed his 'deep sense of grief' at the loss of the contract and noted that 'he had never met a body of people who had shown more willingness and enthusiasm' towards their work.[110]

The final programme from Bristol – *Discs-a-Gogo*, presented by Tony Blackburn – was transmitted on 2 March, and the following day, the final programmes were broadcast from the Pontcanna studios. John Betjeman's eulogy, *Come to an End*, was the final transmission by TWW on 3 March 1968, and it ended by bidding farewell to the company:

The new firm Harlech which will be centred in Cardiff must build up its own personality. Tele Wele you had a warm, friendly and inspiring one. Like many others I am grateful to you. I am sorry to see you go. It's the death of an old friend.[111]

The following day a new era in the history of ITV in Wales began.

9

ITV in Wales, 1968–1997

Introduction

This chapter traces the history of ITV in Wales and, by default, that of Harlech Television/HTV from 1968 until 1997, when HTV was taken over by United News and Media. Due to restrictions on access to material (see chapter 1), the chapter takes a very broad overview of developments during the forty-year period and focuses on the key issues that dominated the history of ITV in Wales in the 1970s, 1980s and 1990s, in turn. The overarching issue during the 1970s was a campaign for a separate Welsh-language channel, spearheaded by Cymdeithas yr Iaith Gymraeg, the Welsh Language Society, but supported by both Welsh and non-Welsh speakers (for different reasons). With the advent of the Welsh-language channel, S4C, in 1982, HTV had to reposition itself and gain a strong English-language audience. The 1980s was a decade of mixed fortunes for HTV, culminating in a large bid for the Wales and west of England licence in 1991 (under a new franchise auction system introduced by the Conservative government of the time). The bid damaged HTV, coming as it did at the start of a recession, and the story of the 1990s is one of cutbacks and eventual takeover.

TWW's last programme was transmitted on 4 March 1968. The company had decided to sell the last five months of the contract (which ran until the end of July 1968) to Harlech for around £500,000. However, Harlech was not in a position to begin transmitting its own programmes and so the ITA put in place a temporary service, 'Independent Television Service for Wales and the West'. Essentially, pre-existing TWW programmes were transmitted, together with ITV network programmes.[1] By May, Harlech Television was in a position to start broadcasting, two months before they were required to do so under the terms of the contract with the ITA. Harlech Television began on the night of 20 May 1968. As it was the first night of the new contractors, it was considered to be the first night of the 'new ITV'. Yet, as Michael Darlow observed: 'It turned out to be a monumental disaster, marked by technical mishaps, climaxing in the non-appearance of the station's two biggest stars – Richard Burton and Elizabeth Taylor. So much for expressions of "cultural patriotism".[2] The ITA's Director-General, Robert Fraser, wrote to Harlech's Managing Director, Tony Gorard, conveying the Authority's 'strong feeling of disappointment at the general standard' of the programme, which had been networked across the UK. The letter ended by noting that the company had 'missed this opportunity to present itself on the network in a more favourable light'.[3] It was not the best of starts for the newcomer.

The 1970s

It took some time for Harlech to recover from the ignominy of the first night, particularly in view of the fact that the Exchequer levy, combined with the adverse economic climate of the time, prevented the company from investing in programming as it had wished.[4] By 1972, the financial situation of HTV had improved and the annual report to shareholders noted a 'substantial increase' in advertising revenue.[5] Two years later, however, the company's fortunes had changed, and the 18 per cent drop in advertising revenue by February 1974 was accounted for by the world economic crisis, which, in turn, had created a situation of industrial unrest and inflation.[6] The following year saw a similar pattern in terms of income. 'The past year', wrote Lord Harlech, 'is easily described. The British economy was in the doldrums and therefore advertising revenue, our lifeblood, was anything but buoyant . . . In a very direct sense, the prospects for Independent Television are tied to the sickness or health of the British economy.'[7] The prospects in the latter half of the 1970s were mixed. In 1976, following reorganisation and diversification into ventures such as the Frost and Reed art galleries, HTV Group Ltd was formed, of which television was a subsidiary.[8] Whilst 1976 saw a slight improvement in advertising revenue, the period 1977–9 was dominated by economic stagnation and a poor world economic climate. Nevertheless, HTV's expenditure on its own programmes increased during the period and by 1978, the company was producing more originated programming than any other regional company in the ITV network, around sixteen hours per week on average.

Indeed, despite the financial stringency of the decade, HTV's programming output continued to expand. In 1971, the company established a Children's Department in Cardiff, with a brief to focus in particular on Welsh-language programmes. The following year, HTV broadcast Welsh-language children's programming, such as *Miri Mawr* and *Cantamil,* in a regular weekday slot for the first time on television in Wales. Other popular programmes later in the decade included the pop music show *Seren Wib* and the quiz programme *Wstibethma.* Educational programmes, such as the music programme *Sain, Cerdd a Chân* and the weekly women's magazine *Hamdden,* also began during this period. Welsh-language drama series like *Y Gwrthwynebwyr* portrayed the lives of those who had rebelled against authority (such as Bertolt Brecht and Dietrich Bonhoeffer). HTV experimented by broadcasting bilingual programmes from the National Eisteddfod in Haverfordwest in 1972 and the Urdd National Eisteddfod in Pontypridd in 1973.[9] Further experimentation took place when a religious programme, *Gwen a Helen a Tim a Marc,* was created, produced and introduced by four pupils from Ysgol Gyfun Rhydfelen in Pontypridd.[10] Perhaps the pinnacle of Welsh-language experimentation came in September 1978, when HTV dubbed the Western Shane into Welsh. The reaction from the public was overwhelmingly negative and, as one Welsh MP, referring to the event, noted in the House of Commons in 2001: 'That experiment has gone down in Welsh history and will never be tried again.'[11]

Writing of the Wales and West region at the beginning of the 1970s, Jeremy Potter argued that:

> Of all the ITV regions Wales and the West of England was the most intricate in terms of engineering and cultural characteristics and therefore the most awkward to satisfy in terms of the provision of a programme service ... the passion and the rhetoric of years of political debate about the future of Welsh broadcasting made this, among all the complexities of the franchise, the dominant issue.[12]

In a similar vein, Richard Last, writing in the *Daily Telegraph* in December 1970, referred to the awkward nature of the HTV franchise, describing it as a 'televisual Austria-Hungary'. Despite the establishment of HTV Wales and HTV West in 1970, together with boards of directors for both 'sub-regions', the ITV licence was for 'Wales and the West'. 'It is difficult not to see the Wales–West marriage as an artificial one', wrote Last.[13] There remained a good deal of antagonism in the west of England during the 1970s, with concerns that HTV was biased towards Wales, particularly towards the Welsh language. In Wales, however, claims of west-of-England dominance in the boardroom led to accusations of an anti-Welsh bias.[14]

By the end of the 1970s a 'Ban Welsh Telly' group had formed in the west of England, with a view to pressing for the removal of Welsh from English screens altogether and splitting the region.[15]

It was the language issue that dominated the broadcasting sector in Wales throughout the 1970s, in particular the call for a fourth television channel, which would be, in effect, a Welsh-language channel. Some were concerned that the BBC and HTV were focusing too much on Welsh-language viewers, at the expense of others. A Labour Party study group report on television in Wales, published in 1973, noted that many non-Welsh speakers in Wales turned their aerials towards the Mendip (HTV West) transmitter, the BBC's Sutton Coldfield transmitter in the Midlands or the transmitter carrying Westward programmes. Television, it argued, had weakened the link between non-Welsh speakers and Wales: 'The present arrangements have tended to create an identity between Welshness and the Welsh language and in so doing have helped to make the language issue a divisive one.'[16] By July 1979, a survey measuring attitudes towards ITV showed that 82 per cent of the population of Wales wanted more programmes in English about the nation.[17] At the same time a vociferous Welsh-language minority, led by the Welsh Language Society, was campaigning for a separate channel that would carry Welsh-language programming. As in the past, the language issue in television had a clear political dimension. It is clear from documents held at the National Archives that both the Conservative and Labour governments of the 1970s were acutely aware of the potential disruption that broadcasting issues could create in Wales, combined as they were with Westminster fears of a rising tide of nationalist sentiment. In July 1972, for example, the Secretary of State for Wales, Peter Thomas, wrote to the Minister for Post and Telecommunications, Sir John Eden, calling for a way forward with regard to a fourth channel for Wales. 'Otherwise', he stated, 'I foresee an intensified campaign to withhold licence fees and carry out other and more disruptive forms of protest.'[18] When Labour came to power in 1974, it is clear that the Welsh Office and its Secretary of State, John Morris, were keen to appease the situation with regard to broadcasting in Wales. Although by this time broadcasting fell under the auspices of the Home Office, Morris was keen to ensure that the Welsh Office voice was heard in all debates.[19]

In 1974, the Report of the Committee on Broadcasting (also known as the Crawford Report, after its chairman, Sir Stewart Crawford) was published. The committee had been charged in May 1973 to consider, *inter alia*, the issue of a fourth television channel. The report recommended that, on the basis of the cultural and social needs of Wales, 'whatever the decision that may be reached about the use of the Fourth Channel in the rest of the United Kingdom, it should in Wales be allotted as soon as possible to a separate service in which Welsh-language programmes should be given priority'. The model suggested was that of the BBC and HTV moving all current Welsh programming to this new channel. This would not only satisfy the demands of Welsh-speaking campaigners, but would also placate non-Welsh speakers, who were keen to remove the irritation of Welsh-language programming from their screens. However, the report also made clear that a Welsh-language channel on the fourth channel should not be introduced at the expense of the extension of UHF coverage in the rest of the UK.[20]

The IBA's Committee for Wales welcomed the committee's recommendation.[21] HTV, however, took a different view and maintained that the best way forward was to give the fourth channel to ITV and to transmit Welsh programmes on both BBC and HTV in Wales.[22] In May 1974, when this viewpoint was put to the Crawford Committee, Jolyon Dromgoole of the Home Office Broadcasting Department wrote to Lord Harris, Minister of State at the Home Office, calling HTV's arguments 'short on originality and long on self-interest'. He also accused HTV of running counter to the broadly unanimous support in Wales for an exclusively Welsh fourth channel.[23] HTV's objection to the Welsh-fourth-channel solution continued in the latter part of the 1970s. For example, when the broadcasting committee under the chairmanship of Lord Annan reported in 1977, recommending that the fourth channel be made available to an Open Broadcasting Authority, and not the IBA, HTV recorded its disappointment.[24] The company's views were further evinced in a pamphlet published prior to the passing of the 1980 Broadcasting Act and after William Whitelaw, the Conservative Home Secretary, had announced the government's intention to increase Welsh-language programming on both the BBC and HTV in Wales (thus reneging on an election promise of establishing a Welsh fourth channel). HTV argued that placing all Welsh-language programmes on one channel would effectively ghettoise the language, and it welcomed the government's decision to give the fourth channel to the IBA, thereby effectively creating ITV2.[25] Reaction to the government's decision outside

HTV was quite different. In October 1979, the Plaid Cymru MP for Meirionydd Nant Conwy, Dafydd Elis-Thomas, wrote to Lord Belstead, the Home Office Minister, pointing out that a succession of government-appointed committees in the 1970s had recommended the use of the fourth channel in Wales for the Welsh language. He referred also to a national broadcasting movement for a Welsh fourth channel which he and two other MPs, Geraint Howells and Geraint Morgan, had established in 1977, and which had the support of a range of national organisations. Finally, and rather pointedly, Elis-Thomas noted that William Whitelaw's statement on the fourth channel had the support of HTV, the IBA and the anti-Welsh Language Freedom Movement.[26] HTV became the object of much criticism from Welsh-language speakers, supporters and campaigners. At its national conference in Llandudno in October 1979, Plaid Cymru ejected HTV's news team from the conference, following accusations of the company's 'treachery' against the people of Wales.[27]

Eventually, the Conservative government decided to honour the manifesto commitment and the Welsh fourth channel formed part of the 1980 Broadcasting Act. This heralded a new era in Welsh and British broadcasting and introduced third and fourth broadcasting forces, in the shape of Channel 4 and Sianel 4 Cymru (S4C).[28] HTV acquiesced, and entered into a partnership with the new channel.

The 1980s

Not only did HTV have to contend with a new broadcaster and negotiate terms for programme supply (see later in this section), but it faced a rival application for the regional licence, which was due for renewal on 31 December 1981. The rival consortium, headed by Lord Hooson, the former Liberal MP for Montgomery, and including David Thomas, Managing Director of the *Western Mail*, called itself Teledu Hafren/Hafren Television/Severn Television. The written application was weak, and the IBA doubted whether or not the company would actually be able to deliver on the promises made; on 28 December 1980, the contract was awarded to HTV.[29]

Financially, the 1980s was a mixed decade. A lengthy industrial dispute at the end of 1979 took ITV off the air for eleven weeks and resulted in a loss of £6 m. for HTV.[30] Although the economy had not revived as much as had been hoped in 1982, by 1983 advertising revenue was up by 17 per cent to £48.2 m.[31] This trend was common across most

ITV companies, with advertising revenues at around 11 per cent above the rate of inflation.[32] The middle of the decade saw profits rise further, and in 1985, the annual report to shareholders recorded 'substantial progress' in financial terms.[33] Many ITV companies, HTV included, diversified their portfolios during the 1980s. HTV purchased the Frost and Reed art gallery in Bristol, the Dataday diary business and, in the latter part of the decade, Christie's Contemporary Arts for £15 m. Unfortunately, the recession which hit the UK at the beginning of the 1990s drastically reduced the value of these holdings, and a group of companies was sold off for only £3 m. in 1992.[34]

The advent of S4C meant that HTV had to relaunch and rebrand itself as an English-language channel. A series of advertisements in Welsh newspapers in October 1982 aimed to persuade viewers that 'HTV Wales speaks your kind of language'.[35] There was a concerted effort to attract non-Welsh-speaking viewers who had turned their aerials to Granada (in the north), Central (in mid Wales) and HTV West (in the south) in order to 'avoid' Welsh-language programmes on HTV Wales. In 1980, the company opened a studio in Mold, in north-east Wales, partly to allow for increased production hours as a result of S4C, but also to gain a foothold in an area which was still considered to be part of 'Granadaland'. HTV also produced its first English-language soap opera, *Taff Acre*. The serial was based in a south Wales valley town and was shown twice a week in Wales. It also had a run of thirteen weeks on the ITV network and, according to the IBA's annual report, 'gave an insight into contemporary Welsh life, its aim being to look frankly at the personal, moral and financial problems besetting a small South Wales community'.[36] English-language co-productions, emanating from HTV's Bristol centre, also increased during the 1980s, and in 1986, HTV was awarded the Queen's Award for Export Achievement in recognition of the overseas sales of television programmes between 1982 and 1985.[37] Not all co-productions were successful, however. *The Curse of King Tut's Tomb* was an expensive project which was beset with problems from the outset and which ran well over budget. It also caused a degree of resentment within the company, with accusations of 'Bristol-based imperialism' coming from employees based in Cardiff. It was also claimed, in an anonymous letter sent from HTV Wales workers to Dafydd Elis-Thomas, that the expensive production had affected HTV Wales's local production in Cardiff.[38]

In the sphere of Welsh-language programmes, the relationship with the Welsh fourth channel did not get off to the most auspicious start. The IBA had requested seven hours per week of programming from HTV, whereas the government had indicated that twelve hours of Welsh-language programming would be required, the 'shortfall' of five hours coming from the independent production sector. Indeed, the building of a new television centre at Culverhouse Cross on the outskirts of Cardiff had been premised on the basis of the latter figure.[39] The discussions over the type of HTV programming and the price to be paid for it were long and protracted – a 'long-running saga', as one Welsh journal commented.[40] Eventually, a deal was struck. Between November 1982 and the summer of 1984, seven hours forty-five minutes per week would be provided by HTV for S4C at a cost of £13.9 m. Once the new studios at Culverhouse Cross had been opened in the summer of 1984, nine hours of programming would be provided for £16.75 m. The deal would end in 1989, when a new round of contracts would be considered.[41] HTV's programming for S4C was varied, but focused on its strengths in current affairs (*Y Byd ar Bedwar*) and light entertainment (for example, *Torri Gwynt*, programmes featuring the talent of all-round entertainer Caryl Parry Jones and a chat show fronted by Elinor Jones). The popular series focusing on Welsh rural life presented by Dai Jones, *Cefn Gwlad*, also gained a large following on the new channel. HTV also produced a soap opera for S4C. Set in Cardiff and based on family rivalry and city life, *Dinas* soon attracted a loyal audience. However, possibly due to the urban (and therefore slightly unfamiliar for many Welsh viewers) setting, it struggled after an initial period of success. Ultimately, though, it could not compete with BBC Wales's well-established soap opera, *Pobol y Cwm*, which had been running since 1974.

By 1985, S4C considered the £7 m. being paid to HTV for 'service and administration costs' on the company's programmes to be excessive, and attempts were made to reduce costs.[42] A further blow to the relationship between HTV and S4C came in May 1987, when the Welsh fourth channel announced that it would be putting the nine hours a week provided by HTV (worth around £20 m. to the ITV company) out to tender after 1989.[43] Owen Edwards, S4C Director, denied that the move was an 'anti-HTV' one; rather, it was allowing all commercial producers to compete on an equal footing.[44] Partly as a result of this announcement and partly as a result of a downturn in the economy, HTV announced redundancies at the end of 1989, fourteen of which were at the Mold studio. The 1980s did not end well for HTV Wales.

Yet more change was to come. The Peacock Report, published in 1986, which focused on financing the BBC, reflected a wider ideological shift in the way in which broadcasting was perceived and signalled a major change in the way in which television, and ITV in particular, was to be regulated. The government's Broadcasting Act, which reached the statute books in 1990, replaced the IBA with a 'light-touch' regulatory body, the Independent Television Commission. One of the first tasks of the ITC was to oversee the licence-renewal process, which, under the terms of the 1990 Act, now took the form of an auction. Once again, HTV faced a challenge.

The 1990s

This time, however, the rules had changed and there were four groups applying for the Wales and west of England licence. HTV faced challenges from Channel 3 Wales and the West Ltd, Merlin Television (whose Director of Programmes was former BBC Wales senior executive Teleri Bevan) and C3W Ltd (which named Euryn Ogwen Williams, Deputy Chief Executive of S4C, as its Controller in Wales). Under the terms of the 1990 Broadcasting Act, in addition to passing a 'quality threshold' in its programming plans, each group had to submit sealed cash bids. On 16 October 1991, it was announced that HTV had retained the licence to broadcast from 1 January 1993 onwards. But at what cost? The HTV board had made a cash bid of £20.53 m. compared with £19.4 m. from Merlin Television, £18.3 m. from Channel 3 Wales and the West and £17.8 m. from C3W.[45] The ITC were happy with HTV's programmes in quality terms, but had reservations about the company's business plan with regard to staffing, expenditure and other 'significant shortcomings'. Louis Sherwood, the HTV Group Chairman, had overestimated the revenue prospects and share of net advertising revenue.[46] To add insult to injury, the economic recession which hit the UK at the beginning of the 1990s resulted in a loss of airtime sales and saw advertising revenue at an all-time low. January 1991 alone saw a 20 per cent decrease on the previous year.[47] The company suffered severe losses.[48] From 1993 onwards, HTV returned to making a profit, aided by a partnership with the UK cable operator, Flextech, which took a 20 per cent stake in HTV.[49]

Independent television was, according to Howard Tumber, turned upside down by the 1990 Broadcasting Act, one of the main effects being a move towards a consolidation of the ITV network.[50] A series of mergers and takeovers, prompted by the Act but encouraged by further regulatory changes in media ownership rules, reduced the number of regionally based companies. Increased competition within the system, heightened by the decision to allow Channel 4 and S4C to compete with the ITV companies for advertising revenue, led to increased commercial pressures.[51] On 24 November 1993, the Secretary of State for National Heritage announced a relaxation of the rules for the ownership of ITV companies. With HTV's profits rising, the company looked ripe for takeover by a larger company or group. Further ownership changes came into being under the terms of the 1996 Broadcasting Act, which allowed mergers to go ahead, providing they did not impact negatively on the quality and range of programmes and the regional identity of companies. In another change to the rules, companies could own as many television stations as they wished, providing their share of the national (UK) audience did not exceed 15 per cent.[52] On 28 June 1997, HTV was taken over by the London-based United News and Media, a company which owned Express Newspapers and which already had a 20 per cent stake in HTV. It marked the end of almost forty years of Welsh-based ITV broadcasting in Wales.

Conclusion

As Kevin Williams has noted, United did not purchase HTV for its regional programming; it bought the company so that it could build up strength to fight its rival media groups, Carlton and Granada.[53] In July 2000, Granada bought Meridian, Anglia and HTV from United, but the rules relating to audience share meant that Granada had to relieve itself of one of the companies. So, on 23 October 2000, Carlton acquired HTV from Granada for £181 m. and Carlton's 20 per cent holding in the ITV company Meridian. When Carlton and Granada merged in 2004 a new company, ITV plc, was formed from all licensees, apart from STV (Central Scotland), UTV (Ulster), CTV (Channel Islands) and Grampian (northern Scotland). The regional identity upon which ITV had been founded in the 1950s was, to all intents and purposes, put to rest, and independent television in Wales was subsequently rebranded as 'ITV Wales'.

The history of HTV in the twenty-nine years of its existence is a mixed one. After a shaky start it soon gathered momentum and made its mark on the region it served. In Wales, the reputation it made for itself amongst Welsh speakers was shaken somewhat by the stance taken over the Welsh fourth channel. The economic downturn, coupled with an extraordinarily high cash bid during the 1991 franchise round, resulted in cutbacks, staff losses and cheap-to-make programming. Despite the profits made from 1993 onwards, the financial upturn had little impact on what appeared on screen.[54] To some, the 1990 Broadcasting Act and the subsequent licence auction was the beginning of the end, or the death knell, for independent television in Wales.[55] Consolidation in the 1990s led to a loss of identity within the regional ITV companies, which prompted the question, 'Whither ITV Wales?'.

10

Postscript

I would like to return to the five themes laid out in the introductory chapter and draw some conclusions from this study of the history of independent television in Wales.

The tension which exists within the ITV companies between a public service remit and the pressures of the commercial sector has created problems over the years for independent television in Wales. Writing in 1979, in response to criticism from the Welsh Language Society, the Director of Programmes at HTV Wales, Aled Vaughan, admitted that HTV was indeed a commercial company, 'and therefore we are obliged to pay our way, and to do this we must make a profit. If we don't succeed in making a profit, we won't be saved by a grant or a helping hand from any public fund.'[1] This dichotomy stemmed from the 1954 Television Act, which established ITV as a commercially funded public service broadcaster. Moreover, ITV companies had clear regional responsibilities, set in place to counter the London-based focus of the BBC at the time. Balancing the needs of shareholders and a desire to maximise profits against its public service obligations has always been a problem for ITV. Since the 1990 Broadcasting Act there has been a marked retreat from these obligations within ITV. An increasingly competitive and globalised media market has led to ITV's public service requirements being considered a burden by many, such as the commercial broadcaster's former Chief Executive, Michael Grade. The situation has been made more complex by the role of the regulator, OFCOM, which, according to Tom O'Malley, has 'provided regulatory cover for ITV's withdrawal from its public service obligations' as part of its review of public service broadcasting in the UK.[2] In Wales for example, OFCOM approved the reduction of ITV news programming from five hours twenty minutes to four hours per week. Non-news programming (including current affairs) has been reduced from four hours to ninety minutes per week (75 per cent of which will be at peak times).[3]

Linguistic tensions have run through the history of ITV in Wales. The 1954 Act ensured that regional ITV companies paid due attention to the specific cultural make-up of the relevant region, and in the case of Wales, this included the Welsh language. As has been seen in preceding chapters, the fact that ITV in Wales had to serve two linguistic communities (and a third community in the west of England as part of the licence) caused tensions and often insurmountable problems, which were only resolved in 1982 with the advent of S4C. The presence of Welsh-language programmes within the schedules of TWW, WWN and HTV prior to 1982 created divisions within Welsh society. Many viewers either turned their aerials to transmitters based on English soil to avoid the programmes or did not 'convert' to TWW/HTV at all.[4] This created a situation where many viewers could not receive programmes about Wales, thereby creating a cultural, social and political deficit. At the same time, it is clear from the evidence that English-language programming about Wales and Welsh issues was a significant weakness, in terms of ITV strategy in Wales. The ITA and its successor, the IBA, regularly drew the attention of the ITV company in Wales to the shortfall in this area.

This matter is closely related to the third 'tension', that of the alliance between Wales and the west of England. The linking of Wales and the West has been traced to two factors as discussed in this book: economics and transmitters. The uneasy marriage created ill-feeling on both sides of the Bristol Channel from the outset, and this continued in the 1970s, despite HTV's virtual separation of the two 'sub-regions' of Wales and the West. In addition to this, many parts of Wales fell into overlap areas with other broadcasters, most notably north-east Wales, mid Wales and south-east Wales. Creating a unified Welsh audience therefore proved to be difficult for the ITV regional contractors in Wales.

In relation to the tension between the regional and the national, Wales has never had a strong identity on the ITV network. TWW programmes which appeared on the network were few and far between. Whilst *Land of Song* may have presented a certain version of Wales and Welshness, *Discs-a-Gogo*, taken by some ITV regional companies, was not inherently 'Welsh'. HTV's successes on the network, such as *Robin of Sherwood* and *Treasure Island*, have tended to emanate from the Bristol studios of the company. In recent times, Wales has been noticeably absent from network production in terms of both programming and representation. The National Assembly for Wales's Broadcasting Committee reported in 2008 that 'Wales is the UK's invisible nation in terms of its place on TV screens ... We feel that if ITV plc wishes to continue as an UK broadcaster, it should reflect the diversity and richness of character of the whole of the UK'.[5] ITV did not spend any of its 'out-of-London' quota in Wales in 2006 or 2007, and ITV Wales's former head of drama, Pete Edwards, has referred to ITV's 'cultural arrogance', accusing the ITV network of undermining attempts to represent Wales on the UK network.[6]

Finally, the popular-vs.-quality tension has manifested itself in the programming of the ITV contractors over fifty years. The whole *raison d'être* of ITV demands the creation of a mass audience and the quickest way to achieve that aim is to provide entertaining programmes. It is not coincidence that ITV chose the slogan '50 years of entertaining the nation' at the time of its anniversary in 2005. However, cultural prejudice against the commercial broadcaster runs deep, and ITV has been tarnished with the image of a cheap and cheerful broadcaster. Whilst ITV companies in Wales *did* provide relatively cheap-to-make programmes, such as quiz shows, they also led the way with news, current affairs and documentary programme-making, as I have shown. There has, however, been a lack of investment in local drama in Wales, a situation that was not properly addressed until the end of the 1990s, with the appointment of Pete Edwards as head of a newly formed drama development department at HTV.

So what of the future of ITV in Wales? Predicting the future in the midst of change is difficult, and even senior managers at ITV Wales are unsure about what will happen to the commercial broadcaster.[7] ITV is necessary to provide a plurality which offers a required balance to the BBC, which has always held a dominant and powerful position in Wales. Whilst OFCOM argue that public service broadcasting on ITV has become financially unsustainable, 91 per cent of the Welsh population believe that regional independent television is essential to the health of a democratic society.

Forty years ago, in Harlech Television's annual report for 1969, Lord Harlech ended his statement to shareholders by issuing a challenge to the ITA and the government. In doing so, he laid out his company's vision of regional independent television:

> The powers that be must decide whether or not they want to see regional television continue and flourish in this country or whether they want to substitute a single uniform national programme . . . We believe in the regional pattern of Independent Television in this country. We believe in it because people in each area have a right to see programmes reflecting

the special character and interests of the society around them. We believe in it because the search for talent and new ideas within each region can add excitement and variety to the total output of television in the nation as a whole.[8]

The same challenge now faces the present government and regulator. History, it seems, is repeating itself.

Notes

1: Introduction

[1] Throughout the book, the terms 'commercial television' and 'independent television' are used interchangeably, depending on source and context. The word 'independent' was used to signal the television service's difference from the BBC, to suggest a certain distance from the State and to use a term that was more acceptable than 'commercial'. 'Independent Television' and 'ITV' are used in reference to the brand – name of the broadcasting group.

[2] 'Minister to hold ITV Wales talks', http://news.bbc.co.uk/1/hi/business/8058042.stm, 19 May 2009 (accessed 5 June 2009).

[3] Bernard Sendall, *Independent Television in Britain. Volume 1. Origin and Foundation, 1946–62* (London, 1982).

[4] Jamie Medhurst, 'Piecing together Mammon's television: a case study in historical television research', in Helen Wheatley (ed.), *Re-Viewing Television History: Critical Issues in Television Historiography* (London, 2007), pp. 127–41.

[5] See, for example, Cathy Johnson and Rob Turnock (eds), *ITV Cultures: Independent Television over Fifty Years* (Maidenhead, 2005), and Rob Turnock, *Television and Consumer Culture: The Transformation of Modernity* (London, 2007).

[6] Wheatley (ed.), *Re-Viewing Television History*, p. 4.

[7] Since completing the research for the book, the archives and records of the Independent Television Authority (ITA), the Independent Broadcasting Authority (IBA) and the Independent Television Commission (ITC) have been deposited at Bournemouth University library and will be available to academic researchers once again.

[8] Tom O'Malley, 'ITV slashes Welsh services', *Free Press*, 166 (2008), 6.

[9] H. H. Wilson, *Pressure Group: The Campaign for Commercial Television* (London, 1961); Burton Paulu, *British Broadcasting in Transition* (London, 1961).

[10] Wilson, *Pressure Group*, dust jacket.

[11] Asa Briggs, *The History of British Broadcasting in the United Kingdom. Volume IV* (Oxford, 1979 [2000 reprint]), p. 825.

[12] Ibid., p. 849.

[13] Wilson, *Pressure Group*, p. 96.

[14] Burton Paulu, *British Broadcasting: Radio and Television in the United Kingdom* (Minneapolis, 1956).

[15] Paulu, *British Broadcasting in Transition*, p. v.
[16] Sendall, *Independent Television in Britain. Vol. 1*, p. iii.
[17] Paulu, *British Broadcasting in Transition*, p. 191.
[18] Ibid., p. 220.
[19] Ibid., pp. 143–4.
[20] Clive Jenkins, *Power Behind the Screen: Ownership, Control and Motivation in British Commercial Television* (London, 1961).
[21] Ibid., p. 12.
[22] Gwynfor Evans and J. E. Jones, *TV in Wales* (Cardiff, 1958).
[23] Jenkins, *Power Behind the Screen*, p. 218.
[24] Ibid., p. 224.
[25] Peter Black, *The Mirror in the Corner: People's Television* (London, 1972).
[26] Ibid., pp. 189–90.
[27] See, for example, Briggs, *History of British Broadcasting. Vol. IV*, pp. 307–8, and *The History of British Broadcasting in the United Kingdom. Volume V* (Oxford, 1995 [2000 reprint]), p. 673.
[28] See, for example, WAC, R34/1144 – 'Should the BBC share a transmitter with W.W.N.', 1 October 1962.
[29] Bernard Sendall, *Independent Television in Britain. Volume 2. Expansion and Change, 1958–68* (London, 1983).
[30] Sendall, *Independent Television in Britain. Vol. 2*, p. 70.
[31] ITA, CW 1 (63), 1 February 1963.
[32] James Curran and Jean Seaton, *Power Without Responsibility: The Press, Broadcasting and New Media in Britain*, 6th edn. (London, 2003).
[33] Curran and Seaton, *Power Without Responsibility*, pp. 193–6.
[34] Ibid., p. 182; Kevin Williams, *Get Me a Murder a Day: A History of Mass Communication in Britain* (London, 1998), p. 162.
[35] Johnson and Turnock (eds), *ITV Cultures*, p. 16.
[36] Ibid., p. 7.
[37] David Barlow, Philip Mitchell and Tom O'Malley, *The Media in Wales: Voices of a Small Nation* (Cardiff, 2005), p. 102.
[38] Williams, *Get Me a Murder a Day*, p. 108; Davies, *Broadcasting*, p. 59.
[39] Medhurst, 'Piecing together Mammon's television', pp. 128–9.
[40] *Western Mail*, 14 January 1958.

2: The Pre-history of Independent Television in Wales

[1] Rowland Lucas, *The Voice of a Nation* (Llandysul, 1981), p. 15.
[2] John Davies, *Broadcasting and the BBC in Wales* (Cardiff, 1994), p. 2.

[3] Gwynfor Evans, 'Hanes twf Plaid Cymru 1925–1995', in Geraint H. Jenkins (ed.), *Cof Cenedl X* (Llandysul, 1995), p. 157.
[4] Aneirin Talfan Davies, *Darlledu a'r Genedl* (London, 1972), pp. 6–8.
[5] Saunders Lewis (1893–1985) was a Welsh poet, dramatist, literary critic and political activist. He was a founder of the Welsh nationalist party, Plaid Cymru.
[6] Davies, *Broadcasting*, pp. 32–3.
[7] *Welsh in Education and Life* (London, 1927), p. 164.
[8] Davies, *Broadcasting*, p. 49.
[9] Lucas, *The Voice of a Nation*, pp. 41–3.
[10] *BBC Handbook 1931* (London, 1932), p. 65.
[11] *Western Mail*, 12 March 1930. Bowen argued that the west of England could easily be served by the BBC's Daventry transmitter. This would 'free' frequencies which could be used to create an all-Wales service via new transmitters in the Brecon Beacons mountains (for south Wales) and from a location in the north.
[12] See, for example, E. G. Bowen, 'Brad diwethaf y BBC', *Y Ddraig Goch* (December 1933), 2.
[13] Davies, *Broadcasting*, p. 53.
[14] 'Gorchfygwn y BBC', *Y Ddraig Goch* (February, 1932), 2 (my translation).
[15] 'Cymru a'r BBC', *Y Ddraig Goch* (September, 1932), 3.
[16] J. E. Jones, *Tros Gymru* (Swansea, 1970), p. 133.
[17] *The Times*, 20 March 1965.
[18] For further details on the contribution of the Bangor studios to broadcasting in Wales, see Dyfnallt Morgan (ed.), *Babi Sam: Yn Dathlu Hanner Can Mlynedd o Ddarlledu o Fangor* (Bangor, 1985).
[19] John Davies, *Hanes Cymru: A History of Wales in Welsh* (London, 1992), p. 567. Reith, however, denied that pressure from Wales had played any part in the BBC's decision to allocate a separate wavelength to allow the establishment of the Welsh Region.
[20] Davies, *Broadcasting*, p. 205.
[21] *BBC Handbook 1939* (London, 1939), p. 41.
[22] Undeb Cymru Fydd, the New Wales Union, was established in 1941 as a result of a merger between two Welsh cultural groups, the National Union of Welsh Societies and the National Conference for Safeguarding Welsh Culture. It soon developed a coordinating role in Welsh cultural life, developing activities connected with the preservation of the linguistic, social, educational and cultural make-up of Wales. It played a key role in the establishment of the 'Parliament for Wales' campaign in 1950, drawing on the old nineteenth-century radical liberalist tradition rather than the new twentieth-century nationalist movement (as in the case of Plaid Cymru).

[23] Gwynfor Evans, *Y Radio yng Nghymru* (Aberystwyth, 1944), p. 7.
[24] Andrew Crisell, *An Introductory History of British Broadcasting* (2nd edn, London, 2002), p. 79.
[25] Kevin Williams, *Get Me a Murder a Day: A History of Mass Communications in Britain* (London, 1998), p. 151.
[26] Asa Briggs, *The History of British Broadcasting in the United Kingdom. Volume IV. Sound and Vision* (Oxford, 1979 [2000 reprint]), p. 120.
[27] Crisell, *An Introductory History of British Broadcasting*, p. 80.
[28] *Report of the Broadcasting Committee, 1949. Appendix H. Memoranda submitted to the Committee. Cmd. 8117* (London, 1951), p. 236.
[29] Briggs, *History of British Broadcasting. Vol. IV*, p. 121.
[30] Grace Wyndham Goldie, *Facing the Nation: Television and Politics 1936–76* (London, 1977), p. 19. See also Lez Cooke, *British Television Drama: A History* (London, 2003), p. 13, and Williams, *Get Me a Murder a Day*, p. 154.
[31] John Corner (ed.), *Popular Television in Britain: Studies in Cultural History* (London, 1991), p. 3.
[32] Bernard Sendall, *Independent Television in Britain. Volume 1. Origin and Foundation, 1946–62* (London, 1982), p. 4.
[33] Quoted in Briggs, *History of British Broadcasting. Vol. IV*, p. 40.
[34] H. H. Wilson, *Pressure Group: The Campaign for Commercial Television* (London, 1961), p. 39.
[35] The report was another milestone in the history of British broadcasting. Jean Seaton, for example, argues that the origins of commercial television can be traced back to the committee. See James Curran and Jean Seaton, *Power Without Responsibility: The Press, Broadcasting and New Media in Britain*, 6th edn. (London, 2003), p. 160.
[36] See Briggs, *History of British Broadcasting. Vol. IV*, pp. 349–51.
[37] *Report of the Broadcasting Committee, 1949. Cmd. 8116* (London, 1951), p. 190.
[38] Ibid. p. 160. For a detailed study of the Beveridge Committee and Wales see Jamie Medhurst, '"Minorities with a message": the Beveridge Report on Broadcasting (1949–1951) and Wales', *Twentieth Century British History*, 19, 2 (2008), 217–33.
[39] Lucas, *Voice of a Nation*, p. 165.
[40] Davies, *Broadcasting*, p. 199.
[41] *Broadcasting: Memorandum on Television Policy. Cmd. 9005* (London, 1953).
[42] See Sendall, *Independent Television in Britain. Vol. 1.*; Briggs, *History of British Broadcasting Vol. IV*; Cathy Johnson and Rob Turnock (eds), *ITV Cultures: Independent Television over Fifty Years* (Maidenhead, 2005).
[43] Briggs, *History of British Broadcasting. Vol IV*, p. 390.

44 Crisell, *An Introductory History of British Broadcasting*, p. 83.
45 For further information on the idea of pressure-group campaigning for commercial television, see Wilson, *Pressure Group*, and Briggs, *History of British Broadcasting. Vol. IV*.
46 Hansard, House of Lords Debates, vol. 176, col. 1297, 22 May 1952.
47 Wilson, *Pressure Group*, pp. 156–7. Among the signatories were Lady Violet Bonham-Carter, Lord Halifax and Lord Waverley.
48 Des Freedman, *Television Policies of the Labour Party, 1951–2001* (London, 2003), pp. 9–10.
49 It should be noted that the BBC had faced competition in radio in the 1930s from stations such as Radio Normandy and Radio Luxembourg. See Sean Street, *Crossing the Ether: Pre-war Public Service Radio and Commercial Competition in the UK* (Eastleigh, 2006), for further details.
50 John Corner, 'General introduction: television and British society in the 1950s', in Corner (ed.), *Popular Television in Britain*, p. 5.
51 *Television Act 1954. Ch.55* (London, 1955), p. 21.
52 *TV Times*, 20 September 1955.
53 Hansard, House of Commons Debates, vol. 521, col. 242, 9 December 1953.
54 Ibid., vol. 522, col. 240, 15 December 1953.
55 Ibid., vol. 522, col. 241, 15 December 1953.
56 Ibid., vol. 525, col. 1505, 25 March 1954.
57 Ibid.
58 Ibid.
59 Ibid., vol. 527, cols. 409–10, 5 May 1954.
60 Ibid., vol. 527, cols. 410–11, 5 May 1954.
61 Ibid., vol. 527, col. 419, 5 May 1954.
62 Ibid., vol. 527, col. 522, 5 May 1954.
63 Sendall, *Independent Television in Britain. vol. 1*, p. 121.
64 Ibid., p. 330.
65 Granada Group Limited, *Directors' Report and Accounts for the Year Ended October First 1960* (London, 1960), p. 1.
66 Davies, *Broadcasting*, pp. 213–14.
67 John Finch (ed.), *Granada Television: The First Generation* (Manchester, 2003), p. 58.
68 Davies, *Broadcasting*, p. 213.
69 Rhydwen Williams, 'Gorau barn . . . gorau chwedl', *Barn* (Ionawr, 1981), 14. Sidney Bernstein was managing director at Granada Television.
70 NLW, Rhydwen Williams Papers 4.
71 Ibid.
72 Ibid.; Granada Television Archive, Boxes 0629 and 0630.

[73] Warren Jenkins was a producer with Granada, and Rhydwen Williams was a former Baptist minister and crowned bard.
[74] Meredith Edwards, *Ar Lwyfan Awr: Atgofion Actor* (Swansea, 1977), p. 97.
[75] NLW, Rhydwen Williams Papers, 4. The paper's claim was a little overstated, as only north Wales and the south Wales belt – those in the areas reached by the Winter Hill and Wenvoe transmitters – could actually receive ITV programmes.
[76] NLW, Plaid Cymru Archive, M50, Cutting.
[77] David Barlow, 'What's in the 'Post'? Mass media as a site of struggle', in Jane Aaron and Chris Williams (eds), *Postcolonial Wales* (Cardiff, 2005), p. 202.
[78] Talfan Davies, *Darlledu a'r Genedl*, p. 6 (my translation).
[79] Michelle Ryan 'Blocking the channels: T.V. and Film in Wales', in Tony Curtis (ed.), *Wales: The Imagined Nation. Essays in Cultural and National Identity* (Bridgend, 1986), p. 185.
[80] Davies, *Broadcasting*, p. 39.
[81] Williams, *Get Me a Murder a Day*, p. 109.
[82] Talfan Davies, *Darlledu a'r Genedl*, p. 11 (my translation)
[83] Paddy Scannell and David Cardiff, *A Social History of British Broadcasting. Volume I. 1922–1939* (Oxford, 1991), pp. 321–2.
[84] This lack of an all-Wales service would dominate debate over broadcasting in Wales for decades.
[85] Talfan Davies, *Darlledu a'r Genedl*, p. 12 (my translation; original italics).
[86] Aled Jones, *Press, Politics and Society: A History of Journalism in Wales* (Cardiff, 1993), pp. 237–8.
[87] See Jamie Medhurst, ' "You say a minority, Sir; we say a nation": the Pilkington Committee on Broadcasting (1960–62) and Wales', *Welsh History Review*, 22, 2 (2004), 109–36.
[88] Benedict Anderson, *Imagined Communities* (London, 1983), pp. 24–5.
[89] Davies, *Broadcasting*, p. 319.

3: Television Wales and the West, 1956–1963: Organisation and Control

[1] Associated-Rediffusion and ABC Television operated at a loss during their first year (see Independent Television Authority [ITA], *Annual Report and Accounts 1955–56* (London, 1956), p. 2).
[2] The levy on advertising revenue was introduced in 1963 as a result of concerns over excessive profits from what was, essentially, a monopoly of advertising. It was paid by ITV companies and was calculated on the basis of

a sliding scale relating to income from advertising. In 1974, the system changed, following a difficult period for ITV (low profits in particular), and the levy became based on profits rather than fluctuating revenue. For further details see Bernard Sendall, *Independent Television in Britain. Volume 2. Expansion and Change, 1958–68* (London, 1983), pp. 190–201.

[3] NLW, Ben Bowen Thomas Papers, G2/1, TWW Limited, *Report 1966* (London, 1966), p. 19.

[4] The history of Wales (West and North) Television is discussed in detail in chapters 5 and 6.

[5] ITA, Minutes 28 (55), 5 April 1955.

[6] For an explanation of the use of Bands, see the explanatory notes at the beginning of this book. ITA, *Annual Report and Accounts 1954–55* (London, 1955), p. 2.

[7] ITA, *Annual Report and Accounts 1955–56* (London, 1956), p. 1.

[8] See chapter 2 for a discussion on linking Wales and the west of England.

[9] Sendall, *Independent Television in Britain. Vol. 2*, p. 210.

[10] Charles Hill, *Behind the Screen: The Broadcasting Memoirs of Lord Hill of Luton* (London, 1974), p. 48.

[11] Ibid. p. 49.

[12] Referring to the St Hilary transmitter in the Vale of Glamorgan that was to serve the region, John Davies wrote, in a somewhat sardonic manner, that 'the area it served was roughly the same as that served by Wenvoe, for the Authority had decided that south Wales and south-western England should constitute a single franchise territory, presumably on the grounds that, as the mistake had been made twice, there was no reason why it should not be made a third time' (John Davies, *Broadcasting and the BBC in Wales* (Cardiff, 1994), p. 214). Wenvoe was the site of the BBC's transmitter which served Wales and the west of England (see chapter 2).

[13] ITA, Minutes 28 (55), 5 April 1955.

[14] ITA, Minutes 42 (55), 6 December 1955.

[15] ITA, *Annual Report and Accounts 1955–56* (London, 1956), p. 1.

[16] Hansard, House of Commons Debates, Written Answers, vol. 549, col. 130, 29 February 1956.

[17] See, for example, *The People*, 15 April 1956.

[18] Rhys was also editor of the influential Anglo-Welsh journal, *Wales*. Eilian was a crowned and chaired bard of the National Eisteddfod and a leading figure in Welsh cultural life at the time; *World's Press News*, 31 August 1956.

[19] *South Wales Echo and Evening Express*, 5 September 1956.

[20] *Y Cymro*, 20 September 1956.

Notes

[21] ITA, *Annual Report and Accounts 1956–57* (London, 1957), p. 7; ITA, Minutes 62 (56), 18 September 1956.

[22] ITC, 130, Wales and West: Note on Fees, 16 October 1956.

[23] *Western Mail*, 16 October 1956.

[24] For a study of the life of Sir Ifan ab Owen Edwards, see Norah Isaac, *Ifan ab Owen Edwards*, 1895–1970 (Cardiff, 1972), and for Huw T. Edwards, see Gwyn Jenkins, *Prif Weinidog Answyddogol Cymru* (Tal-y-bont, 2007).

[25] ITC, 130, Letter from A. W. Pragnell to Goodman, Derrick and Co., solicitors acting on behalf of the TWW group, 24 October 1956.

[26] ITA, Minutes 64 (56), 16 October 1956; ITC, 130, Welsh Contract: Note by the Chairman, 24 October 1956.

[27] *South Wales Echo and Evening Express*, 26 October 1956; *Bristol Evening Post*, 26 October 1956. The headlines differed slightly, however, with the former declaring 'I.T.V. Choice for S. Wales' and the latter announcing 'West Programme group for I.T.A.'.

[28] *Daily Telegraph*, 27 October 1956. See also Lord Roberts of Conwy, *Right From the Start: The Memoirs of Sir Wyn Roberts* (Cardiff, 2006), pp. 62–3.

[29] Derby had to defend his connections with the Popular Television Association (prior to applying for the Wales and West licence) when challenged by Lord Ogmore in the House of Lords in July 1963: 'I would like to make it quite clear . . . that when I first joined the Popular Television Association campaigning for an independent television service I had no intention of going into commercial television myself' (Bernard Sendall, *Independent Television in Britain. Volume 1. Origin and Foundation, 1946–62* (London, 1982), p. 211).

[30] *The Times*, 27 October 1956.

[31] See Huw T. Edwards, *Hewn from the Rock* (Cardiff, 1967), p. 219.

[32] Lord Roberts of Conwy, *Right From the Start*, p. 62.

[33] Wyn Roberts, *Televidetur*, 10 April 1961 (Wyn Robert's personal papers, loaned to the author).

[34] David Barlow, Philip Mitchell and Tom O'Malley, *The Media in Wales: Voices of a Small Nation* (Cardiff, 2005), p. 130; Sendall, *Independent Television in Britain. vol. 1*, pp. 211–12; *Daily Telegraph*, 4 March 1957.

[35] National Archives, BD24/208, 'Claims in regard to television for Wales', Appendix 6.

[36] Edwards, *Hewn From the Rock*, p. 219.

[37] NLW, Huw T. Edwards Papers, A1/237, Letter from Aneurin Bevan to Huw T. Edwards, 6 September 1956. Jack Hylton, a Labour Party sympathiser, had written to Bevan on 3 September saying that he was 'more than keen' to get Huw T. Edwards on board. He went on to say that 'he will

have the chance to exert great influence in Wales through this medium of Commerical Television' (NLW, Huw T. Edwards Papers, A1/237, Letter from Jack Hylton to Aneurin Bevan, 3 September 1956).
[38] Jenkins, *Prif Weinidog Answyddogol Cymru*, p. 218 (my translation).
[39] NLW, Huw T. Edwards Papers, A2/117, Letter from Edwards to Derby, 23 September 1956.
[40] *Western Mail*, 29 October 1956.
[41] *Y Cymro*, 23 January 1958.
[42] NLW, ex 1778, Company Statement (no date).
[43] NLW, Television Wales and the West Ltd, Welsh Board Minutes, 29 November 1956.
[44] ITC, 130, Letter dated 30 October 1956.
[45] ITC, 130, Memo from Robert Fraser to Bernard Sendall, 1 November 1956 (my italics).
[46] ITC, 130, Letter from Sendall to Chapman-Walker, 5 November 1956.
[47] ITC, 130, Letter from Chapman-Walker to Sendall, 6 November 1956.
[48] ITC, 130, Letter from Howard Thomas to Robert Fraser, 10 May 1957.
[49] NLW, Television Wales and the West Ltd, Welsh Board Minutes, 13 February 1957; Sendall, *Independent Television in Britain. Vol. 1*, p. 215.
[50] NLW, Television Wales and the West Ltd, Welsh Board Minutes, 18 March 1957.
[51] ITC, 130, Letter from Fraser to Chapman-Walker, 28 May 1957.
[52] ITC, 130, Letter from Chapman-Walker to Fraser, 31 May 1957.
[53] *Television Act 1954* (London, 1954).
[54] Alban Davies was appointed by the Postmaster General on 4 August 1956 for a period of four years. His term was then extended on 4 August 1960 for a further period of four years, ending on 29 July 1964. See Hansard, vol. 642, col. 40, 13 June 1961.
[55] ITA, Minutes 65 (56), 6 November 1956.
[56] By 1959, the company was producing two hours forty minutes of Welsh-language programming every week and taking an additional forty minutes from Granada during the winter months. See Independent Television Authority, *Annual Report and Accounts 1958–59* (London, 1959), p. 19.
[57] ITA, Minutes 79 (57), 31 August 1957.
[58] NLW, Television Wales and the West Ltd, Welsh Board Minutes, 10 January 1957.
[59] NLW, Huw T. Edwards Papers, A1/312, Letter from Chapman-Walker to Edwards, 19 February 1957.
[60] NLW, Huw T. Edwards Papers, A1/312, Letter from Chapman-Walker to Edwards, 22 February 1957.

61. Sendall, *Independent Television in Britain. Vol. 1*, p. 216. The estimated costs for building the transmitting station were £295,000 (ITA, Paper 101 (56) [no date]).
62. NLW, Television Wales and the West Ltd, Welsh Board Minutes, 13 February 1957.
63. NLW, Television Wales and the West Ltd, Welsh Board Minutes, 29 April 1957.
64. *Daily Telegraph*, 31 October 1957.
65. *Daily Express*, 7 November 1957; NLW, Television Wales and the West Ltd, Welsh Board Minutes, 11 November 1957.
66. ITA, Minutes 82 (57), 5 November 1957.
67. Lord Roberts of Conwy, *Right From the Start*, p. 64; ITC, 131, Memorandum from Sendall to 'P. L. O.', 21 October 1958.
68. BBC WAC, T16/235/2, Memorandum Controller Wales to Director of Television Broadcasting and Director of Sound Broadcasting, 4 October 1957.
69. BBC WAC, T16/235/2, Memorandum Director of Television Broadcasting to Controller Wales, 8 October 1957.
70. BBC WAC, R34/1144, 'Should the B.B.C. share a transmitter with W.W.N?.', 1 October 1962.
71. NLW, Huw T. Edwards Papers, C9, 'Toast to T.W.W. Limited at the Inaugural Lunch Cardiff – 30th October, 1957. Proposed by T. Mervyn Jones'.
72. *Liverpool Daily Post*, 14 January 1958.
73. *The Times*, 14 January 1958.
74. Kenneth Bailey (ed.), *The Television Annual for 1958* (London, 1958), p. 11.
75. *Daily Herald*, 15 January 1958.
76. *Western Mail*, 15 January 1958.
77. *Western Daily Press*, 15 January 1958.
78. *South Wales Echo*, 15 January 1958.
79. *Y Cymro*, 23 January 1958.
80. *Y Ddraig Goch*, xxx (February 1958), 2.
81. *South Wales Argus*, 16 January 1958.
82. *Television Weekly*, 14 February 1958.
83. *Bristol Evening World*, 4 March 1958.
84. NLW, Television Wales and the West Ltd, Welsh Board Minutes, 9 December 1957; NLW, Television Wales and the West Ltd, Welsh Board Minutes, 9 February 1958.
85. *Bristol Evening Post Supplement*, 25 June 1957.
86. NLW, Television Wales and the West Ltd, Welsh Board Minutes, 12 May 1958; ITC 131, Letter from Chapman-Walker to Fraser, 17 June 1958.

[87] ITC, 131, Memorandum from Fraser to Sir Ivone Kirkpatrick (ITA Chairman), 18 June 1958.
[88] *South Wales Echo*, 25 September 1958.
[89] NLW, ex 1778, Press Statement by the Welsh Board of TWW, January 1959.
[90] ITC, 160, Letter from Chairman and Members of the Welsh Board to Fraser, 9 February 1959.
[91] NLW, Television Wales and the West Ltd, Welsh Board Minutes, 6 April 1959.
[92] NLW, ex 1778, *South Wales Evening Post*, 13 June 1959.
[93] NLW, ex 1778, *Advertiser's Weekly*, 28 August 1959.
[94] *Bristol Evening World*, 17 September 1959.
[95] NLW, ex 1778, *Bath Chronicle*, 25 August 1959.
[96] NLW, Television Wales and the West Ltd, Welsh Board Minutes, 13 July 1959.
[97] NLW, ex 1778, *Financial Times*, 20 November 1959.
[98] In fact, TWW had instigated a Retailers' Scheme in March 1959, the first of its kind to be offered by a television company. Retailers were advised well in advance of the products due to be advertised on TWW. They were then given an opportunity to buy a seven-second spot showing that they had the product which was being advertised in stock. By the end of 1960 around 4,000 retailers had joined the scheme (*Report of the Committee on Broadcasting, 1960. Volume I. Appendix E*, p. 716).
[99] NLW, Television Wales and the West Ltd, Welsh Board Minutes, 17 May 1960.
[100] A fuller discussion of the Pilkington Committee can be found in chapter 5, as it overshadowed many of the debates surrounding the formation of WWN.
[101] *Report of the Committee on Broadcasting, 1960. Cmnd. 1753* (London, 1962), p. 1.
[102] James Curran and Jean Seaton, *Power Without Responsibility: The Press, Broadcasting and New Media in Britain*, 6th edn. (London, 2003), p. 171.
[103] Jeffrey Milland, 'Courting Malvolio: the background to the Pilkington Committee on Broadcasting, 1960–62', *Contemporary British History*, 18, 2 (2004), 77–9.
[104] *Report of the Committee on Broadcasting, 1960. Volume I. Appendix E*, p. 711.
[105] Ibid., p. 710.
[106] Ibid., p. 713.
[107] Ibid., p. 713 Robert Fraser had announced the creation of a west and north Wales ITA region on a visit to the National Eisteddfod in Cardiff on 4 August 1960. See chapters 5 and 6 for the history of the west and north Wales licence area.
[108] *Report of the Committee on Broadcasting, 1960. Volume I. Appendix E*, p. 535.

[109] National Archives, HO244/588, TWW interview with the Pilkington Committee, 18 May 1961.
[110] Curran and Seaton, *Power Without Responsibility*, p. 173. Seaton is referring to 'British' culture here.
[111] *Report of the Committee on Broadcasting. Cmnd 1753*, p. 65.
[112] Ibid., pp. 166–7.
[113] Ibid., p. 186.
[114] Independent Television Authority, *Annual Report and Accounts 1962–63* (London, 1963), pp. 13, 59.
[115] ITC, A/A57/0080/1, Independent Television Authority Advisory Committee for Wales, Minutes 1963–1968, 1(63).
[116] See chapter 5.
[117] NLW, Television Wales and the West Ltd, Welsh Board Minutes, 8 April 1962.
[118] See chapter 5 for details.
[119] NLW, Television Wales and the West Ltd, Welsh Board Minutes, 29 August 1960.
[120] Ibid.
[121] NLW, Television Wales and the West Ltd, Welsh Board Minutes, 13 February 1961; ibid., 11 September 1961.
[122] ITC, 166, Letter from Derby to Kirkpatrick, 21 April 1961.
[123] NLW, Television Wales and the West Ltd., Welsh Board Minutes, 12 June 1961.
[124] NLW, Huw T. Edwards Papers, A1/669, Letter from Sir Ifan ab Owen Edwards to Huw T. Edwards, 10 August 1961.
[125] Sendall, *Independent Television in Britain. Vol. 2*, p. 37.
[126] ITC, 166, Letter from Cadbury to Fraser, 14 April 1961.
[127] NLW, Television Wales and the West Ltd, Welsh Board Minutes, 13 November 1961.
[128] Sendall, *Independent Television in Britain. Vol. 1*, p. 221.
[129] Although, in fact, Derby remained as Chairman until the loss of the franchise in 1967–8.
[130] NLW, Huw T. Edwards Papers, A1/672, Letter from Wyn Roberts to Huw T. Edwards, October 1961.
[131] NLW, Huw T. Edwards Papers, A1/684, Letter from Wyn Roberts to Huw T. Edwards, undated.
[132] NLW, Television Wales and the West Ltd, Welsh Board Minutes, 11 January 1962.
[133] NLW, Television Wales and the West Ltd, Welsh Board Minutes, 6 February 1962. It is worth noting the dispute between TWW and the ITA over the former's title in 1956–7.

[134] NLW, Television Wales and the West Ltd, Welsh Board Minutes, 18 April 1962.
[135] ITA, Minutes 158 (62), 8 May 1962.
[136] Hansard, House of Commons Debates, Written Answers, vol. 663, col. 130, 24 July 1962.
[137] ITA, Committee for Wales, CW 1 (63), 1 February 1963.
[138] ITA, Committee for Wales, CW 2 (63), 8 March 1963.
[139] ITA, Committee for Wales, CW 3 (63), 3 May 1963. The May meeting of the committee, for example, suggested that councils in areas where the relay companies were refusing to carry Teledu Cymru programmes should put pressure on them to do so.
[140] NLW, Television Wales and the West Ltd, Welsh Board Minutes, 18 September 1962.
[141] ITC, 131, Extract from the Chairman's Statement, Wales (West and North) Limited, 10 April 1963.
[142] ITC, 131, Letter from Derby to Fraser, 22 April 1963.
[143] *Western Mail*, 22 May 1963.
[144] National Archives, BD 25/140, 'Note of a meeting: Developments in commercial television in Wales', 23 May 1963. Although this is not discussed further, it could refer to the issues raised by the background note with regard to the way in which Teledu Cymru was perceived by its supporters. A takeover could be seen as a slight to Welsh national sentiment. Alternatively, the loss of an ITV company could be politically damaging for a Conservative government which supported the whole notion of commercial television.
[145] This is interesting, especially in the light of a letter sent by Lord Derby of TWW to the Postmaster General on 12 March, when Undeb Cymru Fydd met with the Minister for Welsh Affairs. In the letter, he raised his concern that he had read press reports that discussions were taking place which might affect the ITV Welsh regional structure. He wrote: 'I respectfully express the hope that no decision concerning the future of Independent Television in Wales will be reached without my Company (T.W.W. Limited) being allowed to state its case' (ITC, 131, Letter from Derby to Bevins, 12 March 1963).
[146] National Archives, BD 25/140, 'Note of a meeting: Developments in commercial television in Wales', 23 May 1963.
[147] NLW, Minutes of the Board of Directors of Teledu Cymru, 21 June 1963.
[148] NLW, T. I. Ellis Papers C62, Report on a Meeting at Bristol by Eric Thomas, 28 June 1963.
[149] NLW, T. I. Ellis Papers C59, Letter from Thomas to all directors, 3 July 1963. It could also be that Derby, as a director of the bank, had been aware of WWN's

difficult financial situation for some time and had based his offers of assistance to the ITA on that information. There is, however, no evidence of this.
[150] NLW, T. I. Ellis Papers C62, Notice of meeting, 10 August 1963.
[151] NLW, T. I. Ellis Papers C62, Letter from Goodman to Thomas, 9 August 1963. See also the *Guardian*, 9 August 1963.
[152] NLW, Emrys Roberts Papers 20, Minutes of the Board of Directors of Teledu Cymru, 17 August 1963.
[153] *The Times*, 17 October 1963, 7.
[154] ITC, 131, 'The origination of the Welsh Company': Note by the Director-General, 25 September 1963.
[155] National Archives, BD25/144, Letter from Bevins to Joseph, 4 November 1963.
[156] ITC, A/S/0038/8, 1964 Contract – Applications – J – TWW.
[157] ITC, A/S/0038/9, 1964 Contract – Applications – J – Independent Television Ltd.
[158] ITC, A/S/0038/8, Minutes of the Interview, 4 December 1963.
[159] ITC, A/S/0038/8, Letter from Derby to Hill, 4 December 1963.
[160] Sendall, *Independent Television in Britain*. Vol. 2, p. 221.
[161] ITC, A/S/0038/8, Second Interview, 2 January 1964.

4: Television Wales and the West, 1956–1963: Programming and Critical Issues

[1] Wyn Roberts, *Independent Television in Wales* (Cardiff, 1961). This idea has been echoed by Tim O'Sullivan's work on television audiences in the 1950s and 1960s, which suggests a closer relationship between ITV and its audience than that of the BBC with its audience ('Television memories and cultures of viewing 1950–65', in John Corner (ed.), *Popular Television in Britain: Studies in Cultural History* (London, 1991), pp. 159–81. See also Lord Roberts of Conwy, *Right From the Start: The Memoirs of Sir Wyn Roberts* (Cardiff, 2006), pp. 59–73.
[2] D. H. Culpitt, 'Yr oes olau hon', *Blodau'r Ffair*, 13 (1961), p. 49. Some of the fears and concerns about the impact of broadcasting on Welsh life had been voiced since the early days of broadcasting in Wales (see chapter 2). For further details on particular fears relating to television see chapter 5, in particular the section on the Pilkington Committee.
[3] 'Pêr Ganiedydd' is a reference to the prolific Welsh hymn-writer William Williams, Pantycelyn (1717–91).
[4] ITA, Minutes 66 (56), 20 November 1956.
[5] ITA, Minutes 78 (57), 30 July 1957.
[6] NLW, Television Wales and the West Ltd, Welsh Board Minutes, 9 September 1957.

[7] NLW, Television Wales and the West Ltd, Welsh Board Minutes, 29 November 1956.
[8] NLW, Television Wales and the West Ltd, Welsh Board Minutes, 7 October 1957. Alban Davies argued that this would 'enable the majority of Welsh viewers to see one Welsh programme each week without having to forgo attendance at church' (ITA, Minutes 81 (57), 8 October 1957).
[9] NLW, Television Wales and the West Ltd, Welsh Board Minutes, 11 November 1957.
[10] ITA, Minutes 84 (57), 10 December 1957.
[11] ITA, Minutes 85 (58), 7 January 1958.
[12] *Television Weekly*, 7 March 1958.
[13] NLW, Television Wales and the West Ltd, Welsh Board Minutes, 14 April 1958.
[14] NLW, Television Wales and the West Ltd, Welsh Board Minutes, 8 February 1960.
[15] ITA, Committee for Wales, CW 4 (63), 12 July 1963; ITA, Committee for Wales, CW 5 (63), 6 August 1963; ITA, Committee for Wales, CW 6 (63), 18 October 1963.
[16] BBC, WAC, R34/1144, Copy of letter from Jacob to Fraser, 9 April 1958.
[17] BBC, WAC, T16/235/3, Memorandum from Oldfield-Davies to McGivern, 11 March 1959.
[18] BBC, WAC, T16/235/3. Memorandum from McGivern to Beadle, 24 April 1959.
[19] *Television Weekly*, 29 May 1959.
[20] *Report of the Committee on Broadcasting, 1960. Volume I. Appendix E*, p. 715.
[21] TWW Ltd, *The Regional Accomplishment in Independent Television* (London, 1962), p. 8.
[22] National Archives, HO244/588, TWW interview with the Pilkington Committee, 18 May 1961.
[23] NLW, Television Wales and the West Ltd, Welsh Board Minutes, 9 January 1961.
[24] NLW, Television Wales and the West Ltd, Welsh Board Minutes, 18 April 1962.
[25] Ibid.
[26] See, for example, Huw T. Edwards's comments in NLW, Television Wales and the West Ltd, Welsh Board Minutes, 10 November 1958, 11 July 1960 and 11 September 1961.
[27] For the view of the Pilkington Committee on this issue, see *Report of the Committee on Broadcasting*, pp. 66–7.

[28] ITC, Television Audience Measurement (TAM) Ratings, week ending 14 October 1962.
[29] *Television Weekly*, 10 January 1958.
[30] *Television Weekly*, 23 November 1962.
[31] *Daily Mail*, 5 January 1961.
[32] *South Wales Echo*, 21 March 1963; TWW, Production Panel Minutes, 21 March 1963.
[33] TWW, Production Panel Minutes, 31 May 1962.
[34] *Television Weekly*, 31 August 1962.
[35] NLW, Television Wales and the West Ltd, Welsh Board Minutes, 12 October 1959.
[36] 'T.W.W. and the General Election 1959', confidential internal document.
[37] NLW, Television Wales and the West Ltd, Welsh Board Minutes, 14 April 1958.
[38] NLW, Ben Bowen Thomas Papers G2/1, TWW Limited, *Report 1966* (London, 1967), p. 19.
[39] *Herald of Wales*, 2 February 1963.
[40] ITA, 'Report on Relay Television in South and West Wales', Committee for Wales Paper 4 (63), 18 April 1963.
[41] *Western Mail*, 28 October 1959.
[42] *Western Daily Press*, 29 October 1956.
[43] *Bath Chronicle and Herald*, 30 March 1961.
[44] National Archives, HO244/588, TWW interview with the Pilkington Committee, 18 May 1961.
[45] NLW, ex 1778.
[46] *Parliamentary Debates. Welsh Grand Committee. Broadcasting*, First Sitting, Wednesday 13 December 1961 (London, 1961), p. 16; *Western Daily Press*, 17 September 1963.
[47] The campaign is discussed in chapter 5.
[48] ITC, 166, Letter from Derby to Sir Ivone Kirkpatrick, 21 April 1963.
[49] NLW, Huw T. Edwards Papers, A1/353, Letter from Davies to Edwards, 17 September 1957.
[50] ITA, Minutes, 96 (58), 29 July 1958.
[51] ITA, Minutes, 100 (58), 4 November 1958.
[52] *Evening Advertiser*, 26 August 1959; TWW, Production Panel Minutes, 3 May 1962.
[53] ITC, A/S/0038/8, 1964 Contract – Applications – J – TWW, Report on new contracts, 28 October 1963; ITA Committee for Wales, CW Paper 7 (63), 24 July 1963.

[54] See Kenneth O. Morgan, *Rebirth of a Nation: Wales 1880–1980* (Oxford, 1981), p. 323.
[55] Television Audience Measurement Ltd, Press Release, 13 March 1958.
[56] *Guardian*, 5 October 1961.
[57] *Report of the Committee on Broadcasting, 1960. Volume I. Appendix E*, p. 537.
[58] Hansard, House of Lords Official Report, vol. 252, col. 462, 22 July 1963.
[59] NLW, Ben Bowen Thomas Papers G2/1, *Report 1966*, p. 16.
[60] This point is important in the context of the loss of the licence in 1967; there were longer-term 'issues' which came into play at that point.
[61] Bernard Sendall, *Independent Television in Britain. Volume 1. Origin and Foundation, 1946–62* (London, 1982), p. 219.

5: Wales (West and North) Television, 1956–1962: Formation and Control

[1] For a detailed critical analysis of WWN in the 1959–63 period see Jamie Medhurst, 'Teledu Cymru – Teledu Mamon? Independent television in Wales, 1959–63'(unpublished Ph.D. thesis, University of Wales, 2004).
[2] As is shown later, the same type of language and discourse would be used again in Welsh submissions to the Pilkington Committee in 1960.
[3] *Report of the Broadcasting Committee, 1949. Appendix H. Memoranda submitted to the Committee. Cmd. 8117*, p. 428.
[4] *Undeb Cymru Fydd 1939–1960* (Aberystwyth, 1960), p. 24.
[5] NLW, Jac L. Williams Papers, Undeb Cymru Fydd Joint Television Committee 1958–63 file, Memorandum dated 18 May 1958.
[6] TC, 130, Memorandum from Sendall to Fraser, 4 July 1957.
[7] ITC, 131, Letter from Edward Brownsden (ITA) to Fraser, 7 July 1958.
[8] Ibid.
[9] ITC, 131, Letter from Fraser to Chapman-Walker, 7 July 1958.
[10] BBC, WAC, T16/235/2, Memorandum, 7 July 1958.
[11] John Davies, *Broadcasting and the BBC in Wales* (Cardiff, 1994), p. 218.
[12] NLW, Jac L. Williams Papers, Meeting of Joint Committee Executive, 22 August 1958.
[13] NLW, Television Wales and the West Ltd, Welsh Board Minutes, 8 September 1958.
[14] ITC, 131, Memorandum Fraser to Sendall, 8 September 1958.
[15] Ibid.
[16] ITC, 60, 'Claims in Regard to Television for Wales: memorandum by the office for Welsh Affairs and the Post Office', December 1958. The

memorandum reiterated many of the issues already raised by cultural groups, notably the detrimental effect of television on the Welsh language and culture, should an all-Wales television service not be established.

[17] ITC, 60, Letter from Fraser to Wolverson (GPO), 18 December 1958.
[18] Ibid.
[19] Ibid.
[20] Ibid.
[21] ITC, 60, Note from Kirkpatrick to Fraser (undated).
[22] ITC, 60, Draft letter from Kirkpatrick to Edwards, 8 July 1959.
[23] NLW, Association of Welsh Local Authorities (AWLA) X31, Letter from Jones to Clerks of local authorities in Wales, 23 January 1959.
[24] Ibid.
[25] NLW, Plaid Cymru Archive, A5, Executive Committee minutes, 3–4 April 1959.
[26] Ifan Gwynfil Evans, 'Teledu Cymru: an independent television service for Wales? (1959–1963)', (unpublished MA dissertation, University of Wales, 1997), p. 9.
[27] NLW, Jac L. Williams Papers, National Conference on Television Service for Wales convened by the Rt Hon the Lord Mayor of Cardiff (Alderman Helena Evans, J P) and held in the City Hall, Cardiff, on Friday, 18th September, 1959, Report (October 1959).
[28] NLW, Jac L. Williams Papers, National Conference on Television Service for Wales.
[29] Evans, 'Teledu Cymru', p. 9.
[30] NLW, Jac L. Williams Papers, National Conference on Television Service for Wales.
[31] Ibid.
[32] Ibid.
[33] Ibid.
[34] Ibid.
[35] Ibid. This was a characteristic statement by Gwynfor Evans which was evident again during Plaid Cymru's oral evidence-gathering session of Pilkington.
[36] NLW, Jac L. Williams Papers, National Conference on Television Service for Wales.
[37] Ibid.
[38] NLW, Jac L. Williams Papers, Minutes of the first meeting of the Continuation Committee, 13 November 1959.
[39] NLW, Jac L. Williams Papers, 'Memorandum from the Committee Appointed by the Conference of Local Authorities of Wales and Monmouthshire held at the City Hall, Cardiff on Friday 18th September 1959, (no date).

[40] Evans, 'Teledu Cymru', p. 11. Channel 13 had already been earmarked as a 'free' channel by the government, to be used in south Wales and the west as a channel for a possible third television service.
[41] NLW, Jac L. Williams Papers, 'Memorandum from the Committee Appointed by the Conference of Local Authorities of Wales and Monmouthshire held at the City Hall, Cardiff on Friday 18th September 1959, (no date).
[42] Ibid.
[43] Bernard Sendall, *Independent Television in Britain. Volume 2. Expansion and Change, 1958–68* (London, 1983), p. 75.
[44] Evans, 'Teledu Cymru', p. 11.
[45] NLW, Jac L. Williams Papers, 'Chairman's notes for members of the Continuation Committee of the Welsh National Television Conference' (no date). See also Evans, 'Teledu Cymru', p. 11. Evans notes that the ITA had been considering completing the coverage of Britain by creating a west Wales franchise 'for at least 6 months'.
[46] ITC, 60, Memorandum from Fraser to Sendall, 11 January 1960.
[47] Ibid.
[48] Ibid.
[49] Ibid. (my italics).
[50] This point was reiterated in May 1961, when the four companies competing for the west and north Wales licence area were interviewed by the ITA.
[51] NLW, Jac L. Williams Papers, Letter from Fraser to Traherne, 11 January 1960.
[52] NLW, Jac L. Williams Papers, Letter from Traherne to Fraser, 13 January 1960. Nevertheless, when the Wales Television Association applied for the ITA licence for west and north Wales in May 1961, three members of the continuation committee – Cennydd Traherne, T. I. Ellis and Haydn Williams – were listed as directors and founder shareholders. See National Archives, BD 23/209, 'Application for appointment as programme contractor for west and north Wales by a group now called The Wales Television Association/Teledu Cymru', 1961.
[53] NLW, Jac L. Williams Papers, Letter from Ellis to Jac L. Williams, 18 January 1960.
[54] BBC, WAC, T16/235/4, 'The transmission of BBC television programmes in Wales'. See also Alun Oldfield-Davies, 'Y BBC a Chymru – Cipolwg dros chwarter canrif', *Y Genhinen*, 12, 1 (1961–2), 55.
[55] NLW, Elwyn and Margaret Davies Papers, D5/4, Letter from Bevins to members of the Pilkington Committee, 10 April 1961.
[56] ITC, 60, Memorandum from Fraser to [?], 22 June 1960.
[57] Ibid.

[58] ITA, Minutes 128 (60), 26 July 1960. In fact it was not released until 7 April 1961, by which time the Postmaster General still had not approved the plans for coverage of the whole west and north area.
[59] Sendall, *Independent Television in Britain. vol. 2*, p. 71.
[60] Ibid.
[61] Ibid., p. 72.
[62] ITC, 60, Second letter from Fraser to Wolstencroft, 7 October 1960. As was noted in chapter 3, the ITA had considered locating a station to serve Wales only (see ITA, Minutes 28 (55), 5 April 1955). It is arguable that the pressure for an all-Wales service can be attributed to dissatisfaction with TWW per se, as is suggested by Fraser here.
[63] *Western Mail*, 7 January 1960.
[64] *Baner ac Amserau Cymru*, 7 January 1960.
[65] NLW, Elwyn Roberts Papers 20, 'Television for Wales, Meeting of Sponsors' minutes, 12 September 1960.
[66] Ibid. It should be noted that the ITA's Winter Hill transmitter had been transmitting Granada programmes to the north-east since May 1956.
[67] Ibid. Emrys Roberts, in his copy of the minutes, had underlined this figure, and placed a '?' next to it. There was no evidential basis for this figure, and Roberts appeared to be questioning it. The issue of over-ambitious estimates arose again in 1961.
[68] NLW, Emrys Roberts Papers 21, Letter from Vaughan to Alban Davies, 11 November 1960.
[69] NLW, Emrys Roberts Papers 21, Notes by Emrys Roberts [no date].
[70] NLW, Emrys Roberts Papers 21, Letter from Alban Davies to Roberts, 24 January 1961.
[71] It is unclear, however, as to whether Alban Davies was speaking personally or as the ITA member for Wales.
[72] NLW, Emrys Roberts Papers 23, Notes of Meeting, 16 March 1961.
[73] NLW, Emrys Roberts Papers 23, Letter from Everett Jones to Roberts, 23 March 1961.
[74] NLW, Emrys Roberts Papers 23, Letter from Everett Jones to Vaughan, 27 March 1961.
[75] ITA, Press Notice 141, 'Programme Contracting Arrangements for West and North Wales', 7 April 1961.
[76] Ibid. The ITA's announcement also attracted interest from other ITV companies, but for different reasons. As noted in chapter 2, Peter Cadbury of Westward Television wrote to Fraser asking him if it would be an idea 'to give the programme contract for West and North Wales to TWW? I have had so many letters from people in Bristol pointing out that Bristol and Wales are

uncomplimentary and such a solution might resolve all our difficulties in the West' (ITC, 166, Letter from Cadbury to Fraser, 14 April 1961).
77 ITC, Applications for Contracts, A/S/0035/31. 'Contracts, West and North Wales, 1961–1963'. It did, however, note that there was still uncertainty about the third transmitter in Flint-Denbigh.
78 ITC, Applications for Contracts, A/S/0035/31.
79 Ibid.
80 It is not clear from the evidence as to how this figure was calculated.
81 Quoted in Evans, 'Teledu Cymru', p. 14.
82 NLW, Emrys Roberts Papers 23, Notebook (undated).
83 NLW, Emrys Roberts Papers 20, Minutes of the Meeting of the Wales Television Association Sub-Committee, 12 April 1961.
84 National Archives, BD 23/209, 'Application for appointment as programme contractor for west and north Wales by a group now called The Wales Television Association/Teledu Cymru'. The company was later forced to change its title, following representations to the ITA by TWW, who objected to the implication that the company covered the whole of Wales. The company agreed to change its title to Wales (West and North) Television Limited, but the Welsh title – Teledu Cymru (which translates as Wales Television) – remained in place.
85 National Archives, BD 23/209, 'Application for appointment as programme contractor for west and north Wales by a group now called The Wales Television Association/Teledu Cymru', p. 11.
86 Ibid. pp. 42–6.
87 ITC, 166, 'The West and North Wales Contract: note by Mr J. Alban Davies', 24 May 1961.
88 ITA, Minutes, Annexe to minutes 142 (61), 'Interviews with applicants for West and North Wales contract', 30 May 1961.
89 NLW, Emrys Roberts Papers 23, Letter from Everett to Roberts, 31 May 1961.
90 NLW, Emrys Roberts Papers 20, Report of the Continuation Committee to the Second National Conference on Television for Wales, 7 July 1961.
91 Ibid.
92 Ibid.
93 Ibid.
94 However, I would argue that far from wanting TWW to expand into the west, the ITA were inclined to want to appoint a new contractor. Evidence presented in chapters 3 and 4 suggests a tense relationship between the ITA and TWW from the outset, and ITA documents point towards the opposite of what Williams was arguing. In framing the issue in this way, however, Williams was able to portray the Continuation Committee in a more 'heroic' light.

[95] NLW, Emrys Roberts Papers 20, Report of the Continuation Committee to the Second National Conference on Television for Wales.
[96] Ibid.
[97] Ibid.
[98] NLW, Emrys Roberts Papers 20, Minutes of the meeting of the Welsh Television Association, 20 June 1961. See also ITA, Minutes 143 (61), 20 June 1961.
[99] Sendall, *Independent Television in Britain. Vol. 2*, p. 75.
[100] Ibid.
[101] NLW, Emrys Roberts Papers 20, Minutes of the meeting of the Wales Television Association, 20 June 1961.
[102] NLW, Emrys Roberts Papers 21, Letter from Vaughan to Roberts, 26 June 1961.
[103] NLW, Huw T. Edwards Papers A1/669, Letter from Sir Ifan ab Owen Edwards to Huw T. Edwards, 10 August 1961; original underlining (my translation).
[104] NLW, Sir T. H. Parry-Williams and Lady Amy Parry-Williams Papers LL58, Cutting from the *Western Mail*, 12 August 1961.
[105] Aneirin Talfan Davies [Sodlau Segur], *Teledu Mamon* (Carmarthen, 1962). The author was Assistant Head of Programmes at the BBC in Cardiff.
[106] See Asa Briggs, *The History of British Broadcasting in the United Kingdom. Volume IV* (Oxford, 1979 [2000 reprint]), ch. 7.
[107] Gwynfor Evans and J. E. Jones, *TV in Wales* (Cardiff: Plaid Cymru, 1958), p. 5.
[108] *Teledu Mamon*, p. 9. For a detailed critique of the pamphlet see Jamie Medhurst, 'Wales Television – Mammon's television? ITV in Wales in the 1960s', *Media History*, 10, 2 (2004), 119–31.
[109] Unfortunately, this does not translate easily, but roughly means 'On Tiptoe'.
[110] Ifan Gwynfil Evans, 'Drunk on hopes and ideals: the failure of Wales Television, 1959–63', *Llafur: Journal of Welsh Labour History*, 7, 2 (1997), 91.
[111] *Report of the Committee on Broadcasting, 1960. Cmnd. 1819–1. Volume II. Appendix E* (London, 1962), p. 963.
[112] Ibid.
[113] Ibid.
[114] Ibid. pp. 951–2
[115] Ibid., p. 961.
[116] NLW, Undeb Cymru Fydd 257, Oral evidence, Undeb Cymru Fydd.
[117] *Report of the Committee on Broadcasting, 1960. Cmnd. 1819–1. Volume II. Appendix E*, p. 962. For a similar argument see the '*Teledu Mamon*' pamphlet published in 1962. The author argued that commercial television was undoing all the good achieved by the closing of pubs on Sundays – a long

cherished tradition, a part of the so-called 'Welsh way of life', was being destroyed by ITV.
[118] See, for example, Jeffrey, 'Courting Malvolio: the background to the Pilkington Committee on Broadcasting, 1960–62', *Contemporary British History*, 18, 2 (2004), 76–102, and James Curran and Jean Seaton, *Power Without Responsibility: The Press, Broadcasting and New Media in Britain* 6th edition (London, 2003), chapter 12.

6: Wales (West and North) Television, 1962–1963: Operation, Programming and Demise

[1] The executive committee of WWN were aware of the fact that only one transmitter would be operational at the end of July, but decided to go ahead with the launch as planned on 14 September (see NLW, Emrys Roberts Papers 20, Minutes of the Executive Committee of Teledu Cymru, 20 July 1962.)
[2] NLW, Sir T. H. Parry-Williams and Lady Amy Parry-Williams Papers, LL58, Programme for the Official Opening, 14 September 1962.
[3] *Teledu Cymru*, p. 3, (my translation).
[4] *Western Mail*, 14 September 1962.
[5] Ibid.
[6] NLW, Emrys Roberts Papers 20, Minutes of the Executive Committee of Teledu Cymru, 12 October 1962.
[7] See also John Roberts Williams, *Annwyl Gyfeillion* (Llandysul, 1975), p. 67. I have not encountered any evidence which portrays Hughes in a positive light. Therefore, the picture of Hughes is based on evidence from board directors (T. I. Ellis's diary) and the memoirs of the News Editor (John Roberts Williams).
[8] NLW, T. I. Ellis Papers, C58, Memorandum from the Budgetary and Staffing Committee to the Board of Directors, 21 January 1963. There are no specific examples given in the memorandum, but it is possible that Hughes was aware of the confidential report sent by Havard Gregory to Thomas Parry on 9 January 1963 and the supplementary report sent to Parry on 24 January 1963.
[9] T. I. Ellis, Diary, 22 January 1963.
[10] NLW, Emrys Roberts Papers 20, Memorandum from Thomas Parry to all directors, 23 January 1963. By this time, Parry had received the first part of a confidential report by Havard Gregory, Teledu Cymru Senior Producer, who made accusations against Hughes.

[11] T. I. Ellis, Diary, 19 March 1963 (my translation). No reason is given for Parry's unease.
[12] NLW, Emrys Roberts Papers 22, Letter to Haydn Williams from Emrys Roberts, 27 March 1963.
[13] It has been suggested, for example, that WWN spent £25 on purchasing ashtrays emblazoned with the company logo – a luxury the company could ill afford (see the interview with one former staff member, Iris Jones, at Richard Jones, 'TV heroes: Iris Jones', http://www.transdiffusion.org/emc/TVHeroes/iris).
[14] T. I. Ellis, Diary, 31 May 1963.
[15] Nathan Hughes remained at WWN until the takeover. He then emigrated to the United States, where he worked with several American television companies.
[16] T. I. Ellis, Diary, 10 November 1962.
[17] See correspondence in NLW, T. I. Ellis Papers, C59.
[18] T. I. Ellis, Diary, 30 July 1963, (my translation) Ellis was a person who liked to work at things in a structured, methodical way and do everything 'properly'. In the light of this, his diaries demonstrate a clear frustration with the way WWN was managed.
[19] T. I. Ellis, Diary, 1 August 1963 and 20 August 1963.
[20] T. I. Ellis, Diary, 13 September 1963, (my translation).
[21] NLW, Emrys Roberts Papers 20, Minutes of the Executive Committee of Teledu Cymru, 12 October 1962.
[22] NLW, Emrys Roberts Papers 20, Minutes of the Executive Committee of Teledu Cymru, 10 November 1962.
[23] NLW, Emrys Roberts Papers 20. Minutes of the Executive Committee of Teledu Cymru, 23 November 1962. The set count was an index based on the total number of all those homes whose aerials were aligned to receive the transmissions of a particular mast. The TAM rating was applied to individual programmes, the figure relating to the estimated number of people watching at a given time. The higher the figure in both indexes, the better in terms of advertising revenue.
[24] ITA, Minutes, 169 (62), 18 December 1962.
[25] NLW, Emrys Roberts Papers 20, Minutes of the Board of Directors of Teledu Cymru, 21 December 1962.
[26] ITA, Committee for Wales Minutes, 1 (63), 1 February 1963.
[27] NLW, Emrys Roberts Papers 20, Minutes of the Board of Directors of Teledu Cymru, 1 March 1963.
[28] NLW, Emrys Roberts Papers 20, Minutes of a meeting between Teledu Cymru and the ITA, 7 March 1963.

29. NLW, Emrys Roberts Papers 20, Minutes of the Board of Directors of Teledu Cymru, 28 and 29 March 1963.
30. ITA, Committee for Wales Minutes, 3 (63), 3 May 1963.
31. ITA, Minutes, 176 (63), 9 May 1963; NLW, Emrys Roberts Papers 20, Minutes of the Board of Directors of Teledu Cymru, 14 May 1963.
32. ITA, Committee for Wales Minutes, 1 (63), 1 February 1963.
33. ITA, CW Paper 4 (63), 'Report on Relay Television in South and West Wales – April 1963'. There is a story (told to the author at a meeting of the Cardigan Cymmrodorion on 12 November 2003) that when the company eventually folded, some of the production staff took the WWN sign and held it up in protest, having added 'We Were Novices'.
34. ITA, CW Paper 4 (63), 'Report on Relay Television in South and West Wales – April 1963'.
35. Interview with Nathan Hughes, 6 August 2004.
36. Bernard Sendall, *Independent Television in Britain. Volume 2. Expansion and Change, 1958–68* (London, 1983), p. 79.
37. Interview with John Roberts Williams, 28 February 1998.
38. *Teledu Cymru*, 14–22 September 1962 (my translation)
39. *Teledu Cymru*, 7–13 October 1962 (my translation) The editor answered the comment regarding the timing of the programmes by stating that the company could not afford to broadcast beyond the 6 p.m.–7 p.m. and 10.30 p.m.–11 p.m. slots.
40. *Teledu Cymru*, 7–13 October 1962, p .2 (my translation).
41. *Teledu Cymru*, 21–27 October 1962 (my translation).
42. These figures are derived from copies of the programme journal, *Teledu Cymru*. Granada, however, ceased production of its Welsh programme, *Dewch i Mewn*, when WWN began broadcasting in September 1962.
43. *Teledu Cymru*, 25 November–1 December 1962.
44. *Teledu Cymru*, 6–12 January 1963.
45. Sendall, *Independent Television in Britain. Vol. 2*, p. 79.
46. Interview with John Roberts Williams, 28 February 1998. The programme budget for individual news programmes was often as little as £45, this often coming from the pockets of the staff themselves.
47. *Teledu Cymru*, 31 March–5 April 1963.
48. NLW, Elwyn Roberts Papers 20, Minutes of the meeting of the Board of Directors of Teledu Cymru, 21 December 1962.
49. Ibid.
50. NLW, T. I. Ellis Papers, C59, Memorandum from the General Manager to the Programme Committee, 1 January 1963.
51. *Baner ac Amserau Cymru*, 23 May 1963.

[52] Ibid.
[53] *Western Mail*, 25 May 1963; cutting in NLW, Aneirin Talfan Davies Papers, Box 1 (my translation).
[54] Elain Haf, 'Y ddrama deledu Gymraeg, 1955–1982' (unpublished M.Phil. thesis, University of Wales, 1996) 31. The lack of original television drama was an issue which dogged TWW, particularly during the 1964–8 period (see chapter 8).
[55] A popular ITV quiz programme, presented by Michael Miles, with a substantial cash reward for the winner. As Sendall notes, 'it was regular viewing in thousands of homes and was invariably in the "Top Twenty" charts' (Bernard Sendall, *Independent Television in Britain. Volume 1. Origin and Foundation, 1946–62* (London, 1982), p. 321).
[56] NLW, Sir T. H. Parry-Williams and Lady Amy Parry-Williams Papers, LL58, Memorandum from the General Manager to the Programme Committee, 21 January 1963.
[57] NLW, Sir T. H. Parry-Williams and Lady Amy Parry-Williams Papers, LL58, Memorandum from the General Manager to the Programme Committee, 25 February 1963. This was an attack on Havard Gregory, with whom Hughes had had a long-running disagreement.
[58] NLW, Sir T. H. Parry-Williams and Lady Amy Parry-Williams Papers, LL58, Memorandum from the General Manager to the Programme Committee, 25 February 1963.
[59] *The Times*, 1 June 1963.
[60] See John Davies, *Broadcasting and the BBC in Wales* (Cardiff, 1994), pp. 228–30, and Ifan Gwynfil, 'Teledu Cymru: an independent television service for Wales? (1959–1963)', (unpublished MA dissertation, University dissertation, University of Wales, 1997), 28–30.

7: Television Wales and the West, 1964–1968: Operation and Programming

[1] See Bernard Sendall, *Independent Television in Britain. Volume 2. Expansion and Change, 1958–68* (London, 1983), pp. 81–2, and NLW, Television Wales and the West Ltd, Welsh Board Minutes, 16 June 1964. WWN shareholders were offered a very good deal, in that they would get a £4.25s. investment in a profitable company for every £6 they had invested in what was now a bankrupt company.
[2] NLW, Huw T. Edwards Papers, A3/25, letter from Lyn Evans to John Baxter, 29 January 1964. In fact, the new Channel 7 service for south Wales, which

effectively created an all-Wales ITV service for the first time, did not come into being until 15 February 1965.
[3] Ibid.
[4] TWW Production Panel Minutes, 30 January 1964.
[5] NLW, Television Wales and the West Ltd, Welsh Board Minutes, 16 June 1964.
[6] *Western Mail*, 10 July 1964.
[7] Cited in ITA, Regional Officer for Wales and the West [hereafter ROWW] Monthly Report, July 1964.
[8] ITA, *Annual Report and Accounts 1964–65* (London, 1965), p. 1.
[9] ROWW Monthly Report, July 1964.
[10] NLW, Huw T. Edwards Papers, A2/151, letter from Edwards to Baxter, 24 August 1964. See also Gwyn Jenkins, *Prif Weinidog Answyddogol Cymru* (Tal-y-bont, 2007), p. 222.
[11] NLW, Television Wales and the West Ltd, Welsh Board Minutes, 16 June 1964.
[12] ROWW Monthly Report, October 1964. TWW also produced a one-off programme on Mary Rand, which was transmitted at 10.05 p.m. on 1 September 1964 (*Television Weekly*, 28 August 1964).
[13] The BBC had launched its BBC Wales television service on 9 February 1964; by the autumn of that year, 68 per cent of the Welsh population could receive BBC Wales broadcasts (John Davies, *Broadcasting and the BBC in Wales* (Cardiff, 1994), p. 275).
[14] ROWW Monthly Report, January 1965. The main TWW board stood at five Welsh, eleven English and one American.
[15] Author's interview with Lord Roberts of Conwy, 15 April 2008.
[16] *Guardian*, 15 February 1965.
[17] ITA, *Annual Report and Accounts 1965–66* (London, 1966), p. 25.
[18] NLW, Television Wales and the West Ltd, Welsh Board Minutes, 11 February 1965.
[19] NLW, Television Wales and the West Ltd, Welsh Board Minutes, 8 April 1965 and 13 May 1965.
[20] *The Times*, 20 March 1965.
[21] Confidential memorandum from Wyn Roberts to John Baxter and Bryan Michie, 17 May 1965.
[22] ROWW Monthly Report, March 1965 and April 1965. This figure included TWW's subsidiary companies in addition to its television operation.
[23] ROWW Monthly Report, June 1965.
[24] Western Mail, 2 August 1965.
[25] Western Mail, 6 August 1965.

[26] ROWW Monthly Report, December 1965.
[27] *Guardian*, 17 December 1965.
[28] *Western Daily Press*, 2 June 1966.
[29] *Daily Telegraph*, 21 October 1966.
[30] John Davies, *A History of Wales* (rev. edn, London, 2007), p. 610.
[31] Lord Roberts of Conwy, *Right from the Start: The Memoirs of Sir Wyn Roberts* (Cardiff, 2006), p. 71.
[32] Wyn Roberts, 'The Aberfan Disaster: a personal report', undated (Wyn Roberts's personal papers, loaned to the author)
[33] Lord Roberts of Conwy, *Right from the Start*, p. 71.
[34] ITA, CC Paper 7(66), 'Wales and the West: note by the Director-General', 28 October 1966.
[35] NLW, Television Wales and the West Ltd, Welsh Board Minutes, 10 November 1966.
[36] ITC, 60, Memorandum from Fraser to Hill, 22 November 1966.
[37] *Bristol Evening Post*, 22 December 1966.
[38] *Western Mail*, 16 February 1967.
[39] Although only two applications were received, the ITA's Committee for Wales noted that 'a large number of enquiries had been received' prior to the closing date (ITA, Committee for Wales, CW 28 (67), 23 March 1967).
[40] Letter from W. A. C. Collingwood to G. Bailes, 10 June 1967 (Wyn Roberts's personal papers, loaned to the author).
[41] Independent Television Authority, *Annual Report and Accounts 1964–65* (London, 1965), p. 26.
[42] For the same period, Scottish Television broadcast an average of 10 hours 5 minutes, Ulster 6 hours 34 minutes and Anglia 8 hours 30 minutes. Independent Television Authority, *Annual Report and Accounts 1965-66* (London, 1966), p. 26.
[43] Independent Television Authority, *Annual Report and Accounts 1966–67* (London, 1967), p. 24.
[44] Independent Television Authority, *Annual Report and Accounts 1967–68* (London, 1968), p. 35.
[45] *Television Weekly*, 29 May 1964.
[46] TWW Production Panel Minutes, 24 April 1964. It was noted that the standard of dancing on *Top of the Pops* was poor and that *Discs-a-Gogo* would need to select teenagers who could (and would) dance.
[47] *Daily Telegraph*, 24 April 1964.
[48] ITA, Committee for Wales, CW 9 (64), 22 May 1964. There is no evidence to suggest that any further experiments of this kind took place.
[49] ITA, Committee for Wales, CW 8 (64), 13 March 1964.

50 *Y Cymro*, 8 April 1965.
51 *The Times*, 19 February 1965.
52 TWW Production Panel Minutes, 3 December 1964 (original underlining).
53 Ibid.
54 TWW Production Panel Minutes, 4 November 1965; TWW Production Panel Minutes, 13 April 1967.
55 ITA, *Annual Report and Accounts 1965–66* (London, 1966), p. 40.
56 Interview with Lord Roberts of Conwy, 15 April 2008.
57 See, for example, *Y Faner*, 10 February 1966.
58 ROWW Monthly Report, September 1966.
59 TWW Production Panel Minutes, 30 November 1967.
60 As noted in chapter 6, one of the reasons for the failure of WWN was the extensive overlap in north Wales with the Granada signal from Winter Hill and the fact that viewers in the region had been watching Granada since 1956.
61 *Western Mail*, 30 April 1964.
62 NLW, Television Wales and the West Ltd, Welsh Board Minutes, 16 June 1964.
63 ROWW Monthly Report, October 1964.
64 There was still concern in 1966, when power from the Winter Hill transmitter was increased (NLW, Television Wales and the West Ltd, Welsh Board Minutes, 11 March 1965).
65 Ibid.
66 NLW, Television Wales and the West Ltd, Welsh Board Minutes, 16 June 1964.
67 Ibid.
68 Hansard, House of Commons Debates, vol. 698, col. 54 (Written Answers), 28 June 1967.
69 NLW, Television Wales and the West Ltd, Welsh Board Minutes, 10 September 1964.
70 Ibid.
71 NLW, Television Wales and the West Ltd, Welsh Board Minutes, 14 January 1965. The ITA's plans were outlined in *Report of the Committee on Broadcasting, 1960. Volume I. Appendix E*, p. 540.
72 ROWW Monthly Report, April 1965.
73 ITA, Committee for Wales, CW 16 (65), 4 June 1965; NLW, Television Wales and the West Ltd, Welsh Board Minutes, 13 May 1965.
74 ROWW Monthly Report, June 1965.
75 NLW, Television Wales and the West Ltd, Welsh Board Minutes, 14 October 1965.

76 ROWW Monthly Report, December 1965.
77 NLW, Television Wales and the West Ltd, Welsh Board Minutes, 10 March 1966.
78 ITA, Committee for Wales, CW 21 (66), 12 March 1966.

8: Television Wales and the West: The End of the Road

1 Michael Darlow, *Independents Struggle: The Programme Makers who Took on the TV Establishment* (London, 2004), p. 41.
2 ROWW Monthly Report, October 1964.
3 ITA, Committee for Wales, CW 13 (65), 15 January 1965.
4 ITA, Committee for Wales, CW 22 (66), 14 May 1966; ROWW Monthly Report, September 1966.
5 ROWW Monthly Report, December 1965.
6 ITA, Committee for Wales Paper 13 (66), 26 September 1966.
7 ITA, Committee for Wales, CW 26 (66), 3 December 1966.
8 ITA, Committee for Wales, CW 27 (67), 27 January 1967.
9 ITA, Committee for Wales, CW 29 (67), 7 June 1967.
10 ITA, Committee for Wales, CW 33 (68), 19 January 1968.
11 ROWW Monthly Report, September 1964.
12 For an account of contemporary political, social and economic history, see Kenneth O. Morgan, *Rebirth of a Nation: Wales 1880–1980* (Oxford, 1981), p. 359 *passim*. See also Jamie Medhurst, 'Wales television – mammon's television? ITV in Wales in the 1960s', *Media History*, 10 (2) 2004, 126–8.
13 See Gwilym Prys Davies, *Cynhaeaf Hanner Canrif: Gwleidyddiaeth Gymreig 1945–2005* (Llandysul, 2008).
14 *Television Weekly*, 28 August 1964.
15 *Television Weekly*, 3 December 1964; *Television Weekly*, 26 August 1965.
16 ITA, Committee for Wales, CW 11 (64), 26 September 1964.
17 ITA, Committee for Wales, CW 13 (65), 15 January 1965.
18 NLW, Television Wales and the West Ltd, Welsh Board Minutes, 14 October 1965.
19 Letter from Wyn Roberts to Sir Ifan ab Owen Edwards, 18 October 1965 (Wyn Roberts personal papers, loaned to the author).
20 NLW, Television Wales and the West Ltd, Welsh Board Minutes, 13 May 1965.
21 ITA, Committee for Wales, CW 15 (65), 2 April 1965.
22 ROWW Monthly Report, April 1965.
23 ITA, Committee for Wales, CW 17 (65), 28 July 1965.
24 ITA, Committee for Wales, CW 19 (65), 20 November 1965. In March 1966, he proposed that some Welsh-language programmes might have English

captions so as to 'help bridge the gap between Welsh speaking and English speaking viewers and break down the exclusiveness of Welsh language programmes'. The proposal was not accepted by the committee (ITA, Committee for Wales, Paper 3 (66) 25 February 1966, and Committee for Wales, CW 21 (66), 12 March 1966).

[25] *The Times*, 20 March 1965.
[26] ITA, Committee for Wales, CW 7 (64), 24 January 1964.
[27] NLW, Huw T. Edwards Papers, A3/25, Letter from Lyn Evans to John Baxter, 29 January 1964.
[28] ITA, Committee for Wales, CW 8 (64), 13 March 1964.
[29] ITA, Committee for Wales, CW 10 (64), 3 July 1964.
[30] NLW, Television Wales and the West Ltd, Welsh Board Minutes, 15 July 1964.
[31] ROWW Monthly Report, August 1964.
[32] NLW, Television Wales and the West Ltd, Welsh Board Minutes, 29 October 1964.
[33] NLW, Television Wales and the West Ltd, Welsh Board Minutes, 14 January 1965.
[34] NLW, Television Wales and the West Ltd, Welsh Board Minutes, 8 July 1965.
[35] NLW, Television Wales and the West Ltd, Welsh Board Minutes, 9 September 1965.
[36] ROWW Monthly Report, September 1965.
[37] NLW, Television Wales and the West Ltd, Welsh Board Minutes, 14 October 1965.
[38] ROWW Monthly Report, December 1965.
[39] ROWW Monthly Report, September 1966.
[40] TWW Production Panel Minutes, 6 October 1966.
[41] Bernard Sendall, *Independent Television in Britain. Volume 2. Expansion and Change, 1958–68* (London, 1983), p. 337.
[42] NLW, Television Wales and the West Ltd, Welsh Board Minutes, 20 April 1967.
[43] *Observer Review*, 18 June 1967.
[44] Sendall, *Independent Television in Britain. Vol. 2*, p. 354.
[45] Wynford Vaughan Thomas had been involved with the David Frost–Aidan Crawley group, which was applying for the London weekend contract, but withdrew to work with Morgan on the Wales and West bid.
[46] NLW, Frank Price Jones Papers, Box 67, *The Open Secret*, No. 2 (1969), p. 3.
[47] John Morgan made a special visit to St Raphael in the south of France, where Burton was filming Graham Greene's *The Comedians*, and persuaded him to join the consortium.

[48] Wyn Roberts met Wynford Vaughan Thomas on 1 March 1967 at the opening of the BBC Wales studios in Llandâf, Cardiff. Vaughan Thomas was convinced at that stage that TWW was 'safe'. Yet, within a month, he and John Morgan were working on the application (author's interview with Lord Roberts of Conwy, 15 April 2008).
[49] *Sunday Times*, 18 June 1967.
[50] Sendall, *Independent Television in Britain. Vol. 2*, p. 357.
[51] Contract J, Particulars of Application for Wales and West of England Area – All Week, Harlech Consortium, April 1967 (Wyn Roberts personal papers, loaned to the author).
[52] Ibid.
[53] Sendall, *Independent Television in Britain. Vol. 2*, p. 357.
[54] *Application by Existing Programme Contractor, TWW Limited, for appointment as Programme Contractor to the Wales and the West of England area of the Independent Television Authority (Contract J), to take effect from July 10th 1968*, April 1967, p. 16 (Wyn Roberts personal papers, loaned to the author).
[55] A West of England board had been established in 1964 and was chaired by Lord Derby.
[56] Memorandum from Wyn Roberts to John Baxter, 16 May 1967 (Wyn Roberts personal papers, loaned to the author).
[57] NLW, Ben Bowen Thomas Papers, G2/1, Independent Television Authority Programme Contract Interviews, Friday 19th May 1967, TWW Limited, p. 3.
[58] Ibid., p. 4.
[59] Ibid., p.17.
[60] Ibid., p. 15.
[61] Sendall, *Independent Television in Britain. Vol. 2*, p. 358.
[62] NLW, Ben Bowen Thomas Papers, G2/1, Independent Television Authority Programme Contract Interviews, Friday 19th May 1967, Harlech Consortium, p. 12.
[63] Ibid., p. 19.
[64] Sendall, *Independent Television in Britain. Vol. 2*, p. 357.
[65] NLW, Ben Bowen Thomas Papers, G2/1, Independent Television Authority Programme Contract Interviews, Friday 19th May 1967, Harlech Consortium, p. 26.
[66] Ibid.
[67] Sendall, *Independent Television in Britain. Vol. 2*, p. 358.
[68] Lord Hill, *Behind the Screen*, pp. 50–1.
[69] For further details see Sendall, *Independent Television in Britain. Vol. 2*, pp. 333–66.

[70] *The Times*, 12 June 1967.
[71] *Western Mail*, 12 June 1967.
[72] *Daily Express*, 12 June 1967.
[73] *Financial Times*, 12 June 1967.
[74] *Daily Telegraph*, 12 June 1967.
[75] *Western Daily Press*, 27 April 1967.
[76] *South Wales Echo*, 21 June 1967.
[77] Hansard, House of Commons Debates, vol. 749, col. 458, 28 June 1967.
[78] *Guardian*, 15 June 1967.
[79] *Bristol Evening Post*, 16 June 1967.
[80] *Daily Telegraph*, 19 June 1967. See also a similar letter from A. I. Shenkman, from Somerset, in the *Times*, 19 July 1967.
[81] *The Times*, 23 June 1967.
[82] NLW, Emrys Roberts Papers 25, Letter from Lord Derby to the shareholders of TWW, 16 June 1967.
[83] NLW, Emrys Roberts Papers 25, Letter from Lord Hill to Lord Derby, 19 June 1967.
[84] Lord Hill, *Behind the Screen*, p. 58.
[85] Letter from Lord Derby to Lord Hill, 20 June 1967 (Wyn Roberts personal papers, loaned to the author). Peter Bartholomew, TWW joint Managing Director, told the *Daily Express* that Sir Ben Bowen Thomas had said that he was confident that TWW would continue to serve Wales and the West at the time of the opening of the new Pontcanna studios in October 1966. Sir Ben told the newspaper that at the time he had been satisfied with TWW's performance, but that the Harlech Consortium, not yet formed in October 1966, 'held out prospects of giving a better service' (*Daily Express*, 15 June 1967).
[86] NLW, Emrys Roberts Papers 25, Letter from Emrys Roberts to Lord Derby, 23 June 1967.
[87] Memorandum from Wyn Roberts to Lord Derby, 25 June 1967 (Wyn Roberts personal papers, loaned to the author).
[88] NLW, Television Wales and the West Ltd, Welsh Board Minutes, 7 July and 14 July 1967.
[89] ITA, Committee for Wales, CW 31 (67), 23 September 1964.
[90] Hansard, House of Commons Debates, vol. 749, col. 451–2, 28 June 1967.
[91] For detailed analysis of the reasons for the loss of the licence, see Elain Dafydd, 'Lord Hill's little revolution: dymchwel TWW a buddugoliaeth Teledu Harlech' (unpublished M.Phil. thesis, University of Wales, 2005). See also Elain Dafydd, 'Violent and dramatic overhaul': cwymp TWW a dyfodiad Teledu Harlech', *Cyfrwng*, 2 (2005), 49–65; Jamie Medhurst, 'Servant of two

tongues: the demise of TWW', *Llafur: Journal of the Welsh People's History Society*, 8, 3 (2002), 79–87.

92 Peter Black, *The Mirror in the Corner: People's Television* (London, 1972), p. 190.

93 *Western Mail*, 19 June 1967. Sidney and Cecil Bernstein were founder directors of Granada Television, which served the north-west of England from its Manchester studios. See Ray Fitzwalter, *The Dream That Died: The Rise and Fall of ITV* (London, 2008), for a history of ITV from Granada's perspective.

94 TWW was considered the ITA's 'problem child' (John Davies, *Broadcasting and the BBC in Wales* (Cardiff, 1994), p. 226).

95 David Meredith, *Pwy Fase'n Meddwl* (Llandysul, 2002), p. 69.

96 Dafydd, 'Lord Hill's little revolution', p. 142.

97 *Report of the Committee on Broadcasting, 1960. Cmnd. 1753* (London, 1962), p. 166.

98 Ibid., p. 165.

99 Darlow, *Independents Struggle*, p. 42.

100 *Swansea Evening Post*, 16 June 1967. A minority group of MPs dissociated themselves from the Welsh Labour group and came out in support of TWW (*Western Mail*, 14 June 1967).

101 *Guardian*, 13 June 1967.

102 BBC WRC, Broadcasting Council for Wales minutes, 16 June 1967. However, in his copy of a Harlech Television document, *Accepting the Challenge*, published in 1968, Alun Oldfield-Davies, BBC Wales Controller, had scribbled 'Much ado about nothing' (BBC WRC, ITA File).

103 Memorandum from Wyn Roberts to Lord Goodman, 13 June 1967 (Wyn Roberts personal papers, loaned to the author). In 1960, Alun Llywelyn-Williams had refused to take part in a TWW discussion programme, *Pawb a'i Farn*, as he claimed to oppose commercial television on grounds of principle.

104 Meredith, *Pwy Fase'n Meddwl*, p. 89 (My translation).

105 *Financial Times*, 14 July 1967.

106 Ibid, 8 August 1967.

107 *Western Mail*, 7 November 1967.

108 Ibid, 25 November 1967.

109 NLW, Television Wales and the West Ltd, Welsh Board Minutes, 12 October 1967.

110 Ibid, 15 February 1968.

111 Transcript of *Come to an End* (Wyn Roberts personal papers, loaned to the author).

9: ITV in Wales, 1968–1997

1. This period in ITV's history in Wales has all but disappeared from the history books. Useful information on the service can be found at the Transdiffusion Broadcasting System website, http://www.transdiffusion.org/emc/ident/album/itsww.php
2. Michael Darlow, *Independents Struggle: The Programme Makers Who Took On the TV Establishment* (London, 2004), p. 57.
3. ITA, Paper 70 (68), Harlech Television: a note by the Secretary, 10 June 1968.
4. Jeremy Potter, *Independent Television in Britain. Volume 4. Companies and Programmes 1968–80* (Basingstoke, 1990), p. 172.
5. HTV Ltd, *Annual Report and Accounts 1972* (London, 1972), p. 2. The company's title changed from Harlech Television to HTV in 1970 in order to 'play down' the Welsh credentials of the company, in the face of criticism from the West Country.
6. HTV Ltd, *Annual Report and Accounts 1974* (London, 1974), p. 1. For a summary of the economic situation in the early 1970s see Jeremy Black, *Britain Since the Seventies: Politics and Society in the Consumer Age* (London, 2004).
7. HTV Ltd, *Annual Report and Accounts 1975* (London, 1975), pp. 4, 5.
8. HTV Group Ltd, *Annual Report and Accounts 1976* (London, 1976), p. 4.
9. HTV Ltd, *Annual Report and Accounts 1973* (London, 1973), p. 3.
10. Independent Broadcasting Authority, *Annual Report and Accounts 1976–77* (London, 1977), p. 20.
11. http://www.publications.parliament.uk/pa/cm200001/cmhansrd/vo010424/halltext/10424h02.htm
12. Potter, *Independent Television in Britain. Vol. 4*, p. 171.
13. *Daily Telegraph*, 21 December 1970.
14. Potter, *Independent Television in Britain. Vol. 4*, p. 179. The HTV board, in fact, remained relatively well balanced at this time, showing a slight leaning towards Wales, if anything.
15. *Western Mail*, 6 November 1979.
16. *Television in Wales: Report of a Labour Party Study Group* (Cardiff, 1973), p. 9.
17. Potter, *Independent Television in Britain. Vol. 4*, p. 178.
18. National Archives, HO 256/788, Letter from Peter Thomas to Sir John Eden, 13 July 1972.
19. See, for example, National Archives, HO256/837, 3 May 1974, Letter from John Morris to Roy Jenkins (Home Secretary).

Notes

[20] *Report of the Committee on Broadcasting Coverage. Cmnd. 5774* (London, 1974), pp. 42–3.

[21] IBA, Committee for Wales, 90 (74), 13 December 1974.

[22] This stance was outlined in a letter from Sir Alun Talfan Davies, Chairman of the HTV Wales Board, to Peter Thomas, Secretary of State for Wales, on 1 November 1972 (National Archives, HO 256/789).

[23] National Archives, HO 256/837, Letter from Jolyon Dromgoole to Lord Harris, 23 May 1974.

[24] HTV Group Ltd, *Annual Report and Accounts 1977* (London, 1977), p. 4.

[25] *The Fourth Channel in Wales: A Statement by HTV Wales* (Cardiff, [n.d.]), p. 17.

[26] National Archives, BD 25/328, Memorandum from Plaid Cymru (Dafydd Elis-Thomas) to Lord Belstead, 3 October 1979. A number of authors have written on the struggle for the Welsh fourth channel. See, for example, Angharad Tomos, 'Realizing a dream', in Simon Blanchard and David Morley (eds), *What's This Channel Fo(u)r?: An Alternative Report* (London, 1982), pp. 37–53. For the role of Gwynfor Evans in the campaign see Rhys Evans, *Gwynfor Evans: A Portrait of a Patriot* (trans. Robin Chapman; Tal-y-bont, 2008).

[27] *Financial Times*, 27 October 1979.

[28] For government ministerial perspective at the time of the debate over the Welsh fourth channel see Lord Roberts of Conwy, *Right From the Start: The Memoirs of Sir Wyn Roberts* (Cardiff, 2006), pp. 129–38.

[29] IBA Paper 222 (80), Initial Briefing Material on Wales and the West of England, 18 July 1980; Potter, *Independent Television in Britain. Vol. 4*, p. 180.

[30] *Western Mail*, 28 November 1979.

[31] HTV Group Ltd, *Annual Report and Accounts 1983* (London, 1983), p. 4.

[32] Peter Goodwin, *Television Under the Tories: Broadcasting Policy 1979–1997* (London, 1998), p. 35.

[33] HTV Group Ltd, *Annual Report and Accounts 1985* (London, 1985), p. 3.

[34] Paul Bonner with Lesley Aston, *Independent Television in Britain. Volume 5. ITV and the IBA 1981–92: The Old Relationship Changes* (London, 1998), p. 316.

[35] *Wrexham Leader*, 29 October 1982.

[36] IBA, *Annual Report and Accounts 1981–82* (London, 1982), p. 29.

[37] HTV Group Ltd, *Annual Report and Accounts 1986* (London, 1986).

[38] *Broadcast*, 25 February 1980.

[39] HTV Group Ltd, *Annual Report and Accounts 1980* (London, 1980), p. 5.

[40] *Welsh Nation*, May 1982.

[41] HTV Group Ltd, *Annual Report and Accounts 1982* (London, 1982), p. 4.
[42] *Broadcast*, 29 November 1985.
[43] *Broadcast*, 15 May 1987.
[44] *Meet for Lunch*, BBC Radio Wales, 11 May 1987.
[45] Letter from Louis Sherwood, Chairman, HTV Group plc, to shareholders, 25 October 1991. Compare HTV's bid with Channel Television's £1,000, Scottish Television's £2,000 (with no competition), Border's £52,000 (no competition) and Central's £2,000 (no competition).
[46] Bonner with Aston, *Independent Television in Britain. Vol. 5*, pp. 437–8.
[47] Jamie Medhurst, 'The TV franchise affair', *Planet* (April/May, 1991), 111.
[48] HTV Group plc, *Annual Report and Accounts 1992* (London, 1992), pp. 2–4.
[49] HTV Group plc, *Annual Report and Accounts 1993* (London, 1993), p. 3.
[50] Howard Tumber, '10pm and all that: the battle over UK TV news', in Michael Bromley (ed.), *No News is Bad News: Radio, Television and the Public* (Harlow, 2001), p. 101.
[51] Until the 1990 Broadcasting Act the regional ITV companies had been responsible for selling airtime space to advertisers for Channel 4/S4C.
[52] For further details see Cathy Johnson and Rob Turnock (eds), *ITV Cultures: Independent Television over Fifty Years* (Maidenhead, 2005), p. 29.
[53] Kevin Williams, 'United we fall?', *Planet* (August/September, 1997), 53.
[54] See Kevin Williams, 'Serving the nation? Deterioration in TV programming', *Planet* (April/May, 1993), 111–12.
[55] Interviews with Geraint Talfan Davies and Euryn Ogwen Williams, 12 March 2008.

10: Postscript

[1] *Y Faner*, 20 July 1979 (My translation).
[2] Tom O'Malley, 'ITV slashes Welsh services', *Free Press*, 166 (2008), 6.
[3] *Western Mail*, 26 September 2008.
[4] Many viewers in north-east Wales, for example, considered themselves to be part of 'Granadaland', whilst viewers in south Wales received their signal from the Mendip transmitter.
[5] National Assembly for Wales, Broadcasting Committee, *Report on the Future of Public Service Broadcasting in Wales* (Cardiff, 2008), p. 64.
[6] Ibid., p. 41; *Western Mail*, 26 September 2008.
[7] Interview with Elis Owen, National Director ITV Wales, November 2008.
[8] Harlech Television, *Second Report and Accounts Year Ended 31st July 1969* (London, 1969).

References

Manuscripts and other primary sources

BBC Written Archives Centre
　R34/1144; T16/235/2; T16/235/3; T16/235/4.
BBC Wales Record Centre
　Broadcasting Council for Wales file.
British Film Institute
　Harlech Television (then HTV) Annual Reports and Accounts.
Granada Television Written Archive
　Granada Group Limited, *Directors' Report and Accounts for the year ended October First 1960*.
Independent Television Commission Library and Record Centre (now at Bournemouth University)
　ITA minutes
　ITA Annual Report and Accounts
　ITA Committee for Wales minutes
　ITC Microfilms: ITC 30; ITC 60; ITC 131; ITC 160; ITC 166.
　ITA Press Notices: Press Notice 141, 7 April 1961
　ITC Applications for Contracts: A/S/0035/31; A/S/0038/8; A/S/0038/9.
　ITA Papers: 101 (56); CC 7 (66); CW 4 (63).
　TAM Ratings: Week ending 14 October 1962.
National Archives
　BD 23/209; BD 24/208; BD 25/140; BD25/144; HO 244/588.
National Library of Wales
　Aneirin Talfan Davies Papers: Box 1.
　Association of Welsh Local Authorities (AWLA): X30; X31.
　Ben Bowen Thomas Papers: G2/1
　Elwyn and Margaret Davies Papers: D5/4.
　Emrys Roberts Papers: 20; 22; 21; 23; 25.
　ex 1778
　Frank Price Jones Papers: Box 67.
　Huw T. Edwards Papers: A1/237; A1/312; A1/353; A1/669; A1/672; A1/684; A2/117; A2/151; A3/25; C9.
　Jac L. Williams Papers: Undeb Cymru Fydd Joint Television Committee 1958–63 file; National Conference on Television Service for Wales.

Plaid Cymru Archive: A5; M50.
Rhydwen Williams Papers: Box 4.
Television Wales and the West (TWW) Papers: Television Wales and the West Ltd Welsh Board Minutes.
Sir T. H. Parry-Williams and Lady Amy Parry-Williams Papers: LL58.
T. I. Ellis Papers: C58; C59; C62.
Undeb Cymru Fydd Archive: 257.
OFCOM: IBA Committee for Wales minutes
Diaries of T. I. Ellis (on loan to the author).
Lord Roberts of Conwy Papers (on loan to the author).

Newspapers and journals

Baner ac Amserau Cymru
Bath Chronicle and Herald
Blodau'r Ffair
Bristol Evening Post
Bristol Evening World
Caernarfon and Denbigh Herald
Y Cymro
Daily Express
Daily Herald
Daily Mail
Daily Telegraph
Y Ddraig Goch
Evening Advertiser
Financial Times
Free Press
Y Ford Gron
Y Genhinen
Guardian
Herald of Wales
Liverpool Daily Post
Observer
South Wales Argus
South Wales Echo and Evening Express
Sunday Times

Swansea Evening Post
The People
Teledu Cymru
Television Weekly
The Times
TV Times
Wales
Wales Television
The Welsh Nation
Western Daily Press
Western Mail
Wrexham Leader
World's Press News

Official publications

Broadcasting: Memorandum on Television Policy. Cmd. 9005 (London, 1953).

Hansard, House of Commons Debates.

Hansard, House of Lords Debates.

Memorandum on the Report of the Broadcasting Committee, 1949. Cmd. 8550 (London, 1952).

National Assembly for Wales, Broadcasting Committee, *Report on the Future of Public Service Broadcasting in Wales* (Cardiff, 2008).

Parliamentary Debates, Welsh Grand Committee, Broadcasting, First Sitting, Wednesday 13 December 1961 (London, 1961).

Report of the Broadcasting Committee, 1949. Cmd. 8116 (London, 1951).

Report of the Broadcasting Committee, 1949. Appendix H. Memoranda submitted to the Committee. Cmd. 8117 (London, 1951).

Report of the Committee on Broadcasting, 1960. Cmnd. 1753 (London, 1962).

Report of the Committee on Broadcasting, 1960. Volume II. Appendix E. Memoranda submitted to the Committee (Papers 103–275). Cmnd. 1819–1 (London, 1962).

Report of the Committee on Broadcasting Coverage. Cmnd. 5774 (London, 1974).

Television Act 1954 (London, 1954).

Welsh in Education and Life (London, 1927).

Interviews and correspondence

Cenwyn Edwards, May 2008.
Mrs Mari Ellis, February 2004.
Gwynfor Evans, April 1998.
Christopher Grace, May 2008.
Harvard Gregory, February 2005.
Nathan Hughes, August, September 2004.
Robin Jones, March 2001.
David Meredith, March 2008.
Elis Owen, December 2007, October 2008.
Menna Richards, April 2008.
Lord Roberts of Conwy, August 1999, April 2008.
Geraint Talfan Davies, March 2008.
Dorothy Williams, March 1998.
Euryn Ogwen Williams, March 2008.
John Roberts Williams, February 1998.

Secondary sources

Anderson, Benedict, *Imagined Communities: Reflections on the Origin and Spread of Nationalism* (London, 1983).
Bailey, Kenneth (ed.), *The Television Annual for 1958* (London, 1958).
BBC Handbook 1931 (London, 1931).
Barlow, David, 'What's in the "Post"? Mass media as a site of struggle', in Jane Aaron and Chris Williams, *Postcolonial Wales* (Cardiff, 2005).
Barlow, David, Mitchell, Philip and O'Malley, Tom, *The Media in Wales: Voices of a Small Nation* (Cardiff, 2005).
Black, Jeremy, *Britain Since the Seventies: Politics and Society in the Consumer Age* (London, 2004).
Black, Peter, *The Mirror in the Corner: People's Television* (London, 1972).
Bonner, Paul with Aston, Lesley, *Independent Television in Britain. Volume 5. ITV and the IBA 1981–92: The Old Relationship Changes* (London, 1998).
Bowen, E. G., 'Brad diwethaf y BBC', *Y Ddraig Goch* (December, 1933), 2.
Briggs, Asa, *The History of British Broadcasting in the United Kingdom. Volume IV* (Oxford, 1979 [2000 reprint]).
Briggs, Asa, *The History of British Broadcasting in the United Kingdom. Volume V* (Oxford, 1995 [2000 reprint]).

References

Bromley, Michael (ed.), *No News is Bad News: Radio, Television and the Public* (Harlow, 2001).

Cooke, Lez, *British Television Drama: A History* (London, 2003).

Corner, John (ed.), *Popular Television in Britain: Studies in Cultural History* (London, 1991).

Crisell, Andrew, *An Introductory History of British Broadcasting* (2nd edn, London, 2002).

Culpitt, D. H., 'Yr oes olau hon', *Blodau'r Ffair*, 13 (1961), 49.

Curran, James and Seaton, Jean, *Power Without Responsibility: The Press, Broadcasting and New Media in Britain* (6th edn, London, 2003).

Cymdeithas yr Iaith Gymraeg, *Darlledu yng Nghymru: Cyfoethogi neu Ddinistrio'n Bywyd Cenedlaethol? Broadcasting in Wales: To Enrich or Destroy our National Life?* (Aberystwyth [n.d.]).

'Cymru a'r BBC', *Y Ddraig Goch*, (September, 1932), 3.

Dafydd, Elain, 'Lord Hill's little revolution: dymchwel TWW a buddugoliaeth Teledu Harlech' (unpublished M.Phil. thesis, University of Wales, 2005).

Dafydd, Elain, 'Violent and dramatic overhaul': Cwymp TWW a dyfodiad Teledu Harlech', *Cyfrwng*, 2 (2005), 49–65.

Darlow, Michael, *Independents Struggle: The Programme Makers Who Took On the TV Establishment* (London, 2004).

Davies, Aneirin Talfan, *Darlledu a'r Genedl* (London, 1972).

Davies, Aneirin Talfan [Sodlau Prysur], *Teledu Mamon* (Carmarthen, 1961).

Davies, John, *Broadcasting and the BBC in Wales* (Cardiff, 1994).

Davies, John, *Hanes Cymru: A History of Wales in Welsh* (London, 1992).

Edwards, Huw T., *Hewn from the Rock* (Cardiff, 1967).

Edwards, Meredith, *Ar Lwyfan Awr: Atgofion Actor* (Swansea, 1977).

Evans, Gwynfor, 'Hanes twf Plaid Cymru 1925–1995', in Geraint H. Jenkins (ed.), *Cof Cenedl X* (Llandysul, 1995), pp. 153–84.

Evans, Gwynfor, *Y Radio yng Nghymru* (Aberystwyth, 1944).

Evans, Gwynfor and Jones, J. E., *Television in Wales* (Cardiff, 1958).

Evans, Ifan Gwynfil, 'Teledu Cymru: an independent television service for Wales? (1959–1963)' (unpublished MA dissertation, University of Wales, 1997).

Finch, John (ed.), *Granada Television: The First Generation* (Manchester, 2003).

Fitzwalter, Ray, *The Dream That Died: The Rise and Fall of ITV* (London, 2008).

The Fourth Channel in Wales: A Statement by HTV Wales (Cardiff [n.d.]).

Freedman, Des, *Television Policies of the Labour Party 1951–2001* (London, 2003).

Goldie, Grace Wyndham, *Facing the Nation: Television and Politics 1936–76* (London, 1977).

Goodwin, Peter, *Television Under the Tories: Broadcasting Policy 1979–1997* (London, 1998).

'Gorchfygwn y BBC', *Y Ddraig Goch* (February, 1932), 2.

Haf, Elain, 'Y Ddrama Deledu Gymraeg, 1955–1982' (unpublished M.Phil. thesis, University of Wales, 1996).

Hill, Charles, *Behind the Screen: The Broadcasting Memoirs of Lord Hill of Luton* (London, 1974).

Isaac, Norah, *Ifan ab Owen Edwards 1895–1970* (Cardiff, 1972).

Jenkins, Clive, *Power Behind the Screen: Ownership, Control and Motivation in British Commercial Television* (London, 1961).

Jenkins, Gwyn, *Prif Weinidog Answyddogol Cymru* (Tal-y-bont, 2007).

Johnson, Cathy and Turnock, Rob (eds), *ITV Cultures: Independent Television over Fifty Years* (Maidenhead, 2005).

Jones, Aled, *Press, Politics and Society: A History of Journalism in Wales* (Cardiff, 1993).

Lucas, Rowland, *The Voice of a Nation* (Llandysul, 1981).

Medhurst, Jamie, '"Minorities with a message": the Beveridge Report on Broadcasting (1949–1951) and Wales', *Twentieth Century British History*, 19, 2 (2008), 217–33.

Medhurst, Jamie, 'Piecing together Mammon's television: a case study in historical television research', in Helen Wheatley (ed.), *Re-Viewing Television History: Critical Issues in Television Historiography* (London, 2007), pp. 127–41.

Medhurst, Jamie, 'Servant of two tongues: the demise of TWW', *Llafur: Journal of Welsh Labour History*, 8, 3 (2002), 79–87.

Medhurst, Jamie, 'Teledu Cymru – teledu Mamon? Independent television in Wales, 1959–63' (unpublished Ph.D. thesis, University of Wales, 2004).

Medhurst, Jamie, 'The TV franchise affair', *Planet* (April/May, 1991), 111–12.

Medhurst, Jamie, 'Wales Television – Mammon's television? ITV in Wales in the 1960s', *Media History*, 10, 2 (2004), 119–31.

Medhurst, Jamie, '"You say a minority, Sir; we say a nation": The Pilkington Committee on Broadcasting (1960–62) and Wales', *Welsh History Review*, 22, 2 (2004), 109–36.

Meredith, David, *Pwy Fase'n Meddwl* (Llandysul, 2002).
Milland, Jeffrey, 'Courting Malvolio: the background to the Pilkington Committee on Broadcasting, 1960–62', *Contemporary British History*, 18, 2 (2004), 76–102.
Morgan, Dyfnallt (ed.), *Babi Sam: Yn Dathlu Hanner Can Mlynedd o Ddarlledu o Fangor* (Bangor, 1985).
Morgan, Kenneth O., *Rebirth of a Nation: Wales 1880–1980* (Oxford, 1981).
O'Malley, Tom, 'ITV slashes Welsh services', *Free Press*, 166 (2008), 6.
Paulu, Burton, *British Broadcasting in Transition* (London, 1961).
Paulu, Burton, *British Broadcasting: Radio and Television in the United Kingdom* (Minneapolis, 1956).
Potter, Jeremy, *Independent Television in Britain. Volume 4. Companies and Programmes 1968–80* (Basingstoke, 1990).
Roberts of Conwy, Lord, *Right from the Start: The Memoirs of Sir Wyn Roberts* (Cardiff, 2006).
Ryan, Michelle 'Blocking the channels: T.V. and film in Wales', in Tony Curtis (ed.), *Wales: the Imagined Nation. Essays in Cultural and National Identity* (Bridgend, 1986), pp. 181–96.
Sendall, Bernard, *Independent Television in Britain. Volume 1. Origin and Foundation, 1946–62* (London, 1982).
Sendall, Bernard, *Independent Television in Britain. Volume 2. Expansion and Change, 1958–68* (London, 1983).
Television in Wales: Report of a Labour Party Study Group (Cardiff, 1973).
Tomos, Angharad, 'Realizing a dream', in Simon Blanchard and David Morley (eds), *What's This Channel Fo(u)r?: An Alternative Report* (London, 1982), pp. 37–53.
Tumber, Howard, '10pm and all that: the battle over UK TV news', in Michael Bromley (ed.), *No News is Bad News: Radio, Television and the Public* (Harlow, 2001), pp. 96–108.
TWW Ltd, *The Regional Accomplishment in Independent Television* (London, 1962).
Wheatley, Helen, (ed.), *Re-Viewing Television History: Critical Issues in Television Historiography* (London, 2007).
Williams, John Roberts, *Annwyl Gyfeillion* (Llandysul, 1975).
Williams, Kevin, *Get Me a Murder a Day: A History of Mass Communications in Britain* (London, 1998).
Williams, Kevin, 'Serving the nation? Deterioration in TV programming', *Planet* (April/May 1993), 111–12.

Williams, Kevin, 'United we fall?', *Planet* (August/September, 1997), 50–3.
Williams, Rhydwen, 'Gorau barn ... gorau chwedl', *Barn* (January, 1981), 14.
Wilson, H. H., *Pressure Group: The Campaign for Commercial Television* (London, 1961).

Index

Aberfan 5, 136
Aberystwyth 47
adult education programming 138, 149–50
advertisements 25, 29, 46–7, 74–5
advertising revenue 48, 49
Advisory Committee for Wales (ITA) 9, 52, 56, 63, 74, 116
Agar, Herbert 36, 37
All Good Things 138
Am y Gorau 142
Amser Te 66, 121, 122
Anderson, Benedict 32
Anglesey 13
Annan Committee (1974–7) 5, 18, 32
Appleton, E. R. 16
Arfon transmitter viii, 89, 113
Arnold, Tom 36
Arts Council 151
Associated British Corporation (ABC) Television 28, 37, 64, 92
Associated-Rediffusion (see also Rediffusion) 25, 35
Associated Television (ATV) 13, 28, 37, 160
Attlee, Clement 20
audiences 48, 70–2

Baker, Stanley 154, 158
'Ban Welsh Telly' 172
Bangor 18
Baxter, John 59, 131, 156
BBC viii, 13, 14, 16, 17, 20, 21, 26, 30, 61, 66, 79–80, 87–8, 96, 97, 101, 125–7, 151
BBC2 135
BBC Radio 19
BBC Regional Plan 17, 31
BBC Television 19
BBC Wales 133, 150, 153, 172, 173
BBC Welsh Advisory Council 76, 77
Beadle, Gerald 43
Benn, Tony 135
Bennett, (Sir) Frederic 154
Bernstein, Sidney 29
Berrows Newspapers 37
Berry, R. G. 152
Betjeman, John 138
Bevan, Aneurin 38
Beveridge Committee (1949–51) 18, 21, 32, 76–7, 125
Beveridge Report (1951) 4, 21, 23
Bevins, Reginald 49, 55, 57, 58–9
Black, Peter 8
Blackburn, Tony
Bowen, E. G. 17
Bowen, Roderic 27
Box, Donald 57
Brecon, Lord *see* Lewis, D. V. P.
Briggs, Asa 6, 9
Bristol 46
British Broadcasting Corporation *see* BBC
Broadcasting Act (1980) 173
Broadcasting Act (1990) 177–8, 179

Broadcasting Act (1996) 6, 178
Broadcasting Council for Wales (BBC) 22
Brown, Frank 56, 143
Burton, Richard 129, 154, 158, 170

C3W Ltd 177
Cadbury, Peter 54, 72
Cairns, Alun 1
Calvin, Wyn 69
Camau Cyntaf 68
Cambrian Broadcasting Service 35
Cambrian (North and West Wales) Television 94
Cambrian Television 94
Cantamil 171
Cardiff 16
Carleton Greene, Hugh 87
Carlton Television 6, 178
Carmichael, (Sir) John 57
Carr, (Sir) William 37
Cefn Gwlad 176
Celtic Challenge 69
Central Television 1
Channel 3 Wales and the West Ltd 177
Channel Four 10, 174, 178
Chapman-Walker, Mark 7, 8, 23, 36, 37, 39, 40, 41, 44
children's programmes 170–1
Church in Wales 19
Churchill, Winston 20, 23
Cilcennin, Lord 37, 54
Cip ar Chwarae 122
Cipdrem ar Fywyd 67
Claim to Fame 142
Clwb y Llenor 142
Collins, Norman 8, 20, 23

colour television 135
Come to an End 138, 167
Conservative government 11, 22
Continuation Committee 84–5, 87, 89, 90, 96, 127
Coronation Street 71
Council for Wales and Monmouthshire 19
Crawford Committee (1973–4) 5, 18, 32, 172–3
Croeso Christine 68, 142
Culpitt, David Henry 62
Culverhouse Cross 176
Curran, James 10
Cylch Dewi 16
Cymdeithas yr Iaith Gymraeg 11, 169, 172
Cymmrodorion 78
Cynan (Albert Evans Jones) 131, 152

Darlledu a'r Genedl 30
Davies, Cassie 68
Davies, Eic 152
Davies, Eirwen 137
Davies, Elwyn 50, 67
Davies, Glyn 131
Davies, Gwilym Prys 148
Davies, Islwyn 90
Davies, Jenkin Alban 9, 41, 52, 73, 78, 88, 91, 94–5
Davies, John 10, 16, 19
Davies, Kenneth 90
Davies, T. Glynne 122
Derby, Lord 36, 37, 51, 59, 67–8, 157
Dewch i Mewn 5, 28–30, 65, 67
Dinas 176

Index

Discs-a-Gogo 69, 71, 123, 140, 167, 181
Double Your Money 71
drama 68, 130, 138, 151–3, 157
Dwywaith yn Blentyn 152
Dylan Thomas (TWW documentary film) 129

Eden, (Sir) John 172
Edwards, Huw T. 36, 37, 38, 41, 53, 59, 94, 99, 131–2, 144, 150
Edwards, (Sir) Ifan ab Owen 36, 37, 38, 42, 52–3, 99–100
Edwards, Ness 25
Edwards, Owen 176
Edwards, Pete 182
Edwards, Raymond 95
Eilian, John 35
Elis, Islwyn Ffowc 152
Elis-Thomas, Dafydd 174, 175
Ellis, T. I. 90, 96, 102, 114, 115
Emergency Ward 10 44, 71
Emley Moor transmitter 28, 84–5
Emmanuel, Ivor 142
Evans, Geraint 154
Evans, Gwynfor 8, 19, 58, 83, 90, 100, 116, 137
Evans, J. R. 153
Evans, Lyn 56, 74, 143
Evans, (Lady) Olwen Carey 90

fear of television 62–3
Flextech 177
Flint-Denbigh transmitter viii, 90, 98, 113, 116, 143
Foster, Idris 142
fourth channel debate 172–4
Francis, Alfred 37, 48, 51, 54, 59

Fraser, (Sir) Robert 5, 8, 35, 39, 43, 86, 87

General Election (1959) 70
Gilliat, Sidney 37
Goldie, Grace Wyndham 20
Golwg ar Gymru 122
Goodman, Arnold 51, 59
Gorard, Tony 167, 170
Gower, Raymond 25
Grade, Michael 3, 180
'Granadaland' 28
Granada Television 1, 5, 6, 28–30, 39–40, 43, 52, 65, 66, 92, 145, 178
Gregory, Harvard 113
Grenfell, Joyce 50
Griffith, Moses 90
Griffiths, James 132
Gwlad y Gân see Land of Song

Hafren Television *see* Teledu Hafren
Haley, William 19–20
Hamdden 171
Harlech, Lord 153, 170, 182–3
Harlech Consortium 5, 8, 109, 110, 137–8, 153, 158–9, 160, 161, 163–4, 166–7
Harlech Television 169–70; see also HTV
Hawkins, Walter 154
Heddiw 140
Here Today 69, 139
Heycock, Llewellyn 90, 99
Hill, (Lord) Charles 34, 161–2
Hoggart, Richard 50
Holme Moss transmitter 79

Home Office 172, 173
Hopkin Morris, Rhys 18
Howell, Myfanwy 66
Howells, Geraint 174
HTV 2, 5, 6, 13, 111, 169, 170 *passim*
HTV Group Ltd 170, 177
Hughes, Arwel 18
Hughes, Nathan 53, 113–14, 116, 123, 124
Hughes, T. Rowland 18
Hughes Parry, (Sir) David 90, 99
Hylton, Jack 36, 37, 70, 132

In the News 70
Independent Broadcasting Authority (IBA) 173, 181
Independent Television (ITV) 22, 25, 33, 107
Independent Television Authority (ITA) 25, 28, 33–6, 39, 41, 42, 43, 51, 57, 59, 73, 80–1, 86–7, 88, 98, 101, 125–7, 144–5, 147 *passim*, 181
Independent Television Commission 177
Independent Television News (ITN) 45, 136
Independent Television Service for Wales and the West 169
Isaac, Norah 52, 140
IBA *see* Independent Broadcasting Authority
ITA *see* Independent Television Authority
ITC *see* Independent Television Commission
ITN *see* Independent Television News
ITSWW *see* Independent Television Service for Wales and the West
ITV *see* Independent Television

Jenkins, Clive 7–8
Jenkins, Warren 29
Johnson, Cathy 11
Jones, Enid Watkin 52
Jones, J. E. 8, 18, 81
Jones, Percy 38
Jones, Thomas Mervyn 43
Jones, W. S. (Wil Sam) 152, 153
Joseph, Keith 57, 58

Kelly, Ivor 131
Kirkpatrick, (Sir) Ivone 81

Labour Party 24
Lampeter 71
Land of Song 65–6, 71, 121, 140, 151, 181
Leach, Stanley 167
Lewis, D. V. P. 38, 57, 132
Lewis, Saunders 18
Lichfield transmitter 28, 84–5
Liverpool Daily Post 37, 44
Llandovery 71
Llangollen International Eisteddfod 131, 134–5
Llewellyn, David 27
Llewellyn, Harry 38, 68
Llewellyn, (Sir) Godfrey 36, 37
Llywelyn-Williams, Alun 2, 18, 154, 166–7
Lloyd, Selwyn 23
London Weekend Television 160

Macdonald of Waenysgor, Lord 22, 78
Maxwell, (Sir) Alexander 37
McDonald, Graeme 28
media ownership 178
Mendip transmitter 5, 13
Merlin Television 177
Michie, Bryan 44, 167
Milland, Jeffrey 49–50
Miri Mawr 111, 171
Moel-y-Parc transmitter *see* Flint–Denbigh transmitter
monopoly (of broadcasting) 21–2
Morgan, Elystan 137
Morgan, Geraint 174
Morgan, John 154
Morris, John 172
Movie Magazine 142
Mr and Mrs 140, 142
Myers, Bob 39
Myfyr a Mawl 121–2

National Assembly for Wales Broadcasting Committee 181–2
National Broadcasting Company (NBC) 8, 36, 44
National Eisteddfod 74, 78, 79, 89, 120, 145, 171
national identity 30–2, 77, 82, 101
National Television Conference (1959) 5, 82–4
National Television Conference (1961) 5, 96–8
National Television Council 24
New Airs and Faces 69, 104
News of the World 8, 35, 36, 37
Nye! 141

OFCOM (Office of Communications) 3, 180, 182
Ogilvie, Frederick 21
Oldfield Davies, Alun 43, 66, 78
opt-out system 22–3
Orig yr Ifanc 67
ownership 6, 37–8

parliamentary debate 25–8
Parry, Gwenlyn 153
Parry, Thomas 90, 113–14, 115
Parry-Williams, (Sir) T. H. 90
Paulu, Burton 6, 7
Pawb a'i Bethau 122
Peacock Committee (1985–6) 6
Peacock Report (1986) 177
Philipps, (Sir) Grismond 37, 51, 132
Pickering, Tom 18
Pilkington Committee (1960–2) 5, 6, 18, 32, 49–52, 55, 99, 101–2, 126, 127, 165, 166
Pilkington Report (1962) 51–2
Plaid Cymru 46, 76, 77, 81–2, 94, 98, 99, 101–2, 174
Poeton, William 154
Police 5 141
Pontcanna studios 41–2, 43, 135
Pony Express 140
Post Office 98
Popular Television Association 24, 36
Preseli transmitter viii, 89, 113, 115
Prichard, Caradog 134–5
Probert, Arthur 35
programme production 128, 141
Public Service Broadcasting 11, 12, 143

Pwy Fase'n Meddwl 68, 142

quality 13–14, 182

Radio Éireann 16
reception issues 42, 143–6
Rediffusion 160
regional vs national 13
Reith, (Lord) John 16, 18, 19, 24, 31
relay companies 117–18
Rhys, Keidrych 35
Richards, Dewi 140
Roberts, Emrys 58, 90, 91, 113, 114, 162
Roberts, Goronwy 27, 55, 132
Roberts, Wyn 37, 54–5, 61, 134, 136, 142, 148, 156, 162, 166
Roberts Williams, John 113, 122
Rolling Stones 69
Royal Welsh Show 74

S4C 6, 10, 13, 169, 174, 175–6, 178
Sain, Cerdd a Chân 171
Sarnoff, Robert 44
satellite stations 144
scarcity of wavelengths 17
schools programming 138, 149–50
Scottish Television 40, 160
Seaton, Jean 10, 49, 51
Secombe, Harry 158
Sendall, Bernard 1, 9
Seren Wib 171
Severn Television *see* Teledu Hafren
'Severnside' 74, 155–6, 166
shareholders 48–9
Sherwood, Louis 177

Sianel Pedwar Cymru *see* S4C
Sion a Sian 140
Sports Preview 70
Sports programmes 69–70, 122
St Hilary transmitter viii, 5, 40, 42, 48, 72, 84, 133
Sunday Night at the London Palladium 71
Sutton Coldfield transmitter 22
Swansea 16

Taff Acre 175
Take Your Pick 71
Talfan Davies, Alun 154
Talfan Davies, Aneirin 30, 31
Taro Deg 68, 121, 123
Taylor, Elizabeth 170
Teledu Cymru (journal) 113, 119
Teledu Cymru *see* Wales (West and North) Television
Teledu Cymru service viii, 132, 133, 139, 140, 150
Teledu Hafren 174
Teledu Mamon 100–1, 102, 106
television 19
Television Act (1954) 4, 12, 24, 41, 50, 156
Television Audience Measurement (TAM) 70, 74, 115
Television Programme Contractors' Association 39
Television Wales and the West (TWW) 5, 8, 10, 33 *passim*, 99, 101, 108, 129 *passim*, 147 *passim*, 160
Television Wales Norwest 94, 95
Television Weekly 61, 67, 103
Thames Television 160

The Stars Rise in the West 45, 139
Thomas, (Sir) Ben Bowen 131, 132, 144, 149–50, 157, 167
Thomas, D. R. 52
Thomas, Eric 57, 58, 101, 119
Thomas, Gwyn 137
Thomas, Howard 40
Thomas, Huw 45
Thomas, Iorwerth 113
Thomas, Peter 172
Thomas T. Haydn 97
Thomas, William 90
Thomson, Roy 33, 36
Three Little Words 69
transmitters 144–6, 181
Troeon Gyrfa 67
Traherne, Cenydd 83, 90, 95, 96
Tregampau 142
Trysor o Gân 67
Trysorau Cymru 122
Turnock, Rob 11
TWW *see* Television Wales and the West
TWW Reports 139, 141

UHF (Ultra High Frequency) ix
Undeb Cymru Fydd 19, 73, 76, 78, 82, 96, 97, 98, 102
United News and Media 2, 6, 178
University of Wales 17
University of Wales Television Committee 90
Urdd Gobaith Cymru 78, 101, 102

Vaughan, Aled 167, 180
Vaughan, David 90, 91, 93, 99
Vaughan, Trevor 151

Vaughan Thomas, Wynford 154, 166
VHF (Very High Frequency) ix

Wales and West region (ITV) 12–13, 34, 39, 44, 45, 46, 47, 72–3, 77–8, 130, 132–3, 134, 155–6, 157–8, 161, 171–2, 181
Wales and the West 69
Wales Television 54, 55, 94, 98
Wales Television (journal) 119
Wales Television Association 5, 53, 73, 91–2, 94, 95, 126
Wales (West and North) Television 2, 5, 11, 12, 47, 52, 55, 56–8, 60, 71, 74, 76 *passim* 98, 100, 113 *passim*, 129, 164
Welsh in Education and Life (1927) 16
Welsh culture 62–3, 77, 83, 101, 120, 125, 158–9, 180–1
Welsh-interest programming (in English) 59, 68–70, 93, 113, 121, 122, 140, 141, 150–1, 152, 181
Welsh language 12, 17, 18, 31, 46, 62–3, 77, 83, 101, 113, 120, 125, 172–4, 180–1
Welsh-language programming 23, 27, 29–30, 38–9, 40–1, 52, 59, 61, 63–8, 74, 86, 90, 92, 93, 100, 105, 118, 121, 122–4, 137, 149, 152, 170–1, 176
Welsh Language Society *see* Cymdeithas yr Iaith Gymraeg
Welsh Office 172
Welsh Parliamentary Party 76, 101
Welsh Region (BBC) 17, 18
Welsh Spotlight 122

Western Region (BBC) 17, 31
Wenvoe transmitter viii, 4, 22
Westward Television 52, 54, 72, 74, 117, 161
White, Eirene 26
Whitelaw, William 173
Williams, Emlyn 90
Williams, Euryn Ogwen 177
Williams, Haydn 5, 53, 56, 83, 84–6, 93, 94, 95, 96, 99, 100, 113, 115, 116, 123, 126, 167
Williams, Jac L. 82–3
Williams, Rhydwen 29–30
Williams-Wynne, J. F. 90

Wilson, H. H. 6
Wilson, Harold 8
Winter Hill transmitter 13, 28, 29, 40, 98, 143
Woolton, Lord 23
Wstibethma 171
WWN *see* Wales (West and North) Television

Y Ddraig Goch 18
Y Dydd 137, 140–1, 149, 150
Yorkshire Television